WILD by DESIGN

TWO HUNDRED YEARS OF INNOVATION

AND ARTISTRY IN AMERICAN QUILTS

JANET CATHERINE BERLO

and PATRICIA COX CREWS

With Contributions by CAROLYN DUCEY,

JONATHAN HOLSTEIN, and MICHAEL JAMES

INTERNATIONAL QUILT STUDY CENTER AT THE UNIVERSITY OF NEBRASKA–LINCOLN

IN ASSOCIATION WITH UNIVERSITY OF WASHINGTON PRESS, SEATTLE AND LONDON

Color details: p. ii, Mary M. Hernandred Ricard, **My Crazy Dream** (pl. 18); p. vi, **Pots of Flowers** (pl. 9); p. viii, **Crazy Neckties** (pl. 35); p. xiii, Anna Williams, **LIX: Log Cabin** (pl. 44); p. xiv, Pamela Studstill, **Number 41** (pl. 40); p. 2, Katie Pasquini Masopust, **Painted Canyon** (pl. 47); p. 32, **Wool Crazy Quilt** (pl. 19); p. 35, **Log Cabin, Pineapple Variation** (pl. 24); p. 132, Mary Maxtion, **Log Cabin** (pl. 45); p. 159, Terrie Hancock Mangat, **Fireworks** (pl. 42); p. 161, **Log Cabin, Courthouse Steps Variation** (pl. 14).

Copyright © 2003 by the International Quilt Study Center
Designed by Audrey Seretha Meyer
Composition by Jeanne Gustafson
at Integrated Composition Systems
Printed and bound by C&C Offset Printing Co., Ltd., China

13 12 11 10 09 08 07   6 5 4 3 2

University of Washington Press
PO Box 50096
Seattle, WA 98145-5096, U.S.A.
www.washington.edu/uwpress

Library of Congress Cataloging-in-Publication Data

Wild by design : two hundred years of innovation and
artistry in American quilts / edited by Janet Catherine Berlo
and Patricia Cox Crews ; with contributions by Carolyn
Ducey, Jonathan Holstein, and Michael James.

    p.   cm.
Includes bibliographical references.
ISBN-13: 978-0-295-98309-7
ISBN-10: 0-295-98309-4 (alk. paper)
1. Quilts—United States.   I. Berlo, Janet Catherine.
II. Crews, Patricia Cox.   III. Ducey, Carolyn.
IV. Holstein, Jonathan.   V. James, Michael, 1949–

NK9112.W54 2003
746.46'0973—dc21   2002191905

TO **ARDIS JAMES**, WHOSE DISCERNING EYE AND GENEROSITY

GAVE LIFE TO THE INTERNATIONAL QUILT STUDY CENTER

CONTENTS

FOREWORD

MICHAEL JAMES

I find it a curious sensation to be writing a foreword to an art history in which I and my work figure among the subjects under discussion. How could I possibly feign objectivity? The conundrum is magnified by the fact that I've written and published enough first-person narratives about my own work that I've documented a personal artistic history that now provides source material for books such as the one you hold in your hands.

That we have relatively little primary source material to amplify our understanding of the many thousands of eighteenth-, nineteenth-, and early-twentieth-century quilts, however, is certainly a consequence of the marginalization of women's work, which tended to require neither materials that were precious and rare nor specialized technologies. Domestic practices, especially those involving needle and thread, have suffered in cultural contexts that have valued and conferred legitimacy on the work of "professionals" (historically, well-educated and well-traveled white males).

In the past, few quiltmakers thought their handiwork important or valuable enough to document its making and the conditions and motivations that inspired their range of artistic decisions. Consequently, as Janet Berlo points out, fiction and nonfiction writers alike put words in the mouths of anonymous quiltmakers and helped to create a romance and mystique surrounding historical quilts that has permeated much of the literature on the subject.

Today, fortunately, we know better. This is one reason why, one hundred and more years from now, the current renaissance of quilt design and quilt-related activity will be more thoroughly understood and will likely benefit from more insightful and informed analyses. Documen-

tation will be available in many forms: oral histories; photographic, video, and digital records; and works in print of all sorts. If Lucinda Ward Honstain or Harriet Powers were making their masterpieces today, our culture's sensitivity to the aesthetic value of their quilts would leave future historians with far fewer questions about their work and how it came to exist.

The lucid, balanced, and thoroughly researched scholarship in *Wild by Design* documents and celebrates the rich history of the quiltmaker's art. All the authors and commentators look closely at the quilts themselves to illuminate the stories that they can tell, while at the same time recognizing the gaps in our knowledge and understanding of these works that may never be filled. In her essay, Janet Berlo reconsiders timeworn notions about quilts and the artists who made them, notions that have not held up to the informed research practices and contextual purviews now being brought to bear on these eloquent objects. She recognizes and honors the imagination and invention behind a legacy of artistic expression that appeals across every social divide: gender, class, race, ethnicity, nationality, and political affiliation.

While I came to the making of quilts in a different way than did many of the artists who fashioned the visually dazzling quilt heritage represented in *Wild by Design,* I am convinced that what has kept me active in and committed to this practice over nearly thirty years is something that legions of anonymous makers before me must have been equally sensitive to. What I feel is so essential about a quilt, that characteristic that precedes the resolution of the design on its surface or the strategies used in executing that design, is its tactility.

We humans need many obvious things to survive, but

we know that just surviving isn't enough to nourish our psychic well-being. We crave touch—most importantly, most humanly, skin against skin. But the sensual gratification that flesh-to-flesh contact provides isn't our only source of tactile satisfaction. We love the feel of sand on our bare feet, the sensation of moving our hands through a dense patch of tall grass, the warm comfort of a sheet or towel wrapped around our naked bodies.

So I've come to believe this about the makers and the making of quilts: a love of touching and handling fabric, cloth, precedes and sustains a long and fruitful practice in the medium. I've never met a quiltmaker, traditional or nontraditional, who didn't have difficulty resisting the temptation to reach out and touch a quilt masterpiece in an exhibition, despite proscriptions against doing so. I don't know a quiltmaker who doesn't handle the yardage she may be considering for purchase in a quilt or fabric shop. I don't know a fabric artist who isn't as concerned with the hand and drape and weave of a textile as with the embellishments or reconstructions to which she will submit that same textile.

When I've been too busy or distracted to do any work in my studio, when I've been frustrated by demands on my time that kept me from doing what I most wanted do to, taking a few moments to simply run my hands across stacks of fabric on my worktable was enough to hold me over until I could square some quality time there. This tactile experience of textiles can be enormously soothing and restorative, and I believe that this is the experience of anyone who practices the craft of making quilts. While my own work may look strikingly different from that of Lucinda Honstain, Wini Austin, Pamela Studstill, or "Maker unknown," I know that we all shared a love of the feel of fabric between our fingers. It is the common experience that links everyone who has taken up fabric, needle, and thread in pursuit of creative expression, and it is one of the key underlying impulses of every quilt that we today consider "wild by design."

ACKNOWLEDGMENTS

Many people have aided us in our journey toward the publication and exhibition *Wild by Design*. We are grateful to our colleague Jonathan Holstein, who has offered wise counsel to the International Quilt Study Center (IQSC) since its formation in 1997 and whose enthusiasm for the idea of this book equaled our own. Jon helped choose the forty-eight quilts presented here (a difficult choice among the more than 1,250 quilts that make up the IQSC collections) and generously brainstormed with us through the entire process of writing and editing.

Our other collaborators on the book, Carolyn Ducey and Michael James, are both on the staff at the University of Nebraska–Lincoln. Carolyn, Curator of the IQSC Collections, cheerfully answered all questions relating to the quilts in the collections and participated in the examination of the quilts during which our dialogues were initiated. Michael generously agreed to write the book's foreword and participate in a dialogue on his own quilts.

Other staff members of the IQSC gave their time and expertise as well. Marin Hanson, Assistant Curator of the IQSC Collections, who manages the IQSC electronic database, was invaluable in helping us retrieve and organize information throughout the writing and editing process. In addition, she handled all details associated with conversion of the quilt images to electronic files for this publication. Janneken Smucker, IQSC Curatorial Graduate Assistant, contributed in a variety of ways, from determining through microscopic analyses the fiber content of the multitude of fabrics included in the selected quilts to answering through library research the inevitable questions that arose. Finally, Melissa Jurgena, IQSC Graduate Research Fellow, skillfully completed genealogical research regarding most of the nineteenth-century quiltmakers for whom we had a name. In the process, she uncovered information that helped confirm or corroborate details about the quilts' makers, origins, and dates of production. All of the individuals named above worked hard to make this collaborative project a singular pleasure; for that we express our heartfelt thanks.

Janice Driesbach, Director of the Sheldon Memorial Art Gallery at the University of Nebraska–Lincoln, enthusiastically responded to our inquiries about a possible exhibit of offbeat quilts from the IQSC collections. *Wild by Design* was the inaugural exhibition (February 14– March 31, 2003) after the renovation of the Sheldon, featuring some two dozen of the forty-eight quilts in this book. *Wild by Design* was the second Sheldon exhibition of quilts from the IQSC collections. During the spring of 2001, the Sheldon featured approximately thirty African American quilts from the Cargo Collection, an exhibition for which it received critical acclaim. In the future, other selections from the group of forty-eight *Wild by Design* quilts will travel to other museum venues.

We are grateful to have at the International Quilt Study Center the three principal collections that we drew upon for this book, the Ardis and Robert James Collection, the Robert and Helen Cargo Collection of African American quilts, and the Sara Miller Collection of Amish crib quilts. We are especially grateful to Robert and Ardis James, whose generosity and vision led to the establishment of the International Quilt Study Center at the University of Nebraska–Lincoln.

We would like to acknowledge support of the James Foundation, which provided financial support for the publication of this project.

We are grateful to the staff at the University of Washington Press for their expert work in the publication of this volume. Our greatest thanks go to Naomi Pascal, Editor in Chief, whose enthusiasm for this book sustained us, and to Jacqueline Ettinger, who deftly took the kinks out of our prose and expertly shepherded our manuscript to press.

Patricia Cox Crews
International Quilt Study Center
University of Nebraska–Lincoln

Janet Catherine Berlo
Department of Art and Art History
University of Rochester

WILD BY DESIGN

TWO HUNDRED YEARS OF INNOVATION

AND ARTISTRY IN AMERICAN QUILTS

The International Quilt Study Center Collections

PATRICIA COX CREWS

Ardis and Robert James Collection

I n 1979, Robert and Ardis James of Chappaqua, New York, began collecting quilts. Over the next twenty years they accumulated more than one thousand quilts. The James Collection, world-renowned for its inclusion of both antique and contemporary art quilts, consists of a remarkable range of quilts dating from the late 1700s to the present, made in the United States, Europe, and Japan.

Amish and Mennonite quilts from the late nineteenth century make up one of the largest segments of the collection. Quilts from the New England, Middle Atlantic, and Southern states are among the earliest and most valuable examples, while the majority of the quilts are from Ohio, Indiana, and other Midwestern states. More than one hundred quilts document the studio art quilt movement, including works by Michael James, Nancy Crow, Faith Ringgold, Jean Ray Laury, Jan Myers-Newbury, Terrie Hancock Mangat, and others.

Nationally renowned museums, including the Textile Museum in Washington, D.C.; the Museum of American Folk Art in New York City; the Museum of Our National Heritage in Lexington, Massachusetts; and the Museum of the American Quilter in Paducah, Kentucky, have borrowed quilts from the collection for exhibitions. In 1998, eighty-eight quilts from the James Collection traveled to the Tokyo International Forum where they were seen by more than one hundred thousand people during a three-day exhibition. The desire of museums of this stature to exhibit quilts from the James Collection speaks to its quality and depth. It was named one of "the 100 top treasures" in the United States by *Art and Antiques* magazine in 1998

and was designated by the National Trust for Historic Preservation as an official project of the Save America's Treasures program in 2000.

Robert and Helen Cargo Collection

The Cargo Collection encompasses 156 quilts made by African American women, primarily from Alabama. More than thirty-two quiltmakers are represented, including folk artists Yvonne Wells, Nora Ezell, and Mary Lucas.

Robert Cargo, professor emeritus at the University of Alabama and owner of the Folk Art Gallery in Tuscaloosa, began building his collection of Alabama quilts in the late 1950s after inheriting a number of quilts from his great-grandmother. He decided early to focus his efforts primarily on Alabama quilts and assembled a collection that became widely regarded as one of the most important quilt collections in the United States. Since 1980 Cargo has concentrated more on African American quilts from Alabama, with a few examples from several other states of the Deep South.

The quilts in the Cargo Collection date primarily from the fourth quarter of the twentieth century, but also include a number of significant pre-1950 works. Many of the quilts were purchased directly from the makers, some of whom Dr. Cargo came to know quite well as he visited and photographed them at work in their homes. The Cargo Collection superbly illustrates the ongoing role that African American quiltmakers play in the larger tradition of American quilt history. The Cargo Collection, acquired in May 2000, was a shared donation, with contributions from both Robert and Helen Cargo and Robert and Ardis James.

Selected quilts from this collection have been exhibited at the Museum of American Folk Art in New York, the Sheldon Memorial Art Gallery at the University of Nebraska–Lincoln, the National Humanities Center in North Carolina, and the Smithsonian Institution in Washington, D.C., and have been featured in a number of publications including *Quilts: A Living Tradition* by Robert Shaw.

Sara Miller Collection

In September 2000, Sara Miller's collection of Amish crib quilts was acquired by the International Quilt Study Center through the generous support of Robert and Ardis James. This group of ninety Amish crib quilts was assembled by Sara Miller of Kalona, Iowa, during the early to mid-1980s.

Raised in an Amish household, Ms. Miller wanted to know more about her heritage. Collecting Amish crib quilts became one way for her to do so. Primarily from the Midwest, the collection encompasses many patterns typical of Amish quilts, such as Bars, Nine Patch, and Diamond in the Square. Like full-size Amish bed quilts, most of these small quilts are made in dark, saturated colors, but the collection also includes some quilts in the lighter and brighter colors of the 1930s and 1940s. Most of the small quilts have intricate and expertly stitched designs very much like their full-size counterparts. They represent a significant area of Amish quiltmaking tradition.

With the addition of the Sara Miller Collection of Amish crib quilts and the Cargo Collection, the IQSC's collection is now believed to be the largest public collection in the world, numbering more than 1,250 quilts.

"Acts of Pride, Desperation, and Necessity":

Aesthetics, Social History, and American Quilts

JANET CATHERINE BERLO

Introduction

Collected, saved, and combined materials represented for women acts of pride, desperation, and necessity. Spiritual survival depended on the harboring of memories. Each cherished scrap of percale, muslin, or chintz, each bead, each letter, each photograph, was a reminder of its place in a woman's life, similar to an entry in a journal or diary.

—Miriam Schapiro and Melissa Meyer, *"Femmage" (1978)*

Contemporary artist Miriam Schapiro has described American women's traditional arts, such as needlework, quilts, rugs, and scrapbooks, as "acts of pride, desperation, and necessity." An outpouring of scholarship in the last quarter century has revolutionized our understanding of textiles in general and the formerly undervalued art form of quilting in particular. Quilts have come to be recognized as a fundamental source for understanding women's history; moreover, the study of quilts and quiltmaking practices yields great insight into the subtleties of social interactions among women and economic interrelations among different social classes, industries, and nations.[1]

This revolution in knowledge has resulted in a specialization now known as "quilt studies," an interdisciplinary endeavor in which social history, women's history, textile history, and textile science are well-represented. Information on the lives of individual quilters has been excavated, fabrics and dyes have been researched, and the geometric patterns and visual imagery in quilts have been investigated. Yet one aspect of quilts has remained comparatively understudied since Jonathan Holstein first called attention to it in his ground-breaking exhibit *Abstract Design in*

American Quilts at the Whitney Museum of American Art in 1971: their aesthetic dimensions. Holstein put forth the radical propositions that, in their quilts, nineteenth-century American women were "painting with fabric" and that their works demonstrated "the highest degree of control for visual effects."[2]

The Whitney Museum exhibit and Holstein's books addressed the unique artistry and aesthetics of American quilts. His work caused many of us finally to *see* quilts as what Patricia Mainardi called "the great American art."[3] Yet the subsequent silence about quilt aesthetics may be, in part, because art historical inquiry has turned away from aesthetic and formal issues in the last twenty years, focusing instead on social and epistemological questions. Curiously, few professionally trained art historians have ventured into the specialized subfields of textiles and quilt studies. Folklorists, historians, textile scientists, textile historians, and many non-academics are in the forefront. Seldom are quilts discussed in academic art historical journals, although new scholarly journals and popular magazines have sprung up to serve a widespread interest in quilt studies.

My essay and the catalogue entries that follow examine both the aesthetics and the social history of quilts, principally through close examination of quilts chosen from the International Quilt Study Center for their outstanding visual qualities. Many people think of quilts primarily as exercises in rigorously geometric repeat patterning. Yet a great freewheeling tradition exists in quiltmaking in which improvisation, asymmetry, and experimentation are the norm. It is my thesis that this creative and original artistic impulse can be documented back to the early years of quiltmaking in this country. For at least two hundred

5

years, American women artists have made quilts in which offbeat color placement and manipulation of printed textile patterns have combined with bold experimentation in block formation and appliqué. This has resulted in a body of work that is wild by design. Such quilts are not necessarily the exception; many became normative, as this book demonstrates.

Before looking at their design properties and historical matrices, however, it is useful to examine the multiple relationships that scholars, collectors, makers, and other Americans have had with quilts, and the narratives we have told ourselves about these extraordinary objects from the past.

Nationalism and Feminism: Constructing a Quilt Heritage

The making of patchwork quilts is one of the most picturesque of all the folk arts. It is the only one of the home-craft arts that has withstood the machine age. The beauty which has its expression in the work of our architects, artists, and poets of today oftentimes had its first fling in these humble creations in the hands of our pioneer mothers. Needlework was the one art which women could claim as their own.

—Carrie Hall, *The Romance of the Patchwork Quilt* (1935)

In the past two hundred years, two eras were pivotal to the formation of a narrative about American quilts. The first was the Colonial Revival that began in the late nineteenth century. The second took place in the 1970s, a time of unusual receptiveness in the art world to noncanonical works of art, and, even more importantly, the decade of the full flowering of the so-called "Second Wave" of feminism. To understand the history and historiography of quilts, an understanding of the events of the 1970s is crucial and will be addressed first. In that decade, several diverse events and trends of importance to quilt history occurred, each a stone thrown in a pond, with far reaching ripples.

The biggest stone, with the greatest ripple effect, was the revelatory exhibit already mentioned, mounted in 1971 by Jonathan Holstein and Gail van der Hoof at the Whitney Museum in New York City. *Abstract Design in American Quilts* presented quilts, heretofore seen by most as humble domestic icons, as the logical and bold precursors to the modernist visual statements of abstract painters such as Barnett Newman, Piet Mondrian, and Josef Albers. Setting attendance records at the Whitney, engendering widespread media attention, and touring

North America and Europe for many years, this exhibit, its small catalogue of the same name, and the subsequent book *The Pieced Quilt: An American Design Tradition* (1973) were pivotal in opening the art world's eyes—and those of the general public—to the inherent worth of quilts as art objects of considerable visual eloquence.

Arguing that "an important body of American design had been largely overlooked," Holstein articulated the ways that quilts participated in an American visual tradition that had previously been seen as the singular contribution of modern abstract painters. Discussing quiltmakers' creative manipulation of geometric pattern, and the optical effects they created involving both color and form in a large-scale painterly format, Holstein deduced that "quiltmakers arrived at many visual results similar to those obtained by artists painting as much as a century later."[4]

In 1973, a young art historian, Patricia Mainardi, published her polemical article "Quilts: The Great American Art" in the *Feminist Art Journal*. Much reprinted, this article positioned quilts as the legitimate feminist ancestry that those interested in women's arts in the 1970s were so avidly seeking:

Needlework is the one art in which women controlled the education of their daughters, the production of the art, and were also the audience and critics, and it is so important to women's culture that a study of the various textile and needlework arts should occupy the same position in Women's Studies that African art occupies in Black Studies—it is our cultural heritage. Because quilt making is so indisputably women's art, many of the issues women artists are attempting to clarify now—questions of feminine sensibility, of originality and tradition, of individuality vs. collectivity, of content and values in art—can be illuminated by a study of this art form, its relation to the lives of the artists, and how it has been dealt with in art history.[5]

Elsewhere in this article, Mainardi made some of the same points about quilts that Holstein did, surely drawing from his research in doing so; yet she was scornful of the appropriation of quilts by male scholars and curators who wanted to bring them into the modernist conversation about art. As befitted the separatist notions of feminism common in the 1970s, Mainardi sought to place quilts solely within a female discourse (both historically and in her contemporary use of them) and to reclaim them as a cornerstone of a feminist art history:

Quilts have been underrated precisely for the same reasons that jazz, the great American music, was also for so long underrated—because the "wrong" people were making it, and because these people, for sexist and racist reasons, have not been allowed to represent or define American culture. . . .

In music it became an open scandal that while black jazz and blues musicians were ignored, their second-rate white imitators became famous and rich. Feminists must force a similar consciousness in art, for one of the revolutionary aims of the women's cultural movement is to rewrite art history in order to acknowledge the fact that art has been made by all races and classes of women, and that art in fact is a human impulse, and not the attribute of a particular sex, race, or class.[6]

With the hindsight of three decades, it is easier to see that Holstein and Mainardi were, in at least some respects, making similar claims for the legitimacy of quilts as a great American art form and their makers as unchampioned artists. These two authors spoke to different (though overlapping) audiences, using different vocabularies. The subsequent interest in quilts on the part of Women's Studies scholars rests in part on Mainardi's contribution, which placed women's handiwork within a feminist discourse.[7] The explosion of quilt exhibits and the rise of an interest in collecting quilts derive substantially from Holstein's considerable public achievements.[8] The efforts of many scholars, artists, curators, and critics in the 1970s— Holstein and Mainardi among them—opened the art world to the diverse multicultural expressions we have seen there for the last quarter century, including quilts and other textile arts, folk and outsider arts, and numerous ethnic traditions.

The counterculture and "back to the land" movements of the 1960s and 1970s led many young women, myself included, to seek out handmade, rural, and folk traditions and to emulate historical quilts as we sought to make new ones with our own hands. Mainstream women focused on America's bicentennial celebrations of 1976 to honor the tradition of quiltmaking, which they saw as distinctively American.[9] Many states held exhibits emphasizing the quilt heritage of their regions. Urban quilt guilds made collective quilts, and national quilt contests flourished. There were, for example, an astonishing ten thousand entries in the Museum of American Folk Arts/*Good Housekeeping* magazine bicentennial quilt contest; members of historical societies and numerous local quilt guilds made heritage quilts, often memorializing local landmarks or historical events.[10]

Each of these events claimed quilts as part of a distinct patrimony: Holstein and van der Hoof's exhibits claimed them as part of the landscape of American fine arts; Mainardi claimed quilts as part of a feminist artistic legacy. And in the bicentennial year, women all across

America, even those who might not embrace the language of feminism, identified themselves as sisters or granddaughters in this capacious matrilineage of quilters who had long constructed an American artistic heritage with needle, thimble, and "scraps"—as the mythology would have it.

At this same historical moment, a number of young university-trained artists were seeking alternatives to modern abstract painting, which appeared to them to have run its aesthetic course. Some turned to fabric. California artist Jean Ray Laury, who had been making quilts and other textile arts since the 1950s, published *Quilts and Coverlets: A Contemporary Approach* in 1970. The first important book on quiltmaking in a contemporary vein, it was illustrated with many of the author's and other quilt artists' designs.[11] In 1973, Michael James earned an M.F.A. in painting from the Rochester Institute of Technology and shortly thereafter turned to quiltmaking as his artistic medium of choice. Exposed to Amish quilts through a public lecture by Holstein, James began to experiment with an Amish color palette. His 1975 quilt *Bedloe's Island Pavement* married the aesthetics of Mondrian with those of an Amish quilter.[12] His work also served as a reminder that the language of quilts was not, in fact, simply a female idiom (fig. 1, plate 48).[13]

Fig. 1. Suspended Animation. Michael James (1949–). Somerset Village, Massachusetts, 1992. Pieced and machine-quilted cottons, 90" × 90". IQSC 1997.007.1098.

In California in the 1970s, painter Miriam Schapiro abandoned pigment in favor of the materials of women's lives. She and Judy Chicago created *Doll House* as part of the Feminist Art Program at the California Institute of the Arts in 1971–72. In subsequent works like *Lady Gengi's Maze* (1972), *Anatomy of a Kimono* (1976), and *Mary Cassatt and Me* (1976), she mined the poetics of female domestic iconography, collaging old quilt squares, handkerchiefs, and other fabrics into her works in order to "redress the trivialization of women's experience."[14]

All these currents swirled simultaneously, making waves in the world of art collectors, in the world of studio artists, and in the world of art historians and scholars of Women's Studies like me, a young Yale graduate student at the time. Most importantly, these waves eddied and crashed in the world of ordinary American women who chose this moment to celebrate their female artistic heritage by turning their creative energies to the making of quilts. They gave rise to an artistic and economic phenomenon of astonishing proportions that has continued unabated into the twenty-first century.[15]

As so often happens in the cultural arena, a movement that imagined itself as entirely original was in fact replaying and expanding on similar impulses of a prior generation. Many decades before, an American interest in the Colonial Revival (starting around the time of the American centennial in 1876 and continuing into the 1930s) led museums, collectors, and the general public to reexamine the furniture, samplers, quilts, and other folk arts that were part of the legacy of a "simpler" past. Like the Arts and Crafts movement, this was in part a reaction to the industrial revolution, in the wake of which many urban people felt disenfranchised from the pastoral, the handmade, the domestic, and the "authentic."[16]

American women's needlework was displayed at the Centennial Exposition in Philadelphia in the "Exhibition of Antique Relics." European ideas about the value of needlework first came to America through William Morris and the Arts and Craft movement. In England, the Royal School of Art Needlework had been founded in 1872, and their work, also displayed at the 1876 Centennial Exposition, contributed to the fad for richly embroidered embellishment on Crazy quilts, which were also influenced by the remarkable displays at the Japanese Pavilion at the Exposition.[17]

By the end of the Colonial Revival era, in the period from 1913 to the 1930s, many artists and art collectors, tired of an emphasis on European modernism, turned to quilts and other folk arts as exemplars of all that was best about America and the vitality of the country's artistic traditions. In Ogunquit, Maine, in 1913, a group of artists established the Ogunquit School of Painting and Sculpture. They became well known for their curious practice of decorating their little fishing-shack painting studios along Perkins Cove with weathervanes, textiles, and other inexpensive vernacular objects, finding in these simple and expressive works models for their own modernist explorations.[18] One factor in the enthusiasm for folk arts in the 1920s and 1930s was a belief in the essential "Americanness" of these objects. Europe, weakened after the devastation of World War I, seemed to Americans to be suffering from cultural decline. American artists and intellectuals were in search of a homegrown idiom. As art critic Thomas Craven wrote, "I have exhorted our artists to remain at home in a familiar land, to enter into strong nativist tendencies, to have done with alien cultural fetishes."[19]

John Cotton Dana of the Newark Museum had set the stage for a new way of looking at the American past in his 1914 book, *American Art*, by suggesting that a panoply of expressive forms could be called "American art." An abbreviated version of his list includes "cutlery, table linen, . . . houses, churches, banks, . . . signs and posters; lamp posts and fountains; jewelry; silverware; embroidery and ribbons."[20]

In the 1920s, Electra Havemeyer Webb was acquiring the quilts and other folk arts that would, in 1947, become the collection of the Shelburne Museum in Vermont. By 1929, Henry Ford's museum complex in Dearborn, Michigan, opened. Devoted to the history of American culture, art, and industry, it too came to house a significant collection of quilts. That same year, Edith Halpert opened the American Folk Art Gallery in New York City, which she described as "carrying works chosen because of their definite relationship to vital elements in contemporary American art." Just how vital that relationship was is evident in a glance at the efforts of sculptor Elie Nadelman, a Polish émigré who, with his wealthy American wife, accumulated over fifteen thousand pieces of folk art by the 1930s, a collection later dispersed to many museums.[21]

Within this circle of artists and wealthy collectors, quilts and other folk arts were seen as an art form essentially of the past, but one well worth collecting. The rhetoric of nostalgia for simpler times, when American women made quilts, may have been part of the mythos of quilts for sophisticated artists and collectors, yet in their 1935 book, *The Romance of the Patchwork Quilt*, Carrie Hall and Rose Kretsinger declare that quiltmaking "is occupying the attention of womankind everywhere," and that "the whole country is quilt conscious." Dating the quilt revival to 1915, they claim that "more quilts are being pieced today in the cities and on the farms than at any previous time in the history of America."[22]

In a situation prefiguring the New York art world's love affair with quilts and folk art in the 1970s, metropolitan New York audiences were also inundated by folk art shows in the early 1930s. Most influential was *American Folk Art: the Art of the Common Man in America, 1750–1900*, held at the Museum of Modern Art in 1932, about which a reviewer wrote:

These extraordinary objects. . . . are all alike in springing, untaught and carefree, from a culture that was in the making. . . . It is impossible to regard them . . . without a nostalgic yearning for the beautiful simple life that is no more. Artists who find themselves growing mannered or stale will always be able to renew their appetite for expression by returning to the example of these early pioneers, and for that reason it becomes necessary for our museums to take our own primitives as seriously as they already take those of Europe.[23]

Much of the early rhetoric about folk art glorified ordinary working people and the fruits of their hands. Just as the larger discourse on folk traditions was full of language exalting the "naive," the "primitive," and the "untutored," so too were early-twentieth-century texts about quilts full of celebration for the supposedly untutored needlewomen whose work had not been fully appreciated.

Both in the early twentieth century and in the 1970s, needlework and quiltmaking had a great surge in popularity as women looked to artistic genres of the past to make a statement about the present.[24] As we shall see, a couple of the women writing influential works on quilts in the early twentieth century were ardent feminists who believed that the study of women's folk art would illuminate women's history.[25] As outlined above, another generation replayed this in the 1970s, when art world sophisticates, feminists, and ordinary women alike returned to a celebration of quilts as an important American art form. Both of these eras were fundamental in constructing an American quilt narrative that was equal parts mythology and history, fueled by nationalist ideologies and feminist pride.

Myth Making and Quiltmaking: Piecing a History from Scraps

Did you ever think, child, . . . how much piecin' a quilt's like livin' a life? And as for sermons, why, they ain't no better sermon to me than a patchwork quilt, and the doctrines is right there a heap plainr'n they are in the catechism.

—*"Aunt Jane," in Eliza Calvert Hall, Aunt Jane of Kentucky (1907)*

Quilts are iconic in our American heritage precisely because they represent so many things to so many people. As symbolic objects, quilts give shape to an idealized story about American ingenuity and self-sufficiency in general, and female frugality, secrecy, originality, and artistry in particular. Historian David Lowenthal has observed that "the pasts we alter or invent are as consequential as those we try to preserve."[26] In this section, I shall examine some of the often-told tales about quilts and their makers, in order to unpack the mythic history of quilts.

The legacy of the Colonial Revival in America was an idealized, simplistic story of quilts in which the central figure was an illustrious craftswoman "making do" with scraps. In the early twentieth century, little was known about the actual history of quilts. The earliest authors of book-length quilt histories, Marie Webster (1915), Ruth Finley (1929), and Carrie Hall and Rose Kretzinger (1935), had little to rely on in terms of accurate documentation.[27] They conducted their own original research, made their own collections, and relied on the popular folklore of the day about quilts.

One of the sources on which these authors relied was *Aunt Jane of Kentucky*.[28] Far too often in quilt literature, "Aunt Jane" has been quoted as if she were an ethnographic informant rather than a fictional character devised by Eliza Calvert Hall (1856–1935), an activist for women's rights and a creative writer who lived most of her life in Bowling Green, Kentucky, as the wife of a college professor. Although she published suffragist essays, she is remembered today solely for her best-selling book *Aunt Jane of Kentucky* (1907), an anthology of short stories that had previously appeared in national magazines.[29]

The eponymous heroine of the book is an unmarried eighty-year-old rural elder whose homespun feminism encompasses Protestant theology, the inequality of gender relations, the problems of patriarchal inheritance laws, and the ennobled domestic sphere of women's gardens and needlework. In the most often quoted passage, which appears as this section's epigraph, Aunt Jane rhetorically asks the young female narrator to learn her elder's wisdom. Aunt Jane continues:

Many a time I've set and listened to Parson Page preachin' about predestination and free-will, and I've said to myself, "Well, I ain't never been through Centre College up at Danville, but if I could jest git up in the pulpit with one of my quilts, I could make it a heap plainer to folks than parson's makin' it with all his big words." You see, you start out with jest so much caliker [i.e., calico]; you don't go to the store and pick it out and buy it, but the neighbors will give you a piece here and a piece there, and you'll have a piece left every time you cut out a dress, and you take jest what happens to come. And that's like predestination. But when it comes to the cuttin' out, why, you're free to choose your own pattern. You can give the same kind o' pieces to two persons, and one'll make a "nine-patch" and one'll make a "wild goose chase," and there'll be two quilts made out o' the same kind o' pieces, and jest as different as they can be. And that is jest the way with livin'. The Lord sends us the pieces, but we can cut 'em and put 'em together pretty much to suit ourselves, and there's a heap more in the cuttin' out and the sewin' than there is in the caliker.[30]

Aunt Jane characterizes her quilts as her diaries:

You see, some folks has albums to put folks' pictures in to remember 'em by, and some folks has a book and writes down the things that happen every day so they won't forgit 'em; but, honey, these quilts is my albums and my di'ries, and whenever the weather's bad and I can't git out to see folks, I jest spread out my quilts and look at 'em and study over 'em and it's jest like goin' back fifty or sixty years and livin' my life over agin.[31]

Occasionally the unnamed young narrator of *Aunt Jane of Kentucky* pauses to add her own more sophisticated reflections, in case the reader has missed Aunt Jane's didactic points:

I looked again at the heap of quilts. An hour ago they had been patchwork, and nothing more. But now! The old woman's words had wrought a transformation in the homely mass of calico and silk and worsted. Patchwork? Ah, no! It was memory, imagination, history, biography, joy, sorrow, philosophy, religion, romance, realism, life, love, and death; and over all, like a halo, the love of the artist for his work and the soul's longing for earthly immortality.[32]

In the early twentieth century, the belief that quilts were generally composed of scraps and reused fabrics took hold. Writing in 1915 of pre–revolutionary era quilts (a genre for which we actually have almost no evidence),[33] Marie Webster observed, "After these gay and costly fabrics had served their time as wearing apparel, they were carefully preserved and made over into useful articles for the household."[34] Ruth Finley wrote that a quilt originated in "the grimness of economic need."[35] Hall and Kretsinger took up this theme as well: "[T]he pieced quilt . . . was familiar to most households where economy was a necessity as it was created of scrap material not otherwise of use"; "in mansion house or frontier cabin, every scrap was saved for quiltmaking."[36]

The rhetoric of economy and frugality saturates these early texts.[37] Oddly, the quilts that the authors illustrate seldom support this position. The mythic dimension of

quilts held sway to such an extent that the legend tenaciously persisted, even in the face of all material evidence to the contrary. The vast number of extant nineteenth-century quilts are clearly made of new materials, as shall be discussed more fully in the next section of this essay. Some fabrics were purchased expressly for quiltmaking, while others were pieces of new dressmaking materials.

In the letters she wrote to her family in Vermont, Ellen Spaulding Reed (a New Englander who settled in Wisconsin with her husband in the mid-nineteenth century) repeatedly mentions this use of new fabric. For example, on October 21, 1855, she wrote to her mother: "I have cut and made Willard a pair of pants, and made me a dress, and I will send you a piece."[38] This sending of pieces of new fabric to beloved female friends and relatives was common in the nineteenth century and continues today. Elaine Hedges has documented the fabric that traveled in the mail between Connecticut, New York, Wisconsin, and Nebraska in the 1850s, as Hannah Shaw and her daughters kept in touch by the exchange of such mementos: "I will send you some pieces of my new dresses for patchwork," and "Hear are some peaces for Mary's quilt."[39]

Many nineteenth-century quilts show strong evidence of being made from new fabric probably purchased for that express purpose. It is customary to assume that this reflects the maker's prosperity, but an occasional anecdote reveals the sacrifices a dedicated artist of lesser means made in pursuit of her art. Lucyle Jewett recalled a story about her mother, Della Smith Jewett, and the making of a quilt in the late nineteenth century:

It was material to be used for a new dress, and in those early days, the girls had only one new dress a year, so it was important. But Mamma wanted to use her material to join her quilt, and told Grandma Smith so. "If thee uses thy material to join thy quilt," said Grandma, "thee'll have to wear thy old dress again this year." She left it to Mamma to decide, and stated the consequences. Mamma thought it over and used the material for her quilt and wore last year's dress again that year.[40]

A rural twentieth-century Texas quiltmaker of modest means related another story that sheds light on the use of new materials in quilts. She recalled an instance from her youth in the early twentieth century, when she and her mother traveled to the dry goods store to buy some fabric for her hope chest quilts:

We had picked three pieces of remnant blue and was just fingerin' some red calico. We was jest plannin' on enough for the middle squares from that.

Just then Papa come in behind us and I guess he saw us

lookin'. He just walked right past us like he wasn't with us, right up to the clerk and said, "How much cloth is on that bolt?"

The clerk said, "Twenty yards."

Papa never looked around. He just said, "I'll take it all!"

He picked up that whole bolt of red calico and carried it to the wagon. Mama and me just laughed to beat the band. Twenty yards of red. Can you imagine?[41]

In other instances, individual nineteenth-century quiltmakers had access to a wide range of textiles due to proximity to textile industries, their positions as workers in factories where they were able to buy seconds and sample runs, or membership in a family of textile mill owners or dry goods merchants.[42]

Jonathan Holstein has addressed the "scrap bag myth" of American quilts, ascribing it to an ingrained American preoccupation with a preindustrial golden age of self-reliant ancestors. He points out that

the vast majority of nineteenth-century quilts have backs of whole cloth, new at the time the quilts were made, . . . indicating that material was purchased to make the backs, which normally would not have been seen; if quilts were truly objects in whose formation thrift and utility were the primary motives, the backs would logically have been pieced from scraps left over from home clothes production; and, if the romantic histories were true, of pieces salvaged from worn-out garments. Trust me: there is hardly a quilt maker who ever pieced any part of a quilt from sections of worn-out garments. The finished textiles would not have survived enough washings to justify either the savings on textile costs or the labor involved.[43]

The romanticization of the patchwork quilt and other women's work, like spinning and weaving, was part of a larger discourse about colonial household economies that historian Laurel Thatcher Ulrich has called "one of the central myths of American history." Moreover, she argues,

The mythology of household production gave something to everyone. For sentimentalists, spinning and weaving represented the centrality of home and family, for evolutionists the triumph of civilization over savagery, for craft revivalists the harmony of labor and art, for feminists women's untapped productive power, and for antimodernists the virtues of a bygone age. Americans expressed these ideas in local and national celebrations, in family festivals, and in craft demonstrations.[44]

Virginia Gunn has noted that the scrap bag myth became especially entrenched during the Great Depression: "the tales of early colonial foremothers helping to establish a foothold in a new country by recycling worn

textiles into beautiful quilts sustained women making scrap quilts in hard times."[45] Indeed, the twentieth-century reality of rural quilters and the legacy of depression-era quilters has helped entrench the scrap bag myth. For these women, it is no myth, of course. Nonetheless, the idea that most quilts were made from scraps and recycled materials does not hold true for most nineteenth-century quilts in museums and private collections. Examination of these quilts only strengthens our belief that these are deliberate artistic constructions, composed of the finest materials within the artists' means. Some are profligate in their use of costly silks (plates 14, 18); others clearly show that the maker was not working out of any scrap bag, but from the latest bolts available at the dry goods store (plates 4, 6, 7, 10, 15). While of course scrap quilts were made, and washed, and used up, the use of scraps was neither the defining feature nor the motivating factor in this art form, especially in the nineteenth century.

Just as popular literature like *Aunt Jane of Kentucky* lodged an idea of the romance of the rural quilter in the minds of an early-twentieth-century audience, another influential book, this one nonfiction, captivated modern women's imaginations in the 1970s. To write *The Quilters: Women and Domestic Art, an Oral History,* two Texas women, Patricia Cooper and Norma Bradley Buford, set off in search of the quilt heritage of Texas and New Mexico, interviewing elderly rural woman (average age seventy-three) about their lives as quilters. The resulting book, an engaging and eloquent collage of first-person narratives, went through multiple editions, has been used as a textbook in Women's Studies and American Studies courses, and was transformed into a stage play that has toured the country since 1982.[46]

Cooper and Buford's book (and the play based on it) accurately profiles the very real histories and concerns of one type of American quilter—the rural one of modest means. While not questioning its accuracy or its excellence, I'd like to point out that this book's enthusiastic reception reflects the continuation of that very deep American hunger for narratives about the poetry of poverty, the pride in making-do, and the homespun wisdom of the uneducated. Echoes of Aunt Jane can be heard in the words of one Texas quilter:

You can't always change things. Sometimes you don't have no control over the way things go. Hail ruins the crops or fire burns you out. And then you're just given so much to work with in a life and you have to do the best you can with what you got. That's what piecing is. The materials is passed on to you or is all you can afford to buy . . . that's just what's given to you. Your fate. But the way you put them together is your business. You can put them in any order you like. Piecing is orderly. First you cut the pieces, then you arrange your pieces just like you want them. I build up the blocks and then put all the blocks together and arrange them, then I strip and post to hold them together . . . and finally I bind them all around and you got the whole thing made up. Finished.[47]

The latest voice feeding this hunger for the homespun narrative is the plainspoken African American quilter of the rural South, who gives voice to a different segment of the oppressed American spirit and receives a warm welcome in books for adults and for children.[48] I shall address this issue further, below.

Both at the beginning of the twentieth century and at the end, we find in the discourse on quilts a use of language that seeks to ennoble the women who make them. This is understandable, given how often women's work is ignored or trivialized, both in the popular imagination and in the scholarly literature. Nonetheless, it is worthwhile to follow this central discursive thread to see how it unspools.

As mentioned previously, several early writers on quilts were feminists, who display a gendered pride in this female artistic legacy. Eliza Hall, author of *Aunt Jane of Kentucky*, wrote suffragist essays; Ruth Finley, author of *Old Patchwork Quilts and the Women Who Made Them*, was an investigative reporter who wrote about the tough circumstances in which working women labored.[49] It is no surprise, then, that women's artistry should sometimes be celebrated in terms of gender partisanship in the early quilt books. Ruth Finley talks about quilt designs as stepping "fully into the realm of plane geometry. Ninety-nine percent of all pieced quilts represent the working out of geometrical designs, often so intricate that their effective handling reflects most creditably on the supposedly nonmathematical sex."[50] Carrie Hall concurs: "Who shall say that woman's mind is inferior to man's, when, with no knowledge of mathematics, these women worked out geometric designs so intricate, and co-relate each patch to all others in the block?"[51]

Much of the language of feminist writing of the 1970s to the 1990s likewise sought to ennoble and reclaim the artistic work of women who, in the words of Judy Chicago, had been "written out of history."[52] One aspect of this post-1970 feminist reclamation project was the notion that quilts represented a counter-discourse, a covert female language that said the unsayable in a form of silent public oratory. As Patricia Mainardi wrote,

In designing their quilts, women not only made beautiful and functional objects, but expressed their own convictions on a wide variety of subjects in a language for the most part comprehensible only to other women. In a sense, this was a "secret language" among women, for as the story goes, there was more than one man of Tory political persuasion who slept unknowingly under his wife's Whig Rose quilt.[53]

The latest trend in the mythologizing of quilts is the Afrocentric discourse that regards quilts as a secret language that can be unlocked through the revealing of the codes to a worthy acolyte, or a language in which traces of West and Central African secret scripts survive.[54] Some of these theories were promulgated by scholars trained in African art history, who sought evidence to support a thesis about trans-Atlantic survivals of African traditions.[55] Such survivals, documented in African American music and language,[56] seem less persuasive in some realms of the visual arts, like quilts, in which the surviving material evidence suggests local, unracialized sources for imagery, patterns, and techniques. Some of the creative transmuting of traditional quilt patterns engaged in by twentieth-century African American women of the rural South is well documented and remarkably analogous to the creative distortions prized in black music and language (plate 45). In my opinion, however, the assertions of secret languages and symbols that bear an isomorphic relationship to Central and West African symbol systems is insupportable by the standards of scholarly proof.

The most recent permutation of this, which would seem hardly worth mentioning if it had not been embraced so wholeheartedly by the American public, is put forth in the book *Hidden in Plain View: The Secret Story of Quilts and the Underground Railroad*. The authors assert that a secret "Underground Railroad Quilt Code" was revealed when writer Jacqueline Tobin met quilter Ozella McDaniel Williams in the Old Marketplace in Charleston, South Carolina. Williams told Tobin the following (each italicized term is a quilt block pattern):

The *monkey wrench* turns the *wagon wheel* toward Canada on a *bear's paw* trail to the *crossroads*. Once they got to the *crossroads*, they dug a *log cabin* on the ground. *Shoofly* told them to dress up in cotton and satin *bow ties* and go to the cathedral church, get married and exchange *double wedding rings*. *Flying geese* stay on the *drunkard's path* and follow the *stars*.[57]

The authors purport to unlock the meaning of this with a remarkable mishmash of undigested historical data on African textiles, secret societies, and slave routes. They assert that quilts were literal maps to freedom. Impeccable nineteenth-century firsthand sources like Frederick Douglass and Harriet Tubman show that slave songs could indeed be used to transmit secret information about escape from bondage (and Tobin and Dobard do cite these sources); moreover, it is perfectly plausible to imagine quilts hung on a line to signal safety, danger, or some other simple telegraphic message. But it defies reason to consider the stitches and knots on a tied quilt as "a kind of Morse Code in thread," or a two-inch tied grid as standing for increments of five to ten miles, "the approximate distance that could be traveled by a slave in one day," or the display of a Monkey Wrench pattern as a signal to "gather all the tools."[58] As one critic has pointed out, the fact that the tool we call a monkey wrench was only invented about 1850 makes it unlikely to have been an "honored tool" used by African blacksmiths before arrival on slave ships, as the authors assert.[59] This romantic fairy tale has proved so compelling to the public that it has already become entrenched as historical fact and is taught in grade school workshops.

This looks like a recapitulation in grander, racial terms of the feminist mythologizing of quilts that occurred in the 1970s and 1980s. Too often, claims of influence or continuity from an African past are made with little regard for verifiable data to support such sweeping generalizations. Most quilt scholars recognize, for example, that Harriet Powers's Bible quilts (fig. 12) have more in common with the great tradition of American appliqué quilts made all over the United States during the nineteenth century than with supposedly ancestral African traditions greatly removed in time and space, such as appliqué flags made by the Fon people of West Africa.[60]

The more we know about quilts and nineteenth-century history, the more the so-called secret discourse of quilts seems instead to be a widely shared visual language that crossed many media, was used by both genders and diverse races, and was a constituent part of a visual culture encompassing game boards, the iconography of fraternal organizations, Christian symbols, Pennsylvania Dutch *fraktur* painting, weaving, needlework, Staffordshire plates, printed textiles, and the paintings of itinerant artists, among other things (as discussed later in this essay and in the catalogue entries themselves). Some aspects of quilt iconography may have been purely idiosyncratic or autobiographical, but a comparison of mid-nineteenth-century coverlets woven by male professionals and the quilts pieced and appliquéd by middle-class women of the same era, for example, reveals a great crossover of for-

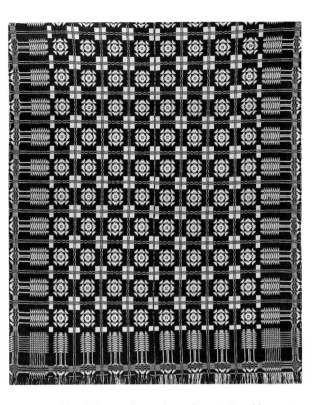

Fig. 2. Double Cloth Coverlet. Maker unknown. Possibly New York, ca. 1825. Cotton and wool, 91″ × 75″. Metropolitan Museum of Art, New York, 1984.330.1.

mal and stylistic elements. I shall examine this in some detail to highlight just one aspect of this widely shared nineteenth-century visual language.

No one has yet rigorously examined the relationships between quilts and woven coverlets.[61] There are documented instances of female textile artists who worked in both mediums, and surely there were many families in which the wives and daughters of professional male weavers were quilters.[62] By the early nineteenth century, American coverlet weavers were creating textiles on multi-harness looms with imagery that looks remarkably like geometric pieced quilts of repeating block designs (fig. 2). Although structurally very different from pieced quilts, coverlets woven on pre-Jacquard looms also rely on a rectilinear design format. Patterns are generally composed of blocks of various sizes and proportions, usually in a two-color scheme. The pattern in figure 2, called Snowflake and Pine Tree, was common to many weavers' workshops and dates back to early-eighteenth-century weavers' pattern books in Germany.[63] (Indeed, many weavers in the United States were German immigrants.) Such coverlets were widely marketed across the United States in the first half of the nineteenth century.

Might quilters have gotten the idea of appliqué pine tree borders from such textiles? One Double Irish Chain quilt with a pine tree border was made in 1854 by Harriet Spicer, a New York quilter who was herself a weaver.[64] Many coverlets are patterned in geometric designs similar to those used in pieced quilts—variants of Four Patch, Nine Patch, Irish Chain, and others, which usually had different names in the weaver's lexicon. In patchwork, of course, the maker readily experimented with color, while most early-nineteenth-century weavings were done in two or three colors.

After 1825, the multiharness Jacquard loom, which could create convincing curved lines and so allowed for an intricate figural repertoire, was introduced to the United States. Between 1825 and the Civil War, there was an explosion of fine coverlets woven by many independent entrepreneurs in New York, Pennsylvania, New Jersey, Ohio, and elsewhere. These textiles often featured central repeating floral designs and a wide array of border patterns, ranging from more naturalistic trees than the earlier double-weave pine trees, to fences, houses, animals, birds, and calligraphic elements. Many motifs, like those in quilts, occurred in the popular iconography of folk painting and carving, embroidery, carpets, fabric prints, and wallpaper.

These highly sought-after "fancy coverlets" were custom produced for a particular client, whose name was often woven into the border (fig. 3).[65] The example illustrated here, made in 1834 by David Haring of Bergen County, New Jersey, for Sarah Ann Outwater, features stars, lush floral motifs, birds, garlands, and other imagery that pervades nineteenth-century appliqué quilts too. Could the woven names of maker and buyer have influenced some women to emblazon more boldly their own names on appliqué and piecework in the mid-nineteenth century? Indeed, could Jacquard coverlets have been a design model for appliqué quilts in general? As Ricky Clark has observed, Jacquard coverlets often consist of

a field of repeated blocks surrounded by a related border. The field patterns are botanical, conventionalized, and radially symmetrical, aligned along vertical, horizontal, and diagonal axes. The field often includes a secondary pattern, as is true of some quilts. . . . Virtually every design structure in classic floral quilts is also found in Jacquard coverlets.[66]

The next two sections of this essay investigate the aesthetics and social history of the appliqué quilt and the pieced quilt, in order to highlight the creative contri-

Fig. 3. Coverlet made for Sarah Ann Outwater. David Daniel Haring (1800–1889). New Jersey, 1834. Cotton and wool, 98 1/2" × 75". Metropolitan Museum of Art, New York, 1988.127.

butions of women to nineteenth-century visual culture and to demonstrate that the quilt aesthetic was one of constant innovation and experimentation, constant openness to new materials and ideas. Indeed, nineteenth-century quiltmakers claimed a greater artistic freedom for themselves than we have given them credit for. It is not my intention to recap within this brief essay the full history of American quilts, which has been carried out so ably elsewhere.[67] I shall make only a few remarks on the tradition within which women were innovating at the beginning of the nineteenth century, before turning my attention to selected examples of their innovations.

Geometric pieced quilts—the kind that most people visualize when they think of an American quilt—afford a nearly limitless range of design possibilities. Yet they tell only part of the story of nineteenth-century women's artistic creativity. Even wilder in design and conception, perhaps, were many of the appliqué quilts made by women who often chose this format to chronicle a personal iconography.

Chronicles in Cloth: Appliqué and Originality

To me it is a precious reliquary of past treasures, a store-house of valuables, . . . a herbarium of withered flowers, a bound volume of hieroglyphics, each of which is a key to some painful or pleasant remembrance.

—*"Annette" in The Lowell Offering (1845)*

Late-eighteenth-century quilts were often whole-cloth quilts of solid colors, in which fine hand-quilting provided the only embellishment, or else "palampores," bed-coverings of fine painted and printed cottons from India (or replicas of such cloth manufactured in Europe), which were backed and hand quilted.[68] By the end of the eighteenth century, women began to fashion central medallions from these high-quality imported fabrics. Called *broderie perse* or cut-out chintz appliqué, this technique of snipping designs from printed fabric and appliquéing them onto a plain fabric ground was an innovative yet less costly way of mimicking an expensive palampore. Sometimes appliquéd flowers, trees, birds, and other imagery cut from European or Indian chintz were mixed with elaborate pieced borders, usually of less costly cloth. This central medallion style (fig. 4) continued into the 1830s, and sometimes beyond. Pieced blocks generally served as a series of enframing borders.

Fig. 4. Central Medallion Chintz Cut-out Quilt. Maker unknown. Probably New England, ca. 1830. Cottons, 107 1/2" × 97 1/2". IQSC 1997.007.0272.

In the nineteenth century, appliqué work was often called "laid work," since fabric shapes were laid atop other fabrics and stitched down, rather than pieced side by side. The appliqué quilt was an opportunity for the textile artist to conceive of her quilt as a canvas onto which she could stitch an ambitious pictorial composition without being bound by the geometric structure of piecework. The elegant and well-known Baltimore Album style of quilt is considered by some to be the epitome of the quilter's art, because of its meticulous hand-stitching and ambitious iconographic program. One of the great regional innovations of nineteenth-century needlework, these laborious works of art—layered, appliquéd, embroidered, and stuffed—seem to have developed as an ingenious way to replicate the appearance of fine imported pictorial chintz using less costly fabrics.[69] The Baltimore Album style took hold in Maryland and Pennsylvania in the mid-1840s. Concurrently, a fad for red and green appliqué quilts developed in the mid-Atlantic region and spread west with migrating settlers. Many red and green quilts were masterpieces of fine needlework, with regular, repeating symmetrical patterns (plate 9). Others are far more idiosyncratic, with unique pictorial narratives or unusual configurations of folk art images (plates 13, 17).[70]

The popularity of and acclaim for the Baltimore Album quilt in the years from 1845 to 1852 may have helped promote the more personalized and idiosyncratic style of pictorial appliqué that was especially popular from the 1850s to the 1870s. Some of these were true album quilts—composed of blocks stitched by a variety of hands, often as a presentation piece for a respected teacher or minister, or a beloved friend departing for westward settlement.[71] Others were more like pictorial autobiographies, presenting themes important to the maker's life and times, as discussed below.

But the roots of these pictorial quilts are far older than the midcentury Baltimore Albums. There are occasional early-nineteenth-century quilts in which the maker has far exceeded the boundaries of conventional style. In 1803, Sarah Furman Warner Williams of New York made an extraordinary pictorial coverlet for her cousin's marriage. She took the conventions of cut-out chintz work in a new direction, depicting an oversize vase of lush flowers flanked by trees in which huge birds roost.[72] Humans and animals frolic in a landscape beneath these trees. Williams's work is more akin to the delicate embroidery popular in her youth than it is to other conventional quilts of the period.

Also inspired by Indian palampores is a pieced and appliquéd counterpane made by Ann Robinson, dated

"Oct 1, 1813 . . . Finished January 27th 1814" (fig. 5). The imagery may be entirely conventional, drawn as it is from Indian bedcoverings, imported chintzes, and needlework samplers. But the artist has composed all of these images into a riotous pictorial scene of great ingenuity. As the nineteenth century progressed, such impulses would become more common and the results even more strikingly original. While these unique appliqués may have been a proportionally small number of the quilts made in the nineteenth century, their originality is remarkable and their influence extends even to the present.

Fig. 5. *Appliqué and Pieced Counterpane. Ann Robinson (dates unknown). Possibly Connecticut, 1814. Cotton and linen, 100" × 97". Shelburne Museum, Shelburne, Vermont, 10–140.*

In the 1830s, Hannah Stockton Stiles of New Jersey enlivened her chintz and calico Tree of Life (a common central motif on quilts since the late eighteenth century) by encircling it with scenes of maritime trade and village activity, giving rise to the title the Trade and Commerce Quilt (fig. 6).[73] Some of the figures are a scant four inches tall, yet the artist has embroidered their facial features and many minute details. She has exploded the notion of a regular, repeating floral border, turning it into a seascape with thirteen large vessels of diverse types, plus several smaller ones. This in turn is surrounded by a border depicting river-port and town life. At the bottom are men and women dressed in fashionable calicoes. On the sides, Stockton appliquéd genre scenes, including a storehouse, grocery, bathhouse, and tavern, and a milkmaid. Unlike

many works of appliqué, especially the meticulously stitched Baltimore Album quilts, the Trade and Commerce Quilt is not a showcase for meticulous needlework. Originality of design and communication of a unique vision were more important to Hannah Stockton Stiles.

Fig. 6. *Trade and Commerce Quilt. Hannah Stockton Stiles (1790–1864). Philadelphia, ca. 1830. Appliquéd and embroidered cottons, 105" × 89". Fenimore Art Museum, Cooperstown, New York, N222.56.*

Numerous original pictorial compositions, some combining piecework and appliqué, have survived from the mid-nineteenth century. In 1843, Elizabeth Roseberry Mitchell of Kentucky devised an ingenious use for a quilt, as both a family record and an object of mourning (fig. 7). She made a pieced quilt in the LeMoyne Star pattern but with an important difference: in the center of the quilt, instead of a larger accent star, she appliquéd a fenced graveyard. A larger fence on the quilt's border echoes this interior enclosure. Although she made this quilt after the deaths of two of her sons, Mitchell clearly envisioned it as a family record—not only of herself, her husband, and their eleven children, but their future families as well. In addition to appliquéing some two dozen coffins (most on the perimeter of her quilt), she hand-stitched the outlines for many more possible coffins along the fencing that borders the quilt. Most have strips of paper or cloth attached to them, labeled with family names. She also embroidered trees and flowering vines around the fencing of the central graveyard, making it a more hospitable place for the coffins that were eventually to be moved there.[74]

Fig. 7. Family Graveyard Quilt. Elizabeth Roseberry Mitchell (1799–1857). Lewis County, Kentucky, ca. 1843. Pieced, appliquéd, and embroidered cottons, 85″ × 81″. Kentucky Historical Society, Frankfort, Kentucky, 59.13.

Some unique pictorial appliqués combine conventional floral blocks with original figurative ones. Betsey Haring's 1859 quilt depicts chairs, horses, and carriages, while other notable examples feature such diverse imagery as baskets used in the New Jersey strawberry trade, equestrian figures, circus performers, and famous race horses.[75] The late-eighteenth-century Tree of Life motif, so common in *broderie perse* and seen in freer form in Hannah Stockton Stiles's quilt (fig. 6) takes a new direction in Abby Bell Ross's Garden of Eden quilt of 1874. A naked Adam and Eve cavort in a landscape full of animals, beneath a Tree of Life containing not only the biblical serpent, but some two dozen exotic birds.[76] One fine silk quilt from the 1870s, probably made by an African American, alternates Log Cabin blocks with appliqués of different types of houses and genre scenes of African American people.[77] All of these quilts provided occasions for the creative needlewoman to stitch autobiography, aspiration, and imagination into her work.

Unique pictorial appliqué quilts also provided the opportunity for women to express political sentiments and organizational affiliations. The nineteenth century was the great age of male fraternal organizations. The Freemasons, the International Order of Odd Fellows, the Improved Order of Red Men, and other societies attracted approximately 20–25 percent of the adult male population. Although meant to exclude women and provide socializing opportunities for the male professional classes, some organizations, under pressure from the wives of members, formed women's auxiliaries. The first to do so, in the early 1850s, was the Odd Fellows.[78] Presumably the many appliqué quilts of the second half of the nineteenth century that display the symbols of these fraternal organizations were made by women's auxiliary members.

Charlotte Gardner's unfinished Odd Fellows Appliqué Top (plate 13) combines common features of midcentury appliqué quilts (a predominantly red and green calico color scheme, eagle and oak leaf borders) with imagery specific to the International Order of Odd Fellows, such as the heart in hand, the three linked rings, and the bows and arrows. That her quilt top reflected her own participation in the women's section, called the Rebekah Degree, is indicated by the beehive, crescent moon, and stars, all emblems of that sisterhood. Like much of the imagery on quilts, fraternal order symbols were widespread in nineteenth-century visual culture; they occur on china, embroidered members' aprons, woven coverlets, and commercially printed textiles, even more than on quilts. Of the many nineteenth-century organizations, Masonic and Odd Fellows imagery appears most often on quilts.[79]

Later in the century, many quilted and pieced banners proclaimed women's political sentiments regarding issues of temperance and feminism. One of the most interesting of these is a Crazy quilt made by Mary Willard in 1889 for her daughter Frances's fiftieth birthday. Frances Willard was the first president of the Women's Christian Temperance Union. Her quilt has more than two dozen biblical sentiments embroidered on it, as well as numerous floral patterns.[80] Just as women pieced quilt blocks with names like Whig Rose, Burgoyne Surrounded, and Clay's Choice to express political beliefs or commemorate historical events, so too did they create pictorial documentation of Confederate or Yankee partisanship during the Civil War, or their appreciation for President Lincoln.[81]

Perhaps the finest social document in needlework of the post–Civil War era is Lucinda Ward Honstain's quilt, with the embroidered notation "Done Nov th. 18, 1867" (plate 12). In forty appliquéd blocks, she combined family biography, political commentary, genre scenes, and conventional decorative motifs common to midcentury appliqué quilts. Recent research on this spectacular work of art has elucidated a great deal about the artist and her social milieu, demonstrating the autobiographical nature of many of the scenes.[82]

Fig. 8. Pictorial Album Quilt. Lucinda Ward Honstain (1820–1904). Brooklyn, New York, dated 1867. Detail of plate 12.

The central rectangular block (taking up the size of three squares) may depict Honstain's home in Williamsburg, an area of Brooklyn, New York (fig. 8). The prosperous-looking red brick house with carefully delineated picket fence, American flag, mullioned windows, fruit trees, and domestic animals anchors the scene. Below, an equestrienne figure riding sidesaddle probably represents her daughter Emma, an accomplished horsewoman. To the right is a three-masted ship from the nearby Brooklyn Navy Yard, where Emma's husband's ship had embarked for its Civil War tour of duty. In the second row from the bottom, one of the blocks depicts a man driving a horse-drawn wagon (fig. 9). Embroidered on the side of the wagon is "W. B. Dry Goods," a reference to Ward and Burroughs Dry Goods, Lucinda's brother's firm.

Honstain was avidly interested in the public events of her era, for she commemorated patriotic, military, and political themes and personages, including Jefferson Davis (plate 12, second row, middle). The famous confederate president had been released from prison in 1867—the year she was working on the quilt—after two years' incarceration for treason. In the third row, left, an eloquent reminder of the result of the Civil War is inscribed in the embroidered message "Master I am free," uttered by a black man facing a white man on horseback (fig. 10). Numerous genre scenes animate the quilt: a washerwoman smoking a pipe next to a hurdy-gurdy man (plate 12, lower right), an African American bootblack (plate 12, bottom row) and ice cream vendor (plate 12, second row, left). Decorative blocks familiar from many midcentury quilts (stars, flowers, baskets, hearts) alternate with more idiosyncratic ones (a fish grill, animal portraits, a bird in a cage).

According to Sara Dillow, the style of appliqué stitch-

Fig. 9. Pictorial Album Quilt. Lucinda Ward Honstain (1820–1904). Brooklyn, New York, dated 1867. Detail of plate 12.

ery differs from block to block in this quilt,[83] suggesting that even if its artistic conception was Lucinda Honstain's alone, she may have had help executing it. Not only was her older sister Sarah a professional dressmaker, but both Lucinda and her daughter were also listed as such in the 1870 census. Presumably Lucinda had worked in her husband's tailoring firm, perhaps even keeping it going while he fought in the war. Between her brother's dry goods firm and her husband's tailor shop, the maker of this quilt clearly had access to a wide range of materials.

Various quilt blocks use techniques of appliqué, reverse appliqué, chain stitch, and other embroidery stitches to emphasize details. While her needleworking skills are superb, Honstain did not seek the crisp perfec-

Fig. 10. Pictorial Album Quilt. Lucinda Ward Honstain (1820–1904). Brooklyn, New York, dated 1867. Detail of plate 12.

tionism of the Baltimore Album style; a freer, folksier effect pervades her work. Though she may have earned her living doing tailoring for others, clearly her love of needlework and her need for personal expression led her to spend many hours making this superlative work of art.

A number of other autobiographical pictorials are known from this era. Most comparable to Honstain's, in its ambitious pictorial program and its combination of autobiographical and genre scenes, is the Burdick-Childs bedcover (1876) in the Shelburne Museum. In thirty-six blocks, its makers commemorate America's centennial and family anecdotes in a snapshot-like style, along with genre and architectural scenes.[84]

In the 1870s and 1880s, more women turned their attention to the making of lavishly embroidered Crazy quilts. Some of these were pictorial, and also had elements of autobiography. On M. M. Hernandred Ricard's quilt, which she titled *My Crazy Dream* (plate 18), a prominent central panel depicts a house with several human figures that might represent her own home and family. She even included a photolithograph of herself (lower right). Leila Utter's Crazy quilt of 1898 contains forty-one portraits of individuals young and old, each wearing distinctive dress.[85] Celestine Bacheller's Crazy quilt contains nine blocks of cityscapes and seascapes depicting the area near Lynn, Massachusetts.[86]

Central to the vitality of American vernacular arts (sometimes called folk or popular arts, for they spring from a personal, community-based impulse for expression rather than from an academic setting where standards of taste and prescribed codes of representation can hamper individuality) is the expression of a unique vision. This singular expression is often given voice through humble means—paper, wood carving, or cloth. All of these appliqué quilts demonstrate such singularity of vision.

Although a small number of nineteenth-century women made professional inroads into such fields as botany and astronomy,[87] much more common were those women who displayed their scientific knowledge— and perhaps even passed it on to others—through the medium of quilts. In 1865, Ernestine Zaumzeil created a unique botanical appliqué in which the vines (more often used as bordering elements on nineteenth-century quilts) take over the entire design field. A half-dozen recognizable varieties of plants are depicted, each carefully delineated as to leaf shape and size.[88] Mennonite quilter Harriet Miller Carpenter, with design input from her husband, created a series of astronomical quilts in the 1880s and 1890s for her grandchildren (plate 20). Ellen Harding Baker is said to have used her appliquéd and embroidered Solar System Quilt (1876) as a visual aid when she gave lectures in Iowa.[89]

Other women expressed their vision of modernity through this old-fashioned medium. Like Hannah Stockton Stiles, Elizabeth Mitchell, and Lucinda Honstain before her, "E.R." of Indiana used cloth to bring to fruition her vision of the centrality of the railroad in late-nineteenth-century life (fig. 11). In a simple dark blue calico appliquéd to white (with a deft enlivening touch of red in the U.S. flag and the female figure's accessories at the bottom), she depicts municipal buildings enclosed within train tracks that border all four sides of the quilt. Two trains, with curly embroidered smoke flowing from their stacks, ride the tracks. This is a vernacular snapshot of the marvels of late-nineteenth-century industry, much as Hannah Stockton Stiles's quilt of half a century earlier celebrated the importance of shipping to the early-nineteenth-century American economy.

African American quilter Harriet Powers's two Bible quilts, one in the Smithsonian (ca. 1886) and the other in the Museum of Fine Arts, Boston (ca. 1895; fig. 12), are among the quilts most widely illustrated and discussed in the last quarter century of scholarship.[90] A seamstress who was born a slave in 1837, Powers completed her two masterworks in her late middle age, using a range of typical fabrics of the time. Most of the work was done by machine. The numerous stars that appear in almost

Fig. 11. Railroad Quilt. Maker unknown ("E.R."). Indiana, 1888. Appliquéd cottons, 71" × 73". Museum of Fine Arts, Boston, 2000.672.

every block of the quilt were individually pieced and inset within the ground cloth using an ingenious style of reverse appliqué (which was probably a neater alternative to turning under the messy edges formed by numerous tiny pieces). The larger figures were machine appliquéd in a free-spirited manner.

Fig. 12. Bible Quilt. Harriet Powers (1837–1911). Athens, Georgia, ca. 1895. Appliquéd cottons, 69" × 105". Museum of Fine Arts, Boston, 64.619. Bequest of Maxim Karolik.

Powers is more concerned with her message than with delicacy of execution, a trait she shares with Hannah Stockton Stiles (fig. 6). For more than a century now, viewers have been impressed with the eloquence of Powers's artistic vision in what she called "the darling

offspring" of her brain.[91] The quilt depicted in figure 12 is composed of fifteen scenes. Ten of these refer to biblical stories, most from the Old Testament, portraying Adam and Eve, Jonah and the whale, Job, and Moses. Only two images (top right and bottom right) derive from the New Testament: John baptizing Christ, and the Crucifixion.[92] Four scenes depict mysterious weather occurrences, among them Black Friday in 1780, when smoke from forest fires caused the sky to darken, and the meteor storms of 1833 and 1846. A fifth tells the story of an "independent hog that ran 500 miles from Georgia to Virginia," possibly a "scarcely veiled reference to the path of runaway slaves of pre–Civil War days."[93]

Like Harriet Miller Carpenter's *God's Night Time Sky* (plate 20), this quilt probably served didactic purposes. After all, Powers herself called her Smithsonian quilt a "sermon in patchwork"; how better to teach the memorable stories of the Old and New Testaments, as well as illustrate God's mysterious powers (as evidenced by shooting stars and other meteorological anomalies), than through pictorial means? The square directly in the center of the quilt depicts the all-night Leonid meteor shower of November 13, 1833. Dismay is signaled by the raised arms of the figures. Eight chrome yellow stars stand out vividly against the blue background. A large white hand is appliquéd to the upper left corner of this central block. Powers said of this event, "the people were fright and thought that the end of time had come. God's hand staid the stars."[94]

It is a pity that these extraordinary works of American vernacular art are almost never contextualized within the history of American quilting or seen as part of the American appliqué tradition under consideration here. Instead, they have been used to establish links with West African textile traditions that almost certainly have nothing to do with them. Folklorist Gladys-Marie Fry was the first to assert these trans-Atlantic links, in 1976. She concedes briefly that "narrative quilts are distinctly an American art form," but illustrates no examples, going on to devote six paragraphs to the supposed relation of Powers's quilts to the West African tradition of appliqué flags made by Fon men in Dahomey and Akan men in Ghana.[95] Regenia Perry says that "there are apparently no American prototypes for Powers's quilt designs." Instead, "the technique of appliqué designs to illustrate a story is most directly related to similar practices in the People's Republic of Benin" (formerly Dahomey). She pronounces the Powers quilts "without parallel in the history of American quilt art."[96]

I would assert, in contrast, that Harriet Powers is a

quintessential American folk artist, using her talent and ingenuity to express her keen interest in Bible stories and wondrous events from oral history and contemporary times. Though poor, she owned a sewing machine and used it to pursue her craft. Her work is no less American in its conception, its imagery, and its execution, than any other appliqué quilt considered here.

Divorcing these important works of art from their American context does an injustice to Harriet Powers both as a self-motivated artist and as a product of her American heritage—a heritage in which she was a devout Christian who exhibited her quilts at regional fairs and sold them to white buyers who valued their remarkable expressiveness. Her Smithsonian quilt was displayed at the 1886 Cotton Fair in Athens, Georgia, and circumstantial evidence suggests that the quilt now at the Museum of Fine Arts, Boston, was displayed at the 1895 Cotton States and International Exposition in Atlanta.[97] As discussed below, such fairs were important to quilters for their dissemination of ideas and art forms. How much more logical that Powers might have been influenced by the culture in which she lived and worked rather than by the cultural forms of West Africans who might or might not have been her ancestors.[98]

As this section has demonstrated, even a small number of examples reveals the wide range of inventiveness in nineteenth-century appliqué quilts. These pictorial and autobiographical impulses continued in twentieth-century quiltmaking, as shall be discussed below.

"Amusing Labors of the Needle": The Nineteenth-Century Pieced Quilt

Amongst the most amusing labors of the needle, that of patchwork will, by many, be accepted as the first. It offers great variety in its progress, producing many striking effects by means of exercising taste in all its combinations. In fact, this parqueterie *of the work-table requires more of the qualities of the artist than might once have been imagined. It demands a knowledge of the power of form and the value of color.*

—*Godey's Lady's Book* (1860)

To return to the words of Miriam Schapiro that opened this essay, quilts more often represent an "act of pride" than an "act of necessity." This was as true in the eighteenth and nineteenth centuries as today. It was as true of pieced quilts as of appliqué quilts. And as the commen-

tator in the popular magazine *Godey's* fully understood nearly a century and a half ago, quiltmaking has always required "the qualities of the artist."[99]

In 1806, Sarah Snell Bryant of Cummington, Massachusetts, drew a number of patchwork patterns in her diary, several of them demonstrating what a creative designer could do with a simple Nine Patch, if only she varied the size and proportion of the blocks or changed the intervening squares from plain ones to strip-pieced ones (fig. 13). Perhaps she was innovating as she drew; perhaps she was recording for later use a new design she had seen at some recent quilting frolic.

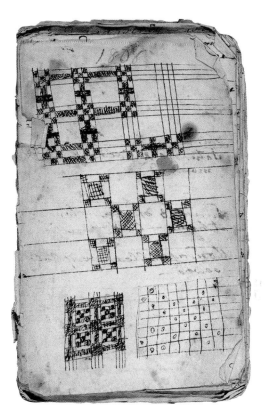

Fig. 13. Patchwork pattern drawn in diary, 1806. Sarah Snell Bryant (1768–1847). By permission of the Houghton Library, Harvard University.

In the early nineteenth century, "quilting frolic" was the name for the communal efforts that later came to be called quilting bees. The British writer Frances Trollope, who lived in Cincinnati during the 1820s, described this event:

The ladies of the Union are great workers, and, among other enterprises of ingenious industry, they frequently fabricate patchwork quilts. When the external composition of one of these is completed, it is usual to call together their neighbours and friends to witness, and assist at the *quilting,* which is the completion of this elaborate work. These assemblings are called "quilting frolics," and they are always solemnized with much good cheer and festivity.[100]

In the early nineteenth century, "bee" was reserved for more mundane tasks, such as the corn husking bee or the fruit paring bee. Frolic, in contrast, suggests the excitement and high spirits present in a gathering of friends and artistic peers. The quilt frolic was the female equivalent of the art academy and the salon (institutions that until the very end of the nineteenth century routinely excluded women, and even then sharply limited their numbers). Women brought their pieced tops to be assembled and hand quilted. These would then be admired, discussed, and used as creative fodder for the next quilts to be made within a community of intimates.

American society in the nineteenth century—more so than in the century before or the century after—was characterized by rigidly maintained gender boundaries. Most women's daily lives were built around female networks. Among their sisters, cousins, and church members, women formed tender and long-lasting friendships. As Nancy Cott elucidates,

A woman discovered among her own sex a world of true peers, in valuing whom she confirmed her own value. In one sense, the female friendships of this period expressed a new individuality on women's part, a willingness and ability to extract themselves from familial definition and to enter into peer relationships as distinct human beings. In another sense, these attachments documented women's construction of a sex-group identity. Women had learned that gender prescribed their talents, needs, outlooks, inclinations; their best chance to escape their stated inferiority in the world of men was on a raft of gender "difference." Female friendships, by upholding such attributes as "heart" as positive qualities, asserted that women were different from but not lesser than—perhaps better than—men.[101]

Quilts demonstrate the power of these female bonds, serving as important markers of emotional intimacy. Women's friendships flourished not only within the home and the church, but within the sewing circle as well, which served as a place of artistic education. At a quilt frolic, one might see the latest fabric purchased in the big city or the most recent clever use of pieced blocks.

As is evident from the illustration in Sarah Snell Bryant's diary, by 1806 women were beginning to make pieced quilts in which various types of blocks, such as

Wild Goose Chase or Four Patch, could be alternated and joined to form a repeating pattern that covered the whole surface of the quilt rather than serving only as enframing borders.[102] This idea spread like wildfire. With its possibility for endless variation and innovation, it became a focus for great artistic activity.

In North America, there are not many examples of true block-style pieced quilts that date unequivocally prior to 1800. The earliest seems to be a quilt in the McCord Museum in Montreal with the year 1726 worked into its design.[103] It is composed of silk, damask, velvet, linen, and cotton. A central eight-pointed star is surrounded by squares of diagonally-quartered and pieced silk. A wide brocaded silk border frames the whole. Another early example is a pieced and appliquéd quilt in the Wadsworth Atheneum in which the central field is composed of squares pieced of four triangles, forming hourglass shapes of light and dark. Around this is a wide border of solid fabric, finely quilted in floral and leaf designs. A central medallion has appliquéd within it, "Anna Tuels her bedquilt given to her by her mother in the year Au 23 1785."[104] In 1793, Mary Johnson surrounded her central medallion of a costly printed Tree of Life with pieced blocks, including Four Patch, Stars, and Flying Geese.[105] In Pittsburgh, N. Virginia Robinson Drum inscribed her name and the date June 16, 1800, on her pieced quilt. In it, the central medallion is a large Variable Star block, surrounded by multiple borders of triangles, hourglasses, rectangles, Flying Geese, and Four Patches.[106]

The shift from quilts in which pieced blocks serve as borders or framing elements to quilts where the interaction of the blocks is itself the focus was a gradual one, occurring during the first third of the nineteenth century. A quilt composed entirely of Flying Geese—no longer just a border, but the sole geometric design in the quilt—illustrates this shift to block style (plate 2). The maker has formed rows of rectangular blocks, set on the diagonal. She has deliberately set off dark triangles against light triangles and oriented her arrow-like "geese" in opposite directions in alternating rows to enliven the design.

Another quilt from the first third of the nineteenth century (plate 1) illustrates the use of pieced squares (a Nine Patch variation called Sheepfold) alternating with One Patch squares of fabric. These strips of Nine Patch and One Patch are then set within large sashes of fine printed fabrics (in substantial enough yardage to indicate that the rose and blue toiles were perhaps purchased specifically for this project). Offsetting these Nine Patches seems to have been a deliberate design ploy. The strips of rose fabric provide the regularity, while the strips of Nine Patch/One Patch offer a slightly offbeat structure for the elegant fabrics.

By midcentury, the pieced block-style had exploded into a storm of visual creativity. Repeating blocks could be as simple as a Four Patch or as complex as the Wild Goose Chase variation in plate 4. Here, each of the sixteen large repeating blocks is painstakingly composed of smaller blocks. Sixty-nine individual pieces make up each large block. The composition gains even more visual interest through the use of pink sashing and wide floral borders. From a distance, the sashing reads as a grid overlaid on the Wild Goose Chase.

I wonder if the use of widely shared patterns, and the supposed conformity to convention that the repeating block style suggests, has blinded some viewers to the staggering creativity that nineteenth-century female artists expressed in their pieced quilts. When artists in other genres (poets, for example, conforming to the unyielding formal conventions of a sonnet or a haiku) work within the "confines" of their chosen medium, it is not judged as a limit on creativity. Why should it be so for the quiltmaker? Indeed, for quilt artist and sonnet writer alike, part of the pleasure of the act lies in the challenge of working both within and against the parameters of the chosen form.

Anyone who has studied nineteenth-century Log Cabin quilts, for example, knows that exact duplication in this pattern is rare. Individual choices in scale, materials, and color palette ensure that each quilt is a unique visual statement. After 1860, more American women began to explore the myriad varieties inherent in its many versions. A limited color selection (fig. 14; plates 11, 23) gives a very different optical effect from a more wild use of fabrics, in which serendipity was part of the design strategy (plate 24).

The interplay of geometrics and optics afforded by the pieced quilt led to experimentation in bold allover designs. Consider the Barn Raising variant of the Log Cabin (fig. 14), in which use of a limited number of fabrics produces a strong design statement, or the crisp geometry of a Four Patch Diamond in the Square (fig. 15), in which the graphic possibilities of a two-color palette (dark blue calico against white) are maximized. In the latter quilt, the artist has successfully played off the different scales of her patterns: the relatively small sawtooth edges that surround each larger square and diamond contrast with the medium-sized diamonds of the border, as well as with the huge central medallion diamond. As in so many mid-nineteenth-century quilts, all of this in turn provides a bold contrast

Fig. 14. *Log Cabin Quilt, Barn Raising Variant. Mennonite; maker unknown. Pennsylvania, ca. 1880. Cottons, 74″ × 74″. IQSC 1997.007.0364.*

to the delicacy of the hand-quilting that covers the surface. Plate 10 provides another example of a strong central geometric design in which small sawtooth edges add a dash of nervous energy to a large-scale motif.

Another complex pattern, the Carpenter's Square (fig. 16) seems to interlace like the Greek fret design used

Fig. 15. *Four Patch Diamond in the Square. Maker unknown. Pennsylvania, ca. 1840–60. Pieced and quilted cottons, 85″ × 85″. IQSC 1997.007.0423.*

in ceramic floor tiles or densely woven carpet patterns. The quilter who made this classic example, in the traditional indigo and white, added three vertical bars at either side for further visual emphasis. In another Carpenter's Square quilt in the IQSC collection, the maker reversed the traditional color scheme, piecing a white geometric design into a dark blue calico background.[107]

Fig. 16. Carpenter's Square. Maker unknown. Indiana, ca. 1890. Pieced and quilted cottons, 79" × 64". IQSC 1997.007.0203.

An expressive yet simple use of pattern as well as color was sometimes the featured aspect of a quilt. The bold optics of the red and white Concentric Squares (plate 30) has a powerful graphic simplicity not seen again in American art until 1960s op art.

In addition to repetitive block designs and experiments in paring down both color and geometry to their simplest elements, the nineteenth-century artist of the pieced quilt also experimented with compositions in which small and large pieces worked together to form central stars (plates 3, 15, 21). It is tempting to call a quilt like the one shown in plate 21 a scrap quilt, since it is composed of more than four thousand one-and-a-quarter-inch squares. But scrutiny of the artist's color and pattern placement reveals extreme deliberation, care, and repetition in her work.

Not all nineteenth-century pieced quilts are rectilinear in design. There is also a great tradition of curved-seam piecework. One of the most celebrated of these patterns is New York Beauty (plate 6). The circles with their sawtooth edges, and the elaboration of that sawtooth design in the sashing, provide one of the great midcentury designs. Robbing Peter to Pay Paul (illustrated here in a later version, plate 25) also experiments with the alternation of

circle and square—a visual conundrum. This example highlights the extravagant color experimentation that occurs in some pieced quilts of the nineteenth century.

The optical effects of all of these quilts are diverse, bold, and wildly experimental. The design achievements of many of them can only be fully appreciated by viewing them from a distance. Yet a number of contemporary feminist authors have criticized the impulse to exhibit quilts on the walls of art museums and to analyze them using the vocabulary of art criticism, especially when the curators and commentators are male.[108] They believe that divorcing quilts from the domestic world of women, within which they were made and used, diminishes rather than enhances our understanding of them. (And indeed displaying *anything* historical in an art museum isolates it from its social context.)

Beverly Gordon, for example, has suggested that a male aesthetic bias has skewed our understanding of quilts. Applying the anthropological notion of proxemics—how people use spatial distance to order their worlds—she proposes that putting quilts on museum walls places them at a "social distance" (four to twelve feet from the viewer) or a "public distance" (twelve to twenty-five feet), which are the proxemic distances in which males are most comfortable. She contends that their female makers intended them to be experienced at an "intimate distance" (from touch to eighteen inches) or a "personal distance" (eighteen inches to four feet), which are female proxemic spaces.[109]

Yet the nineteenth-century makers of Log Cabins (and other quilts that play with our close and far visual apprehension of their surfaces) clearly understood that they were creating patterns that could only be fully appreciated from a social or public distance. So how to explain the fact that although nineteenth-century quilts were principally displayed on beds rather than walls, many of their designs are meant to be appreciated—and can only have been designed—by viewing them from a distance?

Within a household context, quilts would be hung outdoors on a line for airing, providing for the maker and her circle of intimates a long-distance view of their entire design surfaces. Marie Webster noted this in 1915:

To view the real impromptu exhibitions of quilts—for which, by the way, no admission fee is charged—one should drive along any country road on a bright sunny day in early spring. It is this time that the household bedding is given an airing. . . . Of course there is no rivalry between owners, or no unworthy desire to show off, yet, have you ever seen a line full of quilts hung wrong side out?[110]

While few, if any, quilts hung on museum walls in the nineteenth century, many were offered up for public viewing at fund-raising Anti-Slavery Fairs in the 1830s through the 1860s and Sanitary Commission Fairs during the Civil War. Even more widespread were the numerous county, state, and world's fairs held from the early nineteenth century to the present. Barbara Brackman has documented prizes given for quilts as early as 1839 at the Pittsfield, Massachusetts, county fair.[111] Women flocked to these public venues to exhibit their work and to judge the work of their artistic peers, just as male artists flocked to exhibits held at academies, salons, and museums to see their paintings hung on the walls. Many more people visited exhibits at county and state fairs in the nineteenth century than visited museums—hundreds of thousands would attend a large fair like the Ohio State Fair. While fairs continued to have an important role in the twentieth century, new commercial and cultural forces were gathering to shape the making of quilts as that new century began.

Twentieth-Century Quiltmaking and Beyond

Many of us have reinvented ourselves as artists, as art historians, and as women. Taking a new look at history, we have found beauty in unexpected domestic sources. As a result, the sentient, sensual surface of our art has been changed by a profound involvement with the ideas and materiality found in quilts and other useful and decorative arts. The artist-makers of our past have become mentors for women who are now unafraid to see domestic life as a locus for the art-making process.

—Miriam Schapiro, *"Geometry and Flowers"* (1983)

At the beginning of the twentieth century, contradictory messages were transmitted to American women about quilts. In many circles, quilts were passé, old-fashioned, something that grandmothers—not modern young women—made. Yet in 1915, Marie Webster noted a "marked revival of interest in quilts and their making," and in 1935, Carrie Hall commented that more quilts were being made than ever before.[112]

Indeed, the three important quilt books discussed earlier in this essay (Webster's *Quilts: Their Story and How to Make Them*, 1915; Finley's *Old Patchwork Quilts*, 1929; and Hall and Kretsinger's *The Romance of the Patchwork Quilt*, 1935) were not only significant in the construction of quilts as American icons. The designs published in these books also contributed to the literal reconstruction of quilts from the past and the creation of new quilt designs of the present.

Before Webster wrote her book, she achieved fame as a quilt designer. She updated the look of quilts, making them appealing to a new generation. In 1911 and 1912, fourteen of her quilt patterns were published in color in *Ladies Home Journal.* This helped give rise to a modern look: pastel floral appliqué designs in restrained "good taste." Moreover, Webster's work as a designer marked the professionalization of a domestic art.[113] Other designers followed suit; in the 1920s and 1930s, numerous small companies competed for a share of the pattern and kit market. One could buy simple paper patterns, or a sheet of cotton fabric stamped to indicate where to place the appliqué pieces, or even a complete kit with die-cut fabric pieces in a host of "scrap-look" patterns and colors to make one's own Dresden Plate, Double Wedding Ring, or Grandmother's Flower Garden, to name three popular examples.[114] In a situation that prefigured the quilt world of today, early-twentieth-century women could content themselves with working in tried and true patterns established by others, or they could continue to innovate and devise new works of art.

While true creativity in design is harder to document for the first two-thirds of the twentieth century than it is for the nineteenth, there were still some original quiltmakers plying their needles. Early in the century, many rural women continued to piece quilts in the patterns beloved by their mothers and grandmothers: Log Cabin, Bear Paw, and Robbing Peter to Pay Paul among them.[115] Originality of design in geometric piecework in the twentieth century is found most often in the work of Native American, African American, and Amish quilters, as discussed below. The nineteenth-century tradition of original pictorial appliqué has continued unabated into the twentieth century, with extraordinary examples made in all regions.

Some of the twenty-five thousand quilters who submitted their work to Sears Roebuck's Century of Progress Quilt Contest, held in conjunction with the 1933 Chicago World's Fair, chose to create original designs on the Century of Progress theme (although all the top prize winners were either traditional pieced or new floral appliqué designs). Just as nineteenth-century appliqué quilts documented the Philadelphia Centennial and depicted then-modern monuments and buildings, so too did quilt-makers of the 1930s vie with each other to document turbines, telegraphs, airplanes, and the Sears Tower.[116]

Other quilters chose to document history. In 1932, Mildred Jacob Chappell designed her "Settling the West" quilt, depicting the tipis and Conestoga wagons of the old west. Clint Hamilton's appliqué quilt, also on a western theme, depicted Indian villages, a buffalo hunt, the railroad, and other scenes in five horizontal registers.[117]

While inventive quilt design was rather quiescent in the 1940s and 1950s, one art school trained quilter, Bertha Stenge (1891–1957), had what may have been the first solo quilt exhibition at an art museum. The Art Gallery at the University of California–Berkeley exhibited her work in 1941, followed by an exhibit at the Art Institute of Chicago in 1943. Combining traditional piecework on a very small scale and fine appliqué, Stenge was one of the few serious, original quilters to bridge the gap between traditional quilts and the art quilt movement that was to follow.[118]

In the latter part of the twentieth century, there continued to be some vernacular quilters, not linked to the art quilt movement, who made dazzlingly inventive works on a par with the finest nineteenth-century examples of folk appliqué. Laura Lynch (b. 1949), for example, executed panoramic scenes in appliqué that have been exhibited in shows of twentieth-century folk art. Her "textile paintings," as she calls them, depict New York high-rise apartment buildings, parks, and urban beaches, all peopled with scores of small appliquéd and embroidered figures.[119]

Rather than recapping the history of twentieth-century quilting, I shall focus briefly on selected aspects of creativity and originality in twentieth-century quilts, and the ways in which the inherent creativity of many ethnic quilt-making traditions has been documented and appreciated. The late twentieth century has been marked by a deeper understanding and appreciation of ethnic and regional quilting traditions. Hawaiian, Native American, African American, and Amish women made many extraordinary quilts in the twentieth century; these were well documented by the end of the century.[120] The more we understand about the crosscurrents of materials, technologies, meanings, patterns, and imagery in these quilts, the more we can affirm that quiltmaking is indeed the great American art, precisely because it embraces diversity, individuality, and singularity of vision, as well as cooperation, cross-cultural encounter, and democratization. Amish quilters initially learned quilting from their Quaker neighbors and bought fabric from Jewish peddlers. Native

American and Hawaiian quilters adapted and selected those forms that fit comfortably into their cultural categories. African American quilters conjoined their own aesthetic preferences with those of the dominant culture, producing some of the most exuberant designs ever seen in American quilting.

Needlework has long been one mechanism for women of different cultures to share their delight in the pursuit of art. To Victorian missionary women, the sewing circle was also thought of as the place where Christian virtues could be instilled and "savagery" eradicated. Native women, of course, had their own artistic and social agendas. Although both Plains Indian and native Hawaiian women first learned quilting in the nineteenth century, and African American slave women sewed fine textiles on southern plantations, the twentieth-century elaborations of these traditions have received the most attention. I shall briefly examine some aspects of these diverse ethnic traditions.

Plains Indian Quilts.

Taught by nuns and missionaries' wives, Plains Indian women immediately adapted this new art form for their own purposes and to their own aesthetic. While they have used numerous patterns, both traditional and innovative, the eight-pointed star is most representative of twentieth-century quiltmaking among the Lakota and other Plains groups. While their white teachers knew this pattern as Star of Bethlehem or Lone Star, to Plains people the Star quilt rapidly took on indigenous meanings:

The morning star is the first point of light on the horizon, so it's the herald of the new day. The morning star creates the road by which the sun will travel, but then in so doing it extinguishes itself, it's the delineating point that separates dark and the light. So it symbolizes the advent of a new period, a new phase. It's really wonderful to give a star quilt, for me it's giving everybody a fresh start on next year. The morning star represents fulfillment, the release from darkness, ushering in a new day. It's really a wonderful symbol.[121]

The eight-pointed star pattern, composed of hundreds of diamond-shaped patches, has proved to be a limitless format for creativity in the hands of Mennonite, African American, and other women, as seen in plates 3, 15, 28, and 46. The exuberant products of Plains women's needles are no exception. Variations in color, border design, and quilting patterns make each a unique object.[122] Sold to collectors and exhibited at tribal fairs, Plains quilts also maintain an important social function within indigenous societies as a prominent aspect of gift-giving and honoring ceremonies, appearing at powwows, birthdays, graduations, weddings, baby showers, and funerals.[123] Quilts are still displayed during summer Sun Dance ceremonies, as they have been for over a century.[124] In many native communities on the Plains, beadwork and quillwork are much diminished art forms today (compared to what they were in the nineteenth century), but Star quilts are an ever-present symbol of Native women's artistic achievements and ethnic pride. Plains iconography often shines through in Star quilts. The parallelogram structure of each piece is like nineteenth-century wrapped quillwork writ large. The arms of eight-pointed stars are sometimes designed as tipis in a camp circle, while the center of the star may include feather bonnet, buffalo, peace pipe, or eagle designs.[125]

Hawaiian Quilts.

Before contact with outsiders, indigenous women of Polynesia were accustomed to working in two-dimensional soft media such as bark cloth *(tapa)*. Missionary women from New England began to teach quilting as early as 1820.[126] The newcomers chose women of high rank as their apprentices for this new art form, an appropriate action in status-conscious Polynesia. Although the New Englanders may not have grasped the implications of their actions, by introducing needlework to the highest ranking women first, they insured acceptance of quilting among all women. Today, piecework and appliqué are done throughout eastern Polynesia, where each area has a recognizably distinct style. Hawaiian quilt tops are usually constructed of two layers of fabric: a ground of one color and a contrasting cloth for the appliqué (red on white, purple on chrome yellow, dark blue on white, and many other combinations). The cloth to be appliquéd is folded into eighths and cut into elaborate floral or geometric motifs that are then unfolded and painstakingly sewn by hand to the base cloth. This creates an axially symmetrical pattern.

The meticulous appliqué work, which sometimes forms an unbroken design over the entire surface of the textile, is reminiscent of the elegance of some nineteenth-century American appliqué quilts, but the strict two-color format lends a greater sense of abstract rigor to the design. The curvilinear appliqué is accentuated by the quilting stitches, which echo the design in concentric circles about an inch apart. These are referred to as wave patterns, a metaphor befitting a traditionally oceangoing people; the borders are where the waves "go ashore."[127] Throughout Polynesia today, quilts are prestige items, presented at important transitional events such as births, weddings, and funerals.

Amish Quilts.

Art critic Robert Hughes has called Amish quilts "aesthetically radiant objects."[128] To many, they are the quintessential American quilts—simple and bold in their design and color choices, and extravagantly worked in fine hand-quilting stitches (often not apparent in photographs). Paradoxically, Amish quilts are "wild by design" through a process of radical simplification of form paired with an arresting color palette.

An early-twentieth-century Lancaster Amish quilter making a classic Diamond in the Square pattern (plate 33) was drawing on a design prototype that was already more than a century old: the classic center medallion quilt with multiple borders (fig. 4). The Amish quilt's geometry is pared down even further than another of its progenitors, the mid-nineteenth-century Diamond in the Square (fig. 15). The Amish example is the ultimate reduction and distillation of the central medallion style—stripped to its bare bones and then fleshed out through innovative use of color and lavish quilting stitches. This is a circumspect form of innovation, befitting a strict religious order within which worldliness and ostentation are anathema. Amish textile artists delighted in startling color combinations: turquoise and brown; magenta and red; pink and lavender against red and blue-green; vivid blue against black.[129]

In Midwestern Amish quilts, color asymmetry and originality are given freer reign, though still contained within a rigorously geometric format (plate 27). Many Amish quilters of the first half of the twentieth century worked in fine wool fabrics. Jonathan Holstein has pointed out that wool absorbs and reflects light differently than cotton or silk, so that the deep, saturated colors favored by the Amish quilter produce a mysterious luminosity.[130]

Quilts by Mennonite and Church of the Brethren women share some of the aesthetic traits of Amish quilts but are often freer and more inventive. The bold Joseph's Coat pattern, pieced of rainbow-hued stripes, is a Mennonite specialty, as is the Postage Stamp Star, sometimes called the Bowmansville Star because of its singular use in Bowmansville, Pennsylvania (plate 21).[131] Harriet and Uriah Carpenter's astronomical and map quilts are another extraordinary contribution to a turn-of-the-century quilt aesthetic (plate 20).[132]

African American Quilts.

African American women have participated in every quiltmaking trend of the last 150 years; before that they were often accomplished in sewing, as slaves in Southern plantation households.[133] As such, they fashioned clothing and quilts in whatever style was demanded. But in the last twenty-five years, attention paid to African American quilting traditions has been focused principally on quilts made by contemporary working-class women of the rural South.

First discussed by John Vlach in an influential 1976 exhibition, explored in depth by Maude Wahlman in her 1980 doctoral dissertation, and promulgated in subsequent exhibitions, catalogues, and a book,[134] the ideas put forth by Wahlman and others have become popular truisms about African American quilts; indeed, some people now claim that they can determine the race of the maker of a quilt by examining the work alone.

Wahlman suggested that five design principles characterize "most" African American quilts: "the dominance of strips; bright, highly contrasting colors; large design elements; offset designs; multiple patterning."[135] It is clear that these are, in fact, principles that characterize work by many African American women from the rural South (or by those whose family roots lay in the South). But in exhibitions seen all over the country in the 1980s and 1990s, and in a number of influential publications, it was not made clear enough that this represented just one strand of a strong and diverse African American quiltmaking heritage, a strand rooted not only in geography but in class; these quilters are almost all of modest means. As discussed in the dialogues to plates 36, 43, 44, and 45, in the popular imagination "the real African American quilt" has now become essentialized, as if it consists solely of these traits.

As Cuesta Benberry and others have demonstrated more recently, the work of middle-class African American women and those from outside the rural South is often indistinguishable from that of white middle class quilters in the same regions.[136] Benberry, who has long been a serious quilt historian, and as such is deeply familiar with the complexities of all of America's quilting traditions, called this reification of a single African American aesthetic "extremely myopic." She asked,

"How could this small sample of late twentieth century African American quilts represent in its entirety the contribution of thousands of black quiltmakers working at the craft over two centuries? Would the history of blacks in America affirm that they had been a monolithic group without different experiences, environments, customs, and beliefs which would affect their creative efforts?"[137]

If one observes all the cautions, and doesn't assume a single style of expression among all African American quilters, it is possible to celebrate the rural Southern black quilting tradition as one of the great American art forms, akin to the Amish quilting tradition in its singular ability to move the viewer by the sheer power of its artistry.

The Cargo Collection at the International Quilt Study Center, formed principally of works by rural Alabama quilters, contains many innovative quilts that certainly conform to Wahlman's aesthetic principles. Each is wild by design in a distinctive way. Wini Austin's Log Cabin variation, made in the second quarter of the twentieth century, is a playful experiment in color (plate 36); the varied golds and pinks move over the blue surface of the quilt in a syncopated rhythm. So do the letters in Lureca Outland's P Quilt (plate 37), and the squares within squares in Janie Avant's bold, painterly exploration that recalls the late works by Mondrian or Albers (plate 43). Twentieth-century African American quilts from the South are often scrap quilts, but their economy of means is belied by their expressive genius.[138]

The Art Quilt Movement.

As mentioned at the beginning of this essay, many diverse trends came together in the 1970s to cause changes in both the art world and the quilt world. Several artists who are not, strictly speaking, quilters have been influential in destabilizing entrenched ideas about high and low, art and craft, painting and textile work. Miriam Schapiro, one of the founders of the feminist art movement, incorporated old quilt blocks and other domestic textiles into her collages celebrating the domestic world as worthy of artistic consideration. African American artist Faith Ringgold (herself the daughter of a dressmaker and quilter) began in the late 1970s to incorporate textile forms into her art. Many of her mixed-media works of the 1980s and 1990s conjoined acrylic painting and pieced fabric, resisting easy definition as either painting or quilt.[139] Her *French Collection Story Quilt* series of 1991–97 combines figurative painting on canvas, often with quilting stitches running diagonally across the canvas surface. These paintings are framed by running epistolary texts and pieced fabric borders.

In *The Sunflowers Quilting Bee at Arles* (1991), famous African American women (among them Sojourner Truth, Harriet Tubman, and Rosa Parks) work on a sunflower quilt in a field of sunflowers, while Vincent Van Gogh— famous painter of sunflowers—looks on. Part of the narrative written on this quilt says, "The women were finished piecing now. 'We need to stop and smell the flowers sometimes,' they said. 'Now we can do our real art—making this world piece up right.'"[140]

Ringgold and Schapiro were intent on breaking down

barriers of gender and race in the mainstream art world, as well as opening up a dialogue about the "appropriate" media for art at the end of modernism. Concurrently in the developing quilt world, a number of professionally trained artists turned their considerable talents in color and design to the making of quilts.[141] Jean Ray Laury was among the first. Among other significant figures who followed were Therese May, Yvonne Porcella, Terrie Hancock Mangat (plate 42), Jan Myers-Newbury, Pamela Studstill (plate 40), Katie Pasquini Masopust (plate 47), Nancy Crow (fig. 17), and Michael James (fig. 1, plate 48). Many of these individuals went on to become influential teachers and book writers as well as quilters. Nancy Crow

Fig. 17. Crosses. *Nancy Crow (1943–). Baltimore, Ohio, 1976. Pieced cottons, 93 ½" × 95". IQSC 1997.007.1088.*

helped start Quilt National in 1979, the biennial juried exhibit that has become a world-famous venue for contemporary art quilts.

While it is beyond the scope of this essay to fully chart the parameters of the contemporary art quilt movement, I would like briefly to examine two aspects germane to the topic of this book.[142] Among the many ways in which contemporary art quilters push the envelope of the medium, two stand out: work that explores the boundaries of abstraction and geometry, and work that pushes pictorialism to new limits.

Among contemporary quilters who have experimented most successfully with the geometric possibilities of quilts are Nancy Crow and Michael James.[143] Nancy Crow earned an M.F.A. degree in ceramics and textiles from Ohio State

University in 1969. She credits an Ohio Amish Bear Paw quilt with opening her eyes in 1973 to the possibilities of quilts as an artistic medium.[144] By 1976, she was making ambitious quilts, including *Crosses* (fig. 17). Fascinated by Log Cabin variations, she experimented with color and rhythm, coming up with her own version. She is always a bold colorist; here she juxtaposes browns, beiges, oranges, and magentas, framed by black and blue V-shaped forms. Much of her work from the 1970s, like *Crosses,* reflects a visual conversation with traditional quilts. Later she expanded her repertory, finding inspiration in tramp art, Mexican iconography, and African American improvisational quilts, specifically those of Anna Williams (plate 44).[145]

Michael James earned an M.F.A. degree in painting (Rochester Institute of Technology, 1973) before renouncing pigments to embrace the pieced geometry and color play of quilts. In 1978 he wrote *The Quiltmaker's Handbook,* and then participated in jurying the first Quilt National in Ohio in 1979.[146] His work during the late 1970s and 1980s has been characterized as "a playful investigation of the possibilities of strip-piecing combined with a continued exploration of curved versus angular forms to define space and create a sense of movement."[147] He has described his intention in his later works as "dismantling the grid" of the traditional quilt.[148]

In *Suspended Animation* (1992), the quilt structure remains in the long narrow diagonal strips that extend from lower left to upper right, sometimes changing color as many as a dozen times as they progress across the surface of the textile (fig. 1). But this underlying rhythm is contradicted and interrupted by the jagged curves that slice across the surface, providing dramatic changes in color and direction. The artist plays both with and against his medium—here suggesting smashed crockery, puzzle pieces, or, as he has remarked, graffiti. About his own work, Michael James has written, "the curved seam as a design form offers literal fluidity and an organic flexibility that cannot be achieved with the straight seam. Curved seam images have the capacity to pull us more actively into and around the quilt surface."[149]

James, a male working in a creative milieu still populated predominantly by women, is among the most successful contemporary quilt artists. Having had ample opportunity to reflect on gender politics in the art world as well as the quilt world, he takes pride in the title "quilter" and does not seek to be called anything more exalted. Along with a number of feminist artists, he seeks an alternative to the narrow path of so-called mainstream art:

"Since my work deals with color and light, it could be realized in paint. But that isn't all the work is about—only part of it. It's also about an alternative to the mainstream, about choices made so that the personal and the professional, the growing of relationships as well as the growing of a career, could co-exist." Finally, James says, "I like to sew, pure and simple. I like the substance of textiles, their weave and texture, and the way they hold color."[150]

His recent work *Spiritus Mundi* (2000) still avidly explores color, now through simplified formal elements (plate 48). He uses hand-dyed fabrics that play against the uncompromising geometry of the pieced panels with which they are juxtaposed.[151]

Just as in the nineteenth century, when some needle-women sought individuality of expression through the unique pictorial appliqué quilt (figs. 5–12; plates 12, 13), so too, one aspect of today's studio quilt that pushes the boundary of wild design is the pictorial quilt. Therese May was already testing this boundary in 1969, with *Therese's Quilt*. She experimented with machine-appliqué self-portraits, varied and repeated eighty times over the surface in block format.[152] Her subsequent work influenced others to explore both embellishment and pictorial expression. Among the most successful are Wendy Huhn, Jane Bush Cochran, and Terrie Hancock Mangat. All of these women compose scenes that draw inspiration from nineteenth-century Crazy quilts and pictorial appliqués. Like many of those historical quilts, theirs are at least semi-autobiographical; moreover, they draw from the wealth of images available in today's global visual culture. Some are humorous, playing on cultural stereotypes, such as Wendy Huhn's 1950s housewives in *It's a Wonderful Life*, or her iconic images of artists Georgia O'Keeffe, Frida Kahlo, and the Virgin Mary at a picnic in *Georgia, Frida, Mary and Me*.[153]

Jane Burch Cochran and Terrie Hancock Mangat (plate 42) embellish their quilts with a single-minded zealotry that would make a Crazy quilter of the 1880s like M. M. Hernandred Ricard proud (plate 18). Fabrics, buttons, beads, gloves, badges, dresses, artificial flowers, ethnic textiles, sequins, charms, brooches, and other found objects accumulate on their surfaces.[154] Perhaps Mangat's quilts push the boundaries of pictorialism the furthest. Her iconography often refers to Catholic saints, the Virgin of Guadalupe, or a florid Latin American visual sensibility. They combine humor, lush surfaces, and references both to quilt history and to popular culture. They are as accurate a record of the visual excess of our era as the Victorian Crazy quilt was of its era.[155] Overwhelming in both scale and conception, *Fireworks* (plate 42) is at once abstract and pictorial in its evocation of visual explosions in the night sky.

In the cutting-edge works of abstraction as well as in the playful pictorials being made in the art quilt movement today, the work that is most successful is that which remains true to the integrity of the medium of cloth. Quilts that attempt to reproduce an exact photographic verisimilitude seldom achieve more than the status of a curiosity, for they are retrogressive in relation to their era.[156] Yet some art quilters are achieving interesting results using new materials to make references to historic quilt types. Pat Kroth's *Revisiting Jackson* refers both to the history of quilt embellishment and to Jackson Pollock when she fuses, staples, and machine quilts items such as lace, coins, stamps, and candy wrappers onto her quilt; Amy Orr calls her *Twist Tied Log Cabin* a "ritual folly" that pays homage to the Log Cabin in a new iteration requiring more than thirty-five hundred hand-colored twist-ties; Janie Matthews's *American Icon* references global consumerism in an American flag quilt made principally of recycled Coca-Cola cans.[157]

The New Internationalism. Historically, quilts reflected internationalism principally through their materials and sometimes through their patterns. Valuable chintzes from India in the late eighteenth century gave way to replicas made in Britain and France, which gave way in turn to affordable calicoes manufactured in the United States. Costly silks from China used in the eighteenth and early nineteenth centuries were replaced by less expensive silks at the end of the nineteenth century, allowing even middle-class women to be profligate with such materials in their Crazy quilts. Patterns were transmitted through English pattern books, then through *Godey's Lady's Book,* and then through international venues like Philadelphia's Centennial Exposition in 1876, and later World's Fairs, which exposed American women to the latest fads, such as British needlework and Japanese aesthetics.

Today, quilt internationalism is, of course, even broader in scope—it is part of the globalization of culture. The late-nineteenth-century fad for all things "Oriental" has been replaced, at the end of the twentieth century, by an enthusiasm for all things "tribal." Quilters today use fabric evocative of Third World textiles; Latin American, Indonesian, and African textiles themselves are sometimes used in quilts, or their techniques and aesthetics appropriated.[158] I have already mentioned Faith Ringgold, who deliberately paints in the naive style of early-twentieth-century African American folk artists

Fig. 18. Crucifixion. *Yvonne Wells (d.o.b. unknown).*
Tuscaloosa, Alabama, 1986. Pieced and appliquéd cottons,
79" × 68". IQSC 2000.004.0139.

like Horace Pippin, and enframes her quilts with pieced
textiles that reference both Africa and Tibet; there are
other African American art quilters whose work is deliberately neo-primitivizing.[159] Carolyn Mazloomi embraces
African textiles and imagery. Yvonne Wells, although college educated, chooses to make appliqué quilts that are
childlike in their use of rudimentary styles of representation. These powerful, evocative works of art are sometimes mistaken for the work of an untutored folk artist,
so great is that age-old hunger for the "primitive."[160] In
Crucifixion (1986), Wells pays homage to Harriet Powers,
both in the Christian iconography and the referencing of
celestial anomalies (fig. 18). The work of late-twentieth-
century African American quilters is part of the new internationalism too, as their embrace of their roots extends
not only to a rural past in this country but also to a trans-
Atlantic African past and present.[161]

Today we have achieved Marshal McLuhan's ideal of
the "global village." The instantaneous movement of ideas
and images over the Internet means that quilters all over
the world can visit each other's virtual galleries. Excellent
cottons in a dizzying variety of patterns are available
nearly everywhere (and if not, they too can be ordered
over the Internet, whether one is quilting in New York
City, Greenland, or Tokyo).

Today, just as in the nineteenth century, art museums

are not the place of central importance to contemporary
quilt culture. State and county fairs continue to draw tens
of thousands of people, and quilts continue to be shown
at them, but the new populist venue for quilts is the
regional, national, and international quilt show. These
include prestigious juried exhibits such as Quilt National
in Athens, Ohio (begun in 1979), Quilt Visions/San
Diego (begun in 1987), and Heidelberg, Germany's Quilt-
Biennial (begun in 1984). The more broadly based exhibits
such as Houston's International Quilt Festival, Paducah,
Kentucky's American Quilter's Society Annual Show,
Europe's Patchwork and Quilt Expo, and Japan's several
blockbuster exhibits all draw tens of thousands of visitors
for events of very brief duration.[162]

Many American art quilters teach in Europe and
Japan. American quilters buy books by European quilters.
Japanese students come to the International Quilt Study
Center in Nebraska and to the Paducah exhibits, while
Jonathan Holstein and Michael James judge shows in
Tokyo. Europe and Japan both have their own flourishing
quilt movements.[163] The supposedly domestic quilt is a
global industry.

In the nineteenth century, *Godey's Lady's Book* and
other magazines transmitted the latest patterns and ideas
to thousands of women; in the first part of the twentieth
century, *Ladies Home Journal* and a host of other women's
magazines and newspapers printed quilt patterns and
promulgated this art; today, magazines like *Quilter's Newsletter, American Quilter, Art Quilt, New Zealand Quilter,
Quilters' Review* and *The Quilter* (both in Great Britain),
and *Patchiwaku Kiruto Tsushin* and *Quilts Japan* (both
in Tokyo), reach millions of women. So do TV shows,
videos, software programs such as "The Electric Quilt,"
and numerous how-to books published by Rutledge Hill
Press, C & T Publishing, That Patchwork Place, and many
other publishers devoted solely to works of interest to a
quiltmaking public.

At the beginning of a new millennium, the making,
study, and exhibition of quilts continue to preoccupy
us. Quilts continue to serve a number of purposes in
our collective psyche, to link us to the past and to affirm
a female-centered art. Meanwhile, for more than two centuries, American artists have steadfastly continued their
explorations in piecework and appliqué, proving that fabric is an inexhaustible medium for innovation in color,
abstraction, figuration, and other modes of expression.
The selection of works illustrated and discussed here
affirms that American quilt artists' greatest aesthetic
legacy is that their work is, in every sense of the term,
wild by design.

A CATALOGUE OF QUILTS

JANET CATHERINE BERLO, PATRICIA COX CREWS, CAROLYN DUCEY, AND JONATHAN HOLSTEIN

Here follows a catalogue of forty-eight American quilts from the large holdings of the International Quilt Study Center. The selection was made by Janet Catherine Berlo, Patricia Cox Crews, and Jonathan Holstein to illustrate design innovation in two hundred years of American quilts. Our task was a difficult one, simply because so many splendid works of art had to be left out. The quilts chosen reflect the strengths of the IQSC collection: nineteenth-century quilts and twentieth-century African American quilts. There are a number of contemporary art quilts in the collection (approximately one hundred); however, the IQSC contemporary collection represents a slice of the contemporary studio art quilt movement rather than its full scope. Moreover, it was important to us to illustrate that design innovation has been a constant feature in American quilting since its inception more than two hundred years ago, so we chose to focus on historical quilts rather than on the contemporary art quilts that are already widely celebrated for their inventiveness and originality.

Janet Berlo suggested that a conversation about quilts would be a livelier format for sharing our knowledge and insights with others, as an alternative to the more customary formal catalogue entry. These conversations, which were stimulating and illuminating for all of us, took place in front of the quilts in the IQSC storeroom in August and December of 2001 and March of 2002. Our conversations were augmented through communication by e-mail and telephone, and the results edited by Janet Berlo and Patricia Crews, with advice from Jonathan Holstein.

While our dialogues focused on the theme of the book—the artistic innovations of individual quiltmakers—they also ranged through social history, genealogy, textile analysis, and other topics, as germane to each quilt. We hope that these conversations will have something to offer the quilt scholar, the artist, the collector, and the enthusiast. The range of our dialogues suggests some of the many ways that quilts can be analyzed in order to shed light on the history of women, of textiles in particular and of American art in general, and of American culture. Quilts have long been a remarkable locus of artistic achievement in the United States, and their study illuminates many aspects of our history and contemporary culture.

Initials in the dialogue refer to the various contributors to this volume: Janet Berlo, Patricia Crews, Carolyn Ducey, and Jonathan Holstein. Michael James joined us for discussion of his own quilts and one other contemporary quilt.

The catalogue includes basic information (pattern name, quiltmaker name, location made, probable date, dimensions, quilt stitches per inch if hand quilted, and predominant fiber type) for each quilt. If the quilt was titled by the maker, the title is indicated in italics. If it is a conventional pattern name (e.g., Log Cabin), or if we have named it, it is in plain text.

When scanning the caption associated with each quilt, the reader will note that many of the quilts are without solid provenance. Robert and Ardis James assembled their collection primarily by purchase from dealers, who whenever possible supplied them with information about where a quilt was found. Sometimes dealer information is the only clue to the likely place of origin of a particular quilt. Yet the U.S. population has always been a mobile one and we cannot be sure that a quilt was made in the state where it was found by a dealer or collector. Consequently, we very conservatively assigned a place of origin for each quilt in this catalogue.

Some quilt history books and catalogues, especially older ones, have given dates and locations without firm documentation; this approach is not helpful when scholars and collectors try to build on published information as they seek dates and attributions for other quilts. For this reason, more curators and other textile scholars today choose to follow the standard we have used here.

If we have only a dealer's note as to where a quilt was found and no other supporting clues or documentation, we designated its place of origin as "possibly" made in the state where the dealer or the collector indicated the quilt was found. If we identified information—such as stylistic clues within the quilt itself—to support place of origin as being the state where the dealer/collector noted the quilt was found, we designated it as "probably" having been made in that state. If the quilt entered the collection without a dealer's or collector's note on its provenance, then we simply designated it as probably made in the United States.

In some cases, a quilt was accompanied by family information about who made a quilt and where it was made. We endeavored to corroborate this information through genealogical research. If we were successful, we supplied that information in the text or notes. Only then have we listed the place of origin as certain, without a "possibly" or "probably" in front of it.

The names of the makers are known for all the African American quilts in the Cargo Collection, as is the place of origin—usually Alabama. Essential to the integrity of such a collection is knowing the maker's name and racial background. This documentation sets the Cargo Collection apart from most quilt collections, African American or other.

For most of the quilts pictured here, we do not know with certainty when they were made. Once again, the estimated date provided by the dealer or collector was our starting point. We sought additional clues, both in the realm of style and in the realm of scientific evidence, to corroborate or refute those dates. We chose to give a range for the probable date of manufacture, generally a range of at least two decades. Occasionally, the quiltmaker inscribed a date, which we assumed was the date the quilt was completed although we realize it may have commemorated some other significant date in the life of the maker or the intended recipient. We used "circa" in only a few instances, to indicate a probable year that a quilt was made. The term circa is sometimes used to mean a given date plus or minus five years or ten years; we decided to use a date range instead, to be more precise.

The number of quilting stitches per inch (QSPI) is given for each quilt with hand-quilting. We counted the number of stitches in at least three places. When it varied, we listed the range rather than the average, because the former is much more telling than the latter.

The fiber content is also given for each quilt. The predominant fiber is listed first, followed by other fibers if present. Visual inspection provided the initial basis for this information. Microscopic analyses of fibers were performed subsequently whenever selected fabrics used in a quilt did not appear to be of the predominant fiber type and/or whenever the estimated date of a quilt fell just before or during the period when a new manufactured fiber was introduced commercially in the United States. Fiber analyses often provided the determinant clue in estimating the probable date of manufacture.

We hope that the analysis and documentation provided for each catalogue entry, coupled with thoughtful dialogue, will help further strengthen scholarship in the exciting field of quilt studies.

I / NINE PATCH, SHEEPFOLD VARIATION

Maker unknown
Possibly Pennsylvania
1825–45
108" × 97"
Cottons
QSPI: 8
1997.007.0237
International Quilt Study Center,
Ardis and Robert James Collection

JB: People often think of early-nineteenth-century quilts as very fussy and precise, but in fact there are a number of slightly offbeat or irregular quilts in this era, as I discuss in my essay. What I find particularly intriguing about this one is that the quiltmaker has chosen elegant imported fabrics, yet she has used them in an unusual way.

CD: This variant of the Nine Patch, with the oversized central patch, is called either Sheepfold or Puss in the Corner. Strippy designs, a popular choice among quilters throughout the nineteenth century, may derive from whole-cloth toile or chintz quilts first found in Europe and America during the late eighteenth and early nineteenth centuries. Pieces of the same chintz fabric were simply stitched together and then quilted with elaborate representational designs and decorative geometric patterns.[1]

   In the second quarter of the nineteenth century, strips of chintz were alternated with either strips of another chintz, pieced patterns like Wild Goose Chase, or, as in this example, a Nine Patch block.[2] The chintz fabrics often featured vertical arrangements of baskets like those in the monochrome blueprint or architectural pillar prints, a style unique to English textile manufacturers.[3] Strippy quilts continued to be a popular choice for quiltmakers after 1850 and well into the twentieth century.

JB: The pieced bars or strips range from 5 1/4" to 6" wide, and the Nine Patch blocks are set in at imprecise intervals, rather than being arranged with linear precision. This, combined with the rich floral toiles, gives the quilt an exuberant feeling.

PC: The toiles used in this quilt are typical of monochrome roller prints of the period, which are characterized by short vertical repeats, naturalistic flowers, and crowded compositions. The red toile has a 13" vertical repeat and the blue toile a 12 1/2" repeat. According to textile authority Florence Montgomery, a repeat unit of about 12" indicates a cylinder print, whereas a long vertical repeat of about 36" indicates that a piece was copper plate printed.[4] All of the toiles used in this quilt appear to be new. The sheen of the glazed finish is still bright, and there are no signs of fading to suggest the maker recycled this fabric from bed hangings or draperies.

CD: The quilting pattern combines a diamond grid with a floral design. Quilts made in America were typically quilted with an overall geometric pattern, while those made in England were usually extravagantly quilted with representational patterns.[5]

PC: Since this quilt is believed to have been made before the invention of the sewing machine in the mid-1840s, we examined it carefully to see if there was any machine-stitching to disprove the estimated date. We found none. It's hand pieced and hand quilted with eight stitches per inch.

JH: The lack of a border at one end indicates either that the quilt was once longer or that it was made that way. A number of early American quilts were made without a border at the end designated for the top of the bed. Such quilts often had a matching pillow sham that effectively completed the overall design.

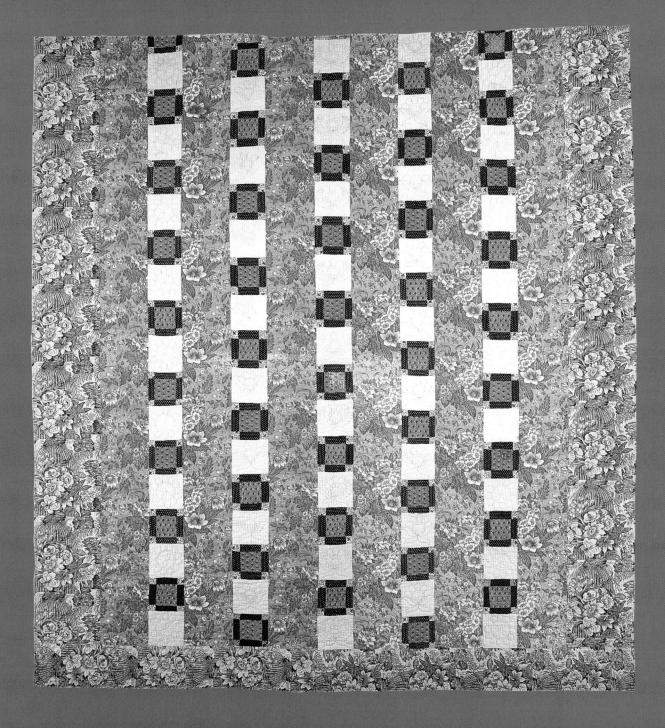

2 / DIAGONAL FLYING GEESE

Sarah K. Headley (1816–1893)
Bucks County, Pennsylvania
Dated 1838
98" × 96"
Cottons
QSPI: 7–8
1997.007.0749
International Quilt Study Center,
Ardis and Robert James Collection

JH: This is a good example of a design that would never have been done in England—an American quilter has taken the idea of a "flying geese" border (pieced and stacked triangles) and has transformed it into a motif for the entire surface by blowing it up and running it diagonally. The large triangles are at least twelve inches wide at the base!

JB: There's a nice alternation of large-scale and small-scale prints that gives movement to the surface.

JH: Another visual trick that gives the surface movement is the alternating rows of light and dark triangles.

PC: The placement of the bold red triangles animates the surface too.

JH: It would be presumptuous for us to infer that this was random. It seems very carefully placed for the best effect.

PC: Although much of the popular folklore about quilts assumes that they were made from scraps of worn clothing, more often the fabrics were new—cuttings left over from dressmaking, or sometimes even new yardage purchased specifically for quiltmaking. When recycled materials were used in quilts made prior to 1850, they usually came from out-of-fashion curtains and bed hangings, rather than worn out clothing.

CD: Yes—this is beautiful, new fabric. It must come from a prosperous household or from a dry goods merchant family; one normally wouldn't see so many different colorways of the same fabric used for dressmaking within one household of modest means.

PC: I agree, unless the maker had access to cloth from a local textile printer. We know that some quiltmakers who lived near a mill or were wives or daughters of mill workers had access to fabric remaining from experiments by cotton fabric printers operating during the 1820s and 1830s. Margaret Ordoñez reports that a quilt documented in the Rhode Island Quilt Project with six different colorways was made by a family in which men from two generations of the family worked at a local textile-printing mill. She notes that it's "a very good document of printers' trying to work out successful color combinations . . . some more successful than others."[1] Some of the fabrics in this quilt, particularly those with very subtle differences in the brown backgrounds, have flaws that suggest they may have been mill trials or factory seconds.

JB: Inscribed on the back in ink is "Sarah K. Headley's 2, 1838." Is this an inventory number, or was it her second quilt that year?

JH: I have seen other instances where an inscription like this clearly meant it was her second quilt.

JB: There are also cross-stitched initials "BRH #1" on the back. The backing may be a reused cotton sheet with its original inventory number embroidered on it.

CD: The initials cross-stitched on the back of the quilt support that theory. Through examination of census records and other public records, we know that Sarah K. Headley was born September 17, 1816, in Falls Township, Bucks County, Pennsylvania, to Benjamin and Rachel Headley. The Headleys were a relatively prosperous farm family. Her mother probably embroidered the inventory number with both parents' initials (BRH) on the sheet. Years later, Sarah may have taken one of the family's old sheets to use as the backing for a quilt she was making in anticipation of her marriage. Sarah married Jesse K. Harper, also a farmer, on March 5, 1840, just two years after she inked the inscription on the back of this quilt. She lived on a farm next-door to her parents in Bucks County until her death in 1893.[2]

PC: Sarah's home in Bucks County was located about thirty miles northeast of Philadelphia. Philadelphia was a notable textile-manufacturing center during the nineteenth century, lending some support to our suspicion that Sarah may have had access to fabrics that were printer's trials or factory seconds from local mills. Regardless of whether the multiple colorways of the fabrics used in this quilt came from mill seconds or were entirely the dressmaking scraps of a prosperous farm wife, they were combined by the maker to create a quilt with extraordinary visual impact.

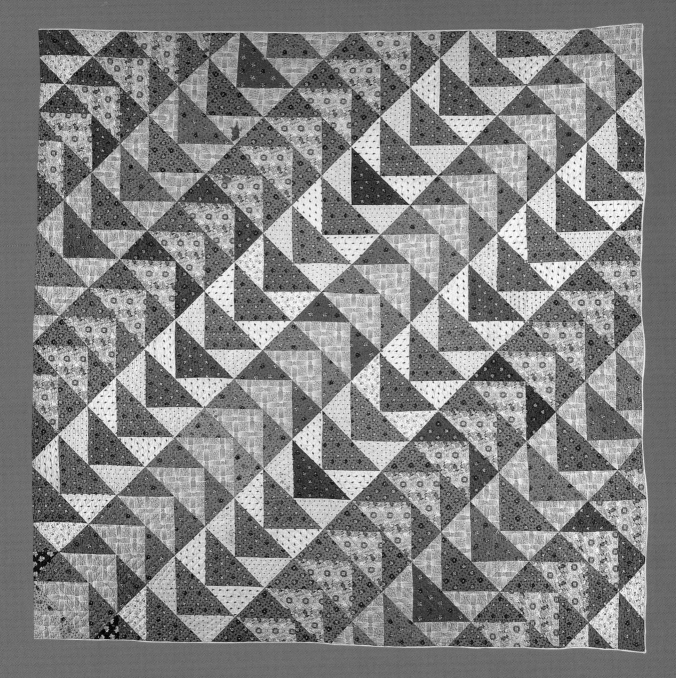

3 / LONE STAR

Maker unknown
Possibly Eastern Pennsylvania
1850–60
114" × 112"
Cottons
QSPI: 5–6
1997.007.0746
International Quilt Study Center,
Ardis and Robert James Collection

JB: The star is one of the most versatile and perhaps the most popular pattern in American quiltmaking.[1] Lone Star, Star of Bethlehem, Feathered Star, LeMoyne Star, Ohio Star—the possibilities are endless. Perhaps that's why star patterns have endured for two centuries. A classic Lone Star is composed of dozens of small diamonds joined into eight large diamonds, each of which becomes one arm of the star. The finished size depends on how many diamonds are joined in each arm. Here, each has 144 diamonds, making 1,152 pieces in the central star alone. This quilt measures more than nine feet on a side. This huge size is characteristic of Lone Stars from the first half of the nineteenth century.[2]

Because of the way a Lone Star is constructed, four relatively large square areas are left in each corner of the quilt. These are often filled with smaller versions of the eight-pointed star, or with floral appliqué, or even, in the early nineteenth century, *broderie perse* designs.

PC: In this example, the same size pieces used in the central star are joined together to make small corner sunbursts, lacking the arms of the star. Half-sunbursts fill the remaining "elbows" of the star. These are appliquéd to the green background rather than pieced within it, an unusual feature.

JB: The four modest calicoes used in this quilt are not very remarkable individually, but when juxtaposed in this serrated pattern, they are transformed. The vivid blue next to the bright yellow really pulsates.

PC: The fabrics are simple, relatively inexpensive roller prints of the type popular from 1830 to 1860. But the olive green quilting thread is 3/2 ply, a type of sewing thread unavailable before 1850,[3] so it would have been quilted after 1850, although it may have been pieced earlier. The hand-quilting echoes the pieced seams. The green background fabric contains a few small hand-quilted stars, which are hard to see on the front of the quilt.

JH: These quilts with echoing stars remind me of bursting fireworks, and perhaps that was an influence. By mid-century, many Americans had seen fireworks; signal and distress rockets bursting against dark night skies over the oceans and lakes were common sights in a seafaring nation.

JB: So perhaps Terrie Mangat's *Fireworks* quilt of 1989 (plate 42) was prefigured well over one hundred years ago by the works of these nineteenth-century quiltmakers!

4 / WILD GOOSE CHASE VARIATION

Maker unknown
Possibly New York
1850–70
80" × 80"
Cottons
QSPI: 5–9
1997.007.0406
International Quilt Study Center,
Ardis and Robert James Collection

JB: This is classic high-Victorian taste, isn't it? Yet the color combinations look rather wild to our eyes.

PC: Yes, these cotton fabrics are in typical colors and patterns of the 1850s and 1860s: the double pinks of the grid, the green vermicular patterns in the triangles, the mineral yellow of the centers of each block, and the subtly printed maroon calico of the background. The wide, blue border fabric features cabbage roses and is a typically Victorian reinterpretation of an eighteenth-century French-style fabric, here in a cretonne (a type of cotton print) rather than a brocade.

JB: Depending on where the viewer stands, this pattern can advance and recede. From some distances it looks like a pink grid superimposed on the diagonal pattern of the flying geese.

JH: We're often startled in quilts of this era by the juxtaposition of extremely complex and busy floral prints with simpler printed fabrics in small patterns or solid colors. This mixed patterning, which is often jarring, didn't really appear again in art until quite recently. The intent of the maker of this quilt, however, was to show off her choice (and expensive) cotton, a kind of display of prestige textiles we see all over the world.

PC: The optical effects of this quilt clearly were important to the maker. She "fussy-cut" the border so that the large figural motif would be the same at the top and bottom, but slightly different on either side.

Several colors of quilting thread were used, white in the white areas, blue in the wide blue border, and maroon in the maroon. The maroon areas are filled with concentric triangles. This seems to have been hand-quilted by more than one person. It ranges from five quilting stitches per inch up to nine.

JB: Perhaps this was put into the quilting frame for a "quilt frolic," and several women took part. Numerous early-nineteenth-century diaries refer to the fun to be had at an all-day quilt frolic. We think of "quilting bee" as the term for such an event, but in the early nineteenth century, "bee" was reserved for prosaic tasks, like a corn-husking bee. "Frolic" more accurately captures the excitement and high spirits of a quilting party.

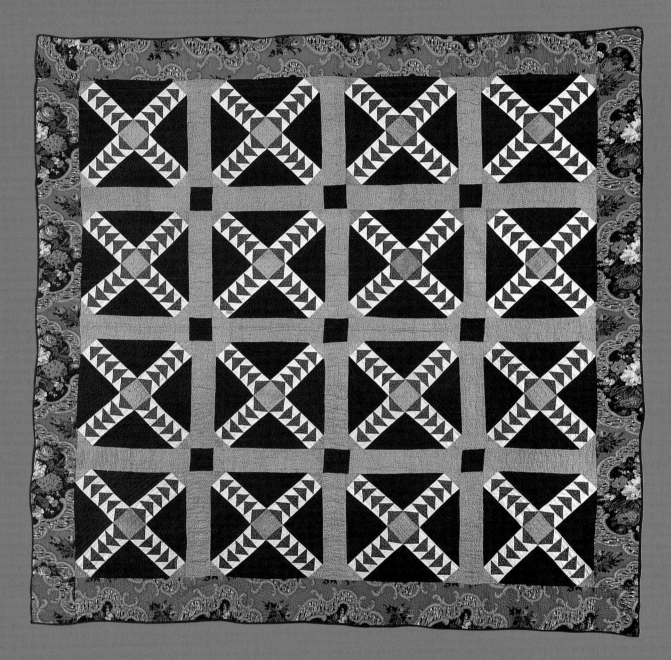

5 / MARINER'S COMPASS

Maker unknown
Probably Pennsylvania
1850–70
86" × 65"
Cottons
QSPI: 9
1997.007.0949
International Quilt Study Center,
Ardis and Robert James Collection

PC: The pattern known as Compass, Mariner's Compass, or Sunburst is a very old one. Yet it's never been very popular, because of its complexity of construction. Those from the early nineteenth century often showcase a great variety of chintzes and calicoes.

CD: The fabrics here include a wide variety of prints typical of the 1830s to 1860s. The use of solid black fabric for the centers and the backgrounds is noteworthy.

JB: The use of chrome orange seems atypical. Most Compass quilts are rather elegant; this one, in contrast, has a folk-art quality to it.

JH: That's because of its characteristic Pennsylvania color choices, much brighter and stronger than we normally see in quilts from other states. Bright colors were very much a part of Germanic folk culture; they still are, in Pennsylvania. Quiltmakers there had the cultural freedom to use the sort of bright colors and visually aggressive combina-tions that might have been frowned on in New England communities. Thank goodness! Our quilt heritage would have been very different without that bold Pennsylvania color sense.

CD: The technique used to make this Mariner's Compass is unusual. It's composed of blocks and background pieces that were completed as individual units. Each circular compass block and curved cross-like background piece was hand-quilted and bound with a narrow, white binding. Each completed unit was then stitched together to create the overall design of the quilt. This technique is found in a few other quilts, including a Civil War era quilt in the International Quilt Study Center's collection.[1] It was a time-consuming process and required excellent needlework skills, which may explain why so few quilts were made like this.

JB: Because it's such a challenging pattern, Mariner's Compass has often been a showcase for fine hand-quilting and appliqué work as well as complex curved piecing, thus showcasing a quilter's fluency with all aspects of her medium.[2] Here the maker's aims were somewhat more modest.

CD: Although she's a good seamstress, with fine, regular stitching and a high number of quilting stitches per inch, her big diamond points don't lay flat.

JB: Nonetheless, she created a memorable ethnic variant on a classic quilting pattern.

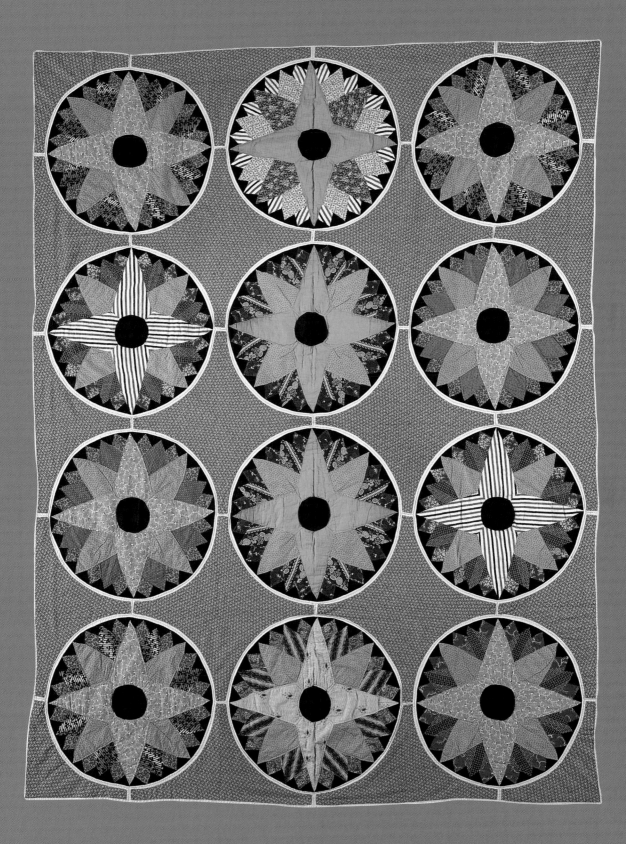

6 / NEW YORK BEAUTY

Maker unknown
Probably Missouri
1850–70
82" × 81"
Cottons
QSPI: 8–9
1997.007.0124
International Quilt Study Center,
Ardis and Robert James Collection

JB: People think of New York Beauty as a classic nineteenth-century quilt design, but the first person who made one was a great innovator! What was she putting together?

JH: This pattern has always amazed me. It's one of the most visually successful in the lexicon of American quilt designs—all those little spikes combined with a strong geometric grid. And we don't have the slightest idea where it came from! There's hardly such a thing as a bad one, and this one is particularly successful. The woman who made it had a very sophisticated sense of scale, design, and color.

I've wondered, without knowing what board games were current in the mid-nineteenth century, if the pattern derived from something like a Parcheesi board; to me, the design has always had the look of a beautifully balanced game board.

JB: Often these quilts have many more complete circles. This one has only four, but it has twelve half- or quarter-circles around the perimeter and a wonderfully inventive hourglass border. The use of the complementary colors of red and green sets up an optical vibration in the viewer's eye.

PC: This optical effect is made even more pronounced by the repetition of thin, elongated triangles.

JH: And she had the graphic design sense to peg down the corners with the bright yellow triangles, which are echoed only in the four squares where the sashings cross. This is an amazing piece of work—a perfect quilt.

PC: This pattern, called Crown of Thorns and Rocky Mountain Road during the nineteenth and early twentieth centuries, became widely known as New York Beauty after Mountain Mist introduced the pattern by that name on its batting wrappers in 1930.[1] This demonstrates how influential Mountain Mist batting and patterns became.

JB: These are its classic colors, but it has a completely different look when executed in indigo on white, for example.[2] It has resonance with contemporary quilters too; though many continue to make classic New York Beauty quilts, Elizabeth Cave has simplified it into an op-art pattern while retaining its New York beat (see plate 41, *Manhattan Heat Wave*).

7 / PRINCESS FEATHER

M. Gingrich
Probably Dauphin County, Pennsylvania
Dated 1854
85" × 84"
Cottons
QSPI: 5–6
1997.007.0774
International Quilt Study Center,
Ardis and Robert James Collection

JH: This is a beautifully designed and orchestrated quilt. Note the very traditional use of the ostrich plumes emerging from a central star figure, a kind of focusing element in the middle of the quilt, and the use of oak leaves as a border. It retains the running vine that we see in so many appliqué quilts, which is, of course, an adoption from earlier Indian textiles. It was transmitted through those textiles, early quilts, and English Adamsesque design, which used a lot of budding vines. The maker has used reverse appliqué in the feathers and the leaves. The feathers have become more like the oak leaves, or the oak leaves have become more like the feathers—whichever way you want to see it.

PC: The hand-quilting is done totally in crosshatch over the central field; in the border, she's used contour or echo quilting that follows the vine.

JH: The crosshatch or diamond grid pattern is very traditional, one of the earliest quilting patterns, and they went on using it in Pennsylvania. The Amish used it right up to the 1940s, the end of the classic period of their quiltmaking. You expect to see that retained grid pattern appear in classic Pennsylvania quilts.

JB: Ricky Clark has pointed out that this plume shape, which we always call Princess Feather and assume to be an ostrich plume, may sometimes be an amaranth plant.[1] When did people start doing the Princess Feather design?

PC: Princess Feather was among the most popular of the floral appliqué patterns. Floral appliqué quilts first appeared in the United States during the 1830s, peaked in popularity about 1850, but continued to be made until the 1890s.[2] Most floral appliqué quilts were done in the complementary colors of red and green on white, rather than in the red and yellow on indigo blue seen here.[3]

According to dealer information, this quilt was made by M. Gingrich in Dauphin County, Pennsylvania.[4] The Pennsylvania attribution is strongly supported by the number of similar works attributed to quiltmakers located in southeastern Pennsylvania. Pennsylvania German women are well known for their bold use of colors in appliqué quilts—reds, blues, chrome yellows, and oranges—at a time when other American quiltmakers were making theirs almost exclusively in red and green on white grounds. And, many Pennsylvania German women made Princess Feather quilts.[5] The top of this one is constructed entirely of cotton solids, but it's backed by a beautiful paisley print.

JB: This quilt is pieced from four blocks and has a border, but one sees a unified design field where neither the border nor the blocks are separate. Princess Feather is one of those patterns in which it's fascinating to see what happens when it's composed in different colors and by different artists.

JH: The term "princess feather" probably comes from the Prince of Wales's heraldic crest—three ostrich plumes—and "princess" is a corruption of "prince's." In the United States, "prince's feather" became "princess feather" through verbal transmission.

JB: The Prince of Wales visited the United States and Canada in the summer of 1860, and many ephemeral objects and decorations incorporating ostrich plumes were made for his visit—items ranging from Native Canadian and Native American women's quillwork to other small-scale commemorative items.[6] It's interesting to speculate whether there might have been a marked increase in Princess Feather quilts subsequent to his visit, which was so widely covered in the popular press.

JH: Many women were influenced by magazines such as *Godey's,* which promoted English notions of elegance, social behavior, and fashion. The lives of the Royal Family were big news, and middle-class women in this country were very aware of them.

8 / PRINCESS FEATHER SAMPLER

Maker unknown
United States
1860–80
80 ½" × 78"
Cottons
QSPI: 8–10
1997.007.0211
International Quilt Study Center,
Ardis and Robert James Collection

PC: Red and green floral appliqué quilts were a popular style in the United States between 1840 and 1880, reaching their peak popularity during the 1850s and 1860s. Women who fashioned quilts in this style typically were creating works that they and their families regarded as exceptional. In many cases, these were used only for special occasions. As a result, many in this style survived.

This maker had a unique vision and created an out-of-the-ordinary quilt inspired by a familiar pattern. She surrounded two large center blocks—one a swirling Princess Feather and the other a pinwheel made of budding Christmas cactus fronds—with smaller appliqué blocks to the left and right of those in the center. In doing so, she combined the two formats generally used in red and green appliqué quilts—the four-block format (see examples in plates 7 and 9) and the multiple (usually six to twelve) block style (see plate 17)—and created an unusual floral appliqué sampler.

CD: Her quilting patterns are also unusual. The maker quilted the green plumes and fronds in the large blocks with a leafed branch design. Hearts, tulips, and other flowers are quilted in the red buds and flowers throughout. A carefully defined hand is stitched within the horn or cornucopia in the lower left block. And she covered the quilt's white background with parallel diagonal lines of quilting about half an inch part, which look as if they were done freehand rather than by following established lines.

PC: The maker used all solid cotton muslins, no calicoes, for this quilt. The bright green fabric of the leaves and trailing vine in the borders appears to have been dyed using a two-step process: dyeing the fabric first with yellow and then over-dyeing with indigo. Prior to the development of synthetic dyes, a two-step process was required to create green colors because no grass green dyes exist in nature.

JH: The maker designated a "top" for this quilt by appliquéing a different border design at one end, an unusual feature. This often meant she wanted it to be placed on the bed so the design would be read in a specific way. This is a particularly appropriate device for asymmetrical quilts that may read better one way than another.

JB: I like the eccentric appliqué borders. This artist's offbeat use of large and small blocks in the center is complemented well by the leaves and vines, which are so different from the many elegant, decorous versions of leaf and vine borders.

The endless inventiveness in nineteenth-century appliqué is a remarkable feature of the American quilting tradition. Whether depicting standard images like flowers and geometric motifs in an unusual way, as this quiltmaker did, or realizing a completely original design like Charlotte Gardner's Odd Fellow's quilt (plate 13), Lucinda Honstain's family history quilt (plate 12), or Harriet Powers's Bible Quilt (fig. 12), the nineteenth-century appliqué artist often pushed the parameters of her medium, either through the virtuosity of her technique or in the originality of her design.

9 / POTS OF FLOWERS

Maker unknown
Probably Ohio
1860–80
81 $\frac{1}{2}$" × 80 $\frac{1}{2}$"
Cottons
QSPI: 11
1997.007.0243
International Quilt Study Center,
Ardis and Robert James Collection

PC: The brilliant red and vibrant green of this quilt's design is a combination that was extremely popular during the second and third quarters of the nineteenth century. Nancy Hornback notes that "red and green were commonly combined for floral motifs in both European and American decorative arts of the period between 1810 and 1840. The ornamentation on stenciled and painted walls, stenciled quilts, furniture, tinware and other household objects that still exist is proof that red and green was a popular color combination in the several decades prior to the appearance of the red and green appliqué quilts."[1]

JB: It's always fascinating to try to figure out not only the interrelationships among the different arts, but more specifically, the relationships among different textile forms. Laurel Ulrich has shown that the so-called "rose blankets" woven and embroidered in the Northeast in imitation of eighteenth-century British imports were objects of domestic manufacture that soon outstripped in excellence the commercial wares they were meant to emulate. Many of the fine embroidered and stenciled blankets and counterpanes of the first half of the nineteenth century surely influenced the trend for floral appliqué, which became so popular by midcentury.[2] This quilt replicates some of the cheerful flowers seen on such blankets.

In my essay (pp. 13–14) I explore the relationship between professionally woven coverlets and quilts. But it's clear that quilters sought artistic inspiration from many sources, including their own gardens. Everything had possibilities as design inspiration for the quilt.

CD: Nineteenth-century women often cultivated ambitious flower gardens that were, in turn, reflected in their quilts. They also found inspiration in the popular press.

According to Susan Curtis, "From gardening publications to ladies' magazines, articles regularly appeared that offered designs and patterns suitable for the quilt-makers' use, and editorials encouraged women to engage in gardening."[3]

Women incorporated grapes, currants, and berries in many of their floral appliqués.[4] I couldn't resist counting the number of berries on this quilt. Though the number of berries clustered around a large flower or lined up on each branch is not always consistent, there are more than 2,800 berries stitched in place!

PC: A lavish quilting design covers the entire surface of this textile. Small, quilted plumed wreathes preside between the large motifs. Triple rows of quilting stretch diagonally across the body of the quilt. Technological advances made this extravagant hand-quilting feasible. As Rachel Maines points out, "It is doubtful that such thread-intensive design strategies . . . appeared before manufactured cotton thread began to be marketed on a national scale about 1820."[5] The stronger thread made possible and likely sparked the stipple quilting, stuffed work, and complicated hand-quilting designs found on quilts of the second quarter of the nineteenth century.

CD: The piping added to the binding edge is a technique that women initially used in constructing clothing. Virginia Gunn attributes many of the various techniques found in quilts to ones women used in nineteenth-century clothing construction.[6] Here, the red piping echoes the vivid blossoms.

JB: While I apprehend this design as an allover pattern, it really is the popular midcentury block style framed by border designs (see plate 17). But because the same red/pink/green color scheme and the same floral imagery are featured in the borders as well as the blocks, it reads as a unified image of a bountiful garden.

JH: I'm often startled by the ability of American quilt-makers to abstract designs in innovative and aesthetically stunning ways. This quilt is a perfect example. Both the urns and the flowers have been simplified and reordered in ways that retain their basic coherence but convert them to elements in a powerful overall design. One doesn't read potted plants here, but is drawn at once into a coherent and unified visual statement of great dignity.

10 / DELECTABLE MOUNTAINS VARIATION

Maker unknown
Probably Lancaster County, Pennsylvania
1865–85
76" × 75"
Cottons
QSPI: 6
1997.007.0398
International Quilt Study Center,
Ardis and Robert James Collection

JB: Delectable Mountains is one of those quilt names, along with Rose of Sharon, Crown of Thorns, and others, that reflect the Christian devotion of many American quilters. This name comes from the seventeenth-century inspirational book *Pilgrim's Progress,* in which it was written, "They went 'til they came to the Delectable Mountains which belong to the Lord."

PC: This one is expertly machine pieced, with the multitude of little triangles perfectly positioned. And the tiny triangles of Turkey red in the center really provide a visual focal point and create movement, a pinwheel effect. The hand-quilting stitches form a two-inch grid over the surface of the quilt, with finer cable quilting in the borders.

JB: Many earlier examples of this pattern feature much finer ornamental quilting. It was popular in the 1840s and 1850s, particularly in Pennsylvania, where this quilt is believed to have originated.[1] Sometimes the earlier ones have a crisp, bold, graphic look, being made of indigo fabric against a white background that really shows off the quilting stitches. This quiltmaker may be playing against that earlier tradition, but in a more relaxed manner.

CD: I find it amazing that its dramatic effect is created entirely with simple triangles in various sizes and colors.

JH: Sometimes, as in this very successful work, we see a quiltmaker playing scale games with a particular visual idea. Here, she has worked together triangles from the very small to the very large in both positive and negative space. We instinctively understand and respond to such manipulations, which are both visual and intellectual. They give the quilt an added dimension and interest.

PC: The design appears at first glance more complicated than it actually is. The light blue and orange triangles create an optical vibration from the juxtaposition of complementary colors.

CD: And the maker's repetition of the large triangular patterns in a smaller version in the quilt's center creates an optical effect that draws the viewer into the center of the quilt. The red sawtooth × in the middle pulls the viewer even further inside.

JB: The light blue and light orange fabrics are different colorways of the same patterned print. Her use of color is interesting. Chrome orange was widely used in Pennsylvania. While this light orange print is not exactly like that, it makes me wonder if the quiltmaker was playing against that tradition too. In this context, the light orange print gives the same bold effect as the chrome orange does in other Pennsylvania quilts.

II / LOG CABIN, PINEAPPLE VARIATION

Maker unknown
Possibly Ohio
1865–85
77" × 68"
Wools and wool/cotton mixtures
QSPI: 5–6
1997.007.0551
International Quilt Study Center,
Ardis and Robert James Collection

JB: This is what I would call a "planned random" use of fabric. The maker is composing her design with numerous prints and solids, but in an intentional layout. The blues and greens, as well as the red polka dots and plaids, are all laid out horizontally, while the busy prints are all oriented vertically.

PC: Many different fabrics have been brought together, to a marvelous effect. There are diverse wool delaines, plaids, dobbies, serges, and gabardines. The somber, brownish-green fabric used as background in the majority of the blocks is woven with a dark green yarn in one direction and a chocolate brown in the other. This creates an iridescent effect that adds to the movement of the design.

JB: This looks hand pieced. And it's very heavy.

PC: It was foundation-pieced, which adds another layer to an already bulky top. In addition, the maker placed cotton batting behind the red square in the middle of each block, emphasizing the glowing center on which the Pineapple pattern is built. For the backing, she chose a black and red floral print that's a cotton and wool mixture.

CD: Most Log Cabin quilts are tacked or tied rather than quilted because of their bulkiness, but this maker chose to hand-quilt her creation. Quilting stitches outline the center square and are then used sparingly "in the ditch" of the third or fourth "log" and between each completed block.

JH: Many quilt patterns don't work visually as well in wools as they do in cotton. But Log Cabin quilts are among those that can be made very successfully in wool, sometimes achieving more interesting and arresting effects than might have been possible in cottons. This quilt shows why: the particular intensity or glow of deeply dyed wools gives an added depth to a busy, small-piece design.

JB: When one stands back from this quilt, it's evident that the choice of paisleys and plaids has added an extra visual dimension of vibration and movement beyond what one normally achieves in a Pineapple pattern, as if these blades are really whirring. It's one big vibrating grid, anchored by the small, glowing red diamonds in the center of each Log Cabin block. The resulting effect is completely different from the same pattern in plate 24, which is much more haphazard in its design.

12 / PICTORIAL ALBUM QUILT

Lucinda Ward Honstain (1820–1904)
Brooklyn, New York
Dated 1867
96" × 86"
Cottons
QSPI: 7–8
2001.011.0001
International Quilt Study Center,
Ardis and Robert James Collection

PC: Recent research by Melissa Jurgena, a graduate research fellow at the International Quilt Study Center, has revealed a remarkable amount of data about this quilt-maker and the meaning of her imagery.[1] Born in Ossining, New York, Lucinda Ward moved to lower Manhattan at age five and remained in the area for the rest of her life. She married John Honstain, a Brooklyn tailor who served as an officer in the Civil War. She made this quilt in her mid-forties, when she was living in the Williamsburg section of Brooklyn.

JB: The stylistic roots of this quilt are to be found in the popular Baltimore Album quilts of the 1840s and 1850s (although, as I discuss in my essay, unique pictorial appliqués predate that well-known genre). In most album quilts, different women stitched the individual blocks. This quilt is an album not in the sense of being a collection put together by diverse women, but as a series of vignettes of the artist's family life and her social milieu.

JH: The format is seven by six blocks, which should lead to forty-two different scenes, but Lucinda Honstain wasn't afraid to break out of the rigid grid to provide a more ample space (the size of three quilt squares) for a depiction of her prosperous-looking home. This oversize scene is in the center of the quilt, but set slightly to the left, giving a more dynamic feel to the composition. In some blocks, she composes the typical floral or geometric appliqués found on many midcentury quilts, while others are unique genre scenes.

JB: "The Reconciliation Quilt" was the nickname given to this quilt, which was published a number of times before it came to the IQSC.[2] Presumably its previous owners gave it this name because of the portrait of Confederate President Jefferson Davis, who was released from prison the year it was made. But this quilt is so much more than that—it's a social snapshot of American society right after the Civil War. The artist expresses an avid interest in topics both personal and political.

PC: The topic of emancipation, for example, was both personal and political to Lucinda Honstain. Her family owned slaves when she was a child. By the time she was seven, all slaves in New York became free under the state's gradual emancipation law. It appears from census records that the family's freed slaves may have continued to live nearby. So she probably continued to have contact with them. Lucinda's childhood memories of these transitions and continued interactions with freed slaves may account for her depiction of African Americans in a number of the blocks of her unique quilt.

JB: In addition to the marvelous block in which a large African American man proclaims to a white man on horseback, "Master I am free," she has composed several scenes in which emancipated blacks ply their trades: at the bottom, a bootblack or cobbler sits on a three-legged stool. In the upper left, an ice cream truck is attended by an African American man.

JH: America had just emerged from the national nightmare of the Civil War when this quilt was made, and things military were still very much in the air. The number of blocks with patriotic and military motifs is quite striking. There are two images of Zouaves (second row from top, far right; second row from bottom, third from left), infantry units that dressed in baggy pants, the kind we call "harem" pants, short jackets, and caps in an eastern style. The Fifth New York Volunteer Infantry regiment was a Zouave outfit and one of the most renowned infantry units of the Civil War. The image of the windmill is interesting too. In the mid-nineteenth century there were still windmills operating on Long Island, and perhaps in Brooklyn.

PC: The maker's father and brother were dry goods merchants, and her husband was a tailor. Perhaps that's why she had access to the remarkable range of fabrics used here. In the center, one row up from the bottom, a man drives a cart with the inscription "W.B. Dry Goods," which stands for Ward and Burroughs Dry Goods. Could this be a portrait of her brother, Thomas Ward?

JB: Melissa Jurgena's fine genealogical research on the family of the artist reveals how much data is available to elucidate the material culture of the nineteenth century. Lucinda Ward Honstain's quilt is one of the masterworks of that century's popular art.

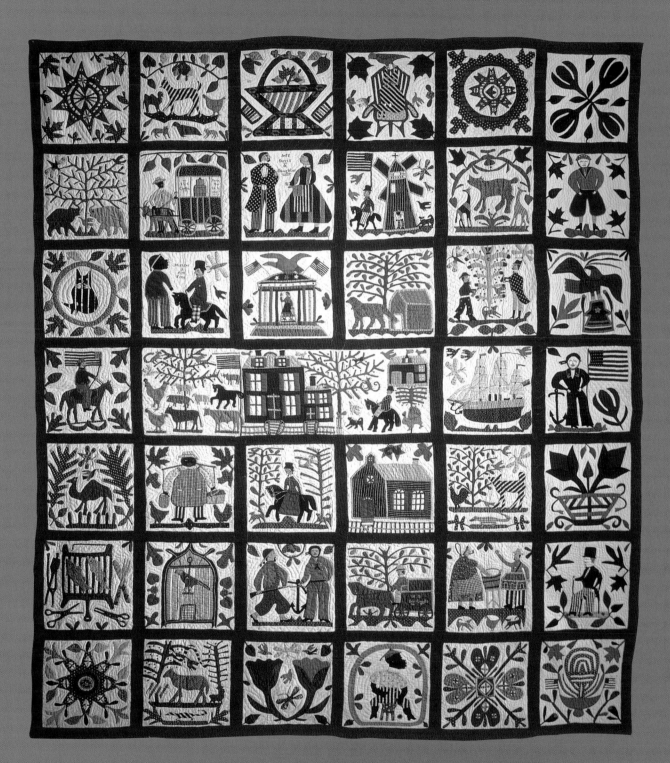

13 / ODD FELLOWS APPLIQUÉ TOP

Charlotte Gardner (~1858–?)
Probably New York or New Jersey
1870–90
104" × 92"
Cottons
Unquilted top
1997.007.0739
International Quilt Study Center,
Ardis and Robert James Collection

JB: This appliquéd quilt top is a lexicon of secret symbols associated with the Independent Order of Odd Fellows (IOofOF on the quilt), one of the most popular fraternal organizations of the nineteenth century. In the medallion area of the quilt, four bows and arrows (emblems of preparedness) point toward the other symbols, including the three chain links (friendship, love, and truth), the axe (progress), and the heart in hand (greeting brethren with affection).[1]

PC: That last sentiment may explain one of the three successive enframing borders—all those pairs of men greeting each other, with outstretched hands. Below them is a patriotic border of the kind that appears on many mid-century appliqué quilts: American eagles and stars. Closer to the center, above the men's heads, is an inner border composed of oak leaves appliquéd to rail-straight vines. The three predominant fabrics are a Turkey red, a double-pink, and a bright yellow-green, all calicoes typical of the 1860s through the 1880s. The eagles cut from the bright red calico boldly frame the design and direct the viewer's eye inward to the central field.

JH: This is an example of the sort of intense visual busyness that was sometimes worked into such appliqué quilts, as if the makers wanted to be sure that everything appropriate to their themes was included. The wonderful figura-tive borders are the most distinguishing visual element of this work, very unusual and effective.

JB: The information that came with this quilt indicated that it was made by Charlotte Gardner as part of her dowry.[2] At first I thought this was unlikely, since the iconography concerns a fraternal organization, and quilts with these types of symbols were sometimes made as presentation pieces or fund-raisers.[3] But as I read more about the Odd Fellows and looked more carefully at the symbols on the quilt top, I came to understand how this could be so. In the 1850s, a woman's auxiliary known as the Rebekah Degree was instituted. Since it was conferred only on women whose husbands were members, we can hypothesize that Charlotte Gardner was marrying an Odd Fellow. In addition to all the male secret symbols she has so carefully appliquéd in the center, there is a bee-hive under the "t" in "charity" and a crescent moon under the "h" in "hope." These, along with seven stars, are the emblems of the Rebekah Degree. Rather than sewing only seven stars, Charlotte Gardner has scattered sixty of them on her quilt top.

PC: So in this instance, historical research seems to support the information that accompanied the quilt.

JB: Everyone associates the "heart in hand" with nineteenth-century quiltmaking, but I didn't know it was an Odd Fellows symbol until researching this work of art. It was also carved on canes and painted on other implements used in Odd Fellow rituals.[4]

JH: Note that in the center of the quilt an appliquéd piece of cloth is shaped into a book with the words "Holy Bible" embroidered on it. This was to remind the nineteenth-century viewer that these fraternal organizations, which wielded so much power over social relationships, were, above all, Christian fraternities.

14 / LOG CABIN, COURTHOUSE STEPS VARIATION

Maker unknown
Possibly Ohio
1870–90
74" × 56"
Silks
Tied/Tufted
1997.007.0934
International Quilt Study Center,
Ardis and Robert James Collection

JH: This Log Cabin variant is called Courthouse Steps because it mirrors the façade of the classical-style municipal buildings that were going up all over the United States in the mid-nineteenth century. The component strips, differentiated by color, read as frieze, steps, and columns, with the so-called doorway being the little central square, often red as in other Log Cabins.

JB: Here, however, the central squares are black, as are the sashings and borders. Little silk tufts of different colors anchor the central black squares, harmonizing with the colors of the fabrics used as the building blocks of the courthouse: green, blue, orange, magenta, and so forth. To further enliven the surface, the maker has attached more tufts in the black sashing between the rows, at the points where the blocks join. She has arranged her silk blocks to form diagonal rows of color, but there is enough variety in her hues of green, blue, purple, gold, orange, and other colors that the diagonal coloration doesn't succumb to a fully predictable pattern. Instead, there's a syncopation of color across the surface.

PC: This gives it a particularly lively feeling. The quilt is both bold and delicate. Her finished log strips are very narrow, ranging from three-eighths of an inch to half an inch in width. She's made 140 blocks, and placed a sashing between them in just one direction. All of the blocks are hand pieced, but the long, narrow borders, including the wonderful strip-pieced borders, are machine stitched.[1]

JB: This is clearly a parlor quilt, made for show. Even the back is beautiful. The maker has affixed rose-colored tufts to punctuate the design of the teal blue striped taffeta she's chosen for her backing.

PC: Silk show quilts, both Crazy quilts and Log Cabin quilts, rose in popularity throughout North America as domestic production of silk accelerated during the last quarter of the nineteenth century. By 1900, American mills produced two-thirds of the world's silk fabric, woven from silk yarn imported from China.[2]

All the silks in this quilt top are in excellent condition, leading me to believe that they were not weighted, or were not heavily weighted. The weighting of silks involved impregnating the fabric with a metallic salt. This process improved the body and draping qualities of the fabric and also created a distinctive rustle when worn. It was developed by the textile industry to meet the demands of fashion. Unfortunately, the metallic salts, when added in excessive amounts (more than 10 percent of the fabric's original weight), weakened the fabric and led to the splitting (or shattering) of silk fabrics so often observed in silk quilts of the late nineteenth and early twentieth centuries.[3]

JH: Silk fabrics were not suitable for many pieced quilt patterns. They worked wonderfully, however, in Log Cabin–style blocks, especially, as here, in small-scale blocks. The intense silk colors and the visual movement gained from the use of little strips and small blocks occasionally produced a real visual gem. The movement of light across the surface of this quilt is particularly fine.

In the last decades of the nineteenth century, there was a great interest in things Japanese. Oriental design motifs, particularly Japanese ones, appeared in many quilts.

JB: So perhaps it's deliberate that these Courthouse Steps look like Japanese lanterns.

JH: The maker was smart enough to add some really strong containing borders. She's consciously designed it as if it were a painting within a wooden frame—at least that's the way I read it. Courthouse Steps is a wonderful pattern. Most of the ones made during the nineteenth century are visually very successful. One hardly ever sees a bad one!

15 / BLAZING STAR

Maker unknown
Possibly Missouri
1875–95
93" × 84"
Cottons
QSPI: 7
1997.007.0405
International Quilt Study Center,
Ardis and Robert James Collection

JH: A large central star composed of parallelogram-shaped pieces has been a standard in American quiltmaking for more than a century and a half. Visually it is always powerful. Often, as here, it is pulsing and radiant. The so-called "cheddar" color (more properly called chrome orange) was popular in the last quarter of the nineteenth century, particularly in Pennsylvania.

PC: This quilt, composed of all solid-color cotton muslins in a variation of the beloved Lone Star pattern, is hand pieced. Its hand-quilting was accomplished in dark thread with seven stitches per inch. The maker may have been Mennonite or Amish, since the quilt has several characteristics typical of their work—the use of solids rather than prints, very fine quilting, and the use of a dark quilting thread. While her expert quilting stitches hold the cotton batting securely in place, she did not select a stitching pattern that sets off her bold Lone Star. Instead she quilted it all over in a simple fan pattern common on Midwestern quilts.

JB: The optics here are spectacular. The orange and red work very effectively against the two shades of green—light sage and dark spruce. The blue in the center and near the points of the Lone Star and in the smaller stars punctuates the design in a rhythmically balanced way.

JH: Such central star designs work best in a square or almost square format because of the way they radiate visually from the center.

JB: Bordering just two sides of the quilt with the chrome orange and sage zigzag frames it in an intriguing manner. The central star is integrated so fully with its complex background that it takes a while to discern the eight points of the star.

CD: Yes, one's eye focuses on the orange ring of diamonds, set between rings of dark green diamonds, which frame the star's pulsating center. The eight points of the star simply act as fillers between the smaller stars that circle the center ring. As if the complexity of the interlocking star pattern wasn't enough, the maker added a zigzag border and bound the quilt in bright red!

JH: Often, as here, there are echoing, smaller stars in the corners or surrounding the main star, a stylistic retention from the pattern's birth in the 1830s. The integration of parts and the color choices in this quilt obscure the (normal) eight arms of the central star, which are, as Janet observed, usually more distinct. In this quilt, they are hiding among the other stars of the galaxy.

PC: The striking orange pieces so satisfactorily positioned throughout were probably colored with chrome orange, which was a mineral dye. By treating potassium dichromate with an alkali, nineteenth-century dyers discovered that they could produce this distinctive color. It became commercially available in America around 1840[1] and remained popular (though not as popular as chrome yellow) from the mid-nineteenth century until the end of the century.

Star patterns are favorites of American quiltmakers across time and place. They were the most prevalent pattern found in Nebraska quilts between 1870 and 1990.[2] The Broken Star, a variation of the large single-star format, was a favorite of Midwestern quiltmakers of the early twentieth century. Ricky Clark notes that the Broken Star is a "particularly favored pattern" of the Ohio Amish.[3]

JB: The star takes on local flavor wherever it is made, whether by Amish or Mennonite quilters, African American quilters, or Native American quilters. Among Plains Indian quilters, where the Lone Star has been popular for well over one hundred years now, it's called the Morning Star, and often the points or the minor stars are turned into tipis, or the star becomes an eagle design. In that context, its hundreds of diamond-shaped pieces recall the complex patterning of Plains Indian quillwork.

PC: The quilt is backed with a beautiful red and black paisley print—a clue that supports its estimated date because black paisley designs on a red ground were a new style that appeared toward the end of the nineteenth century.[4]

16 / THE HATTIE BURDICK
TILE QUILT TOP

Made by Minnie Burdick (1857–1951), Elvira Mixer, Annie
Adams McKee, and (or for) Hattie Burdick (1861–1923)
New London, Connecticut
Circa 1876
80" × 81"
Cottons
Unquilted
1997.007.0163
International Quilt Study Center,
Ardis and Robert James Collection

JB: These so-called Tile quilts intrigue me. They're given
that name because irregular pieces of printed fabric are
appliquéd onto muslin in such a way that the muslin
backing looks like the grout of a tiled surface.

PC: At first glance, Tile quilts resemble Crazy quilts,
but they're constructed entirely differently. Crazy quilts
are made of random pieces of fabric (usually silks) overlapped and attached to a foundation square with fancy
embroidery stitches, whereas Tile quilts are made by
appliquéing random shapes to a white foundation square,
leaving a space between the pieces.

JH: Such Crazy-style work, here beautifully harnessed to
an overall grid pattern, grew out of the asymmetrical design influences, chiefly Asian, that affected Western arts
in the later nineteenth century.

JB: One published Tile quilt is dated circa 1870 and attributed to Edith Montgomery.[1] It's of particular interest to
compare it to this one because both have some blocks
that feature square or rectangular "brick-work" as well as
irregular, shard-like crazy squares. Other quilts like it are
given the name Boston Pavement. I don't know of very
many of them, but several published examples are said
to be from varying geographic locales and with dates that
range from 1870 to 1900.[2]

PC: Few Tile quilts survive, perhaps because so few were
ever made. And, unlike most Crazy quilts, all surviving
Tile quilts are made of cotton and eschew the lavish
embroidery that distinguishes Crazy quilts. The only Tile
quilt with a date inscribed on it (of which I'm aware) is
one owned by the Shelburne Museum with the date 1873
appliquéd in the center block and believed to have been
made in Connecticut.[3] This indicates that Tile quilts pre-

date the Centennial Exposition in Philadelphia, an event
credited with sparking a Crazy quilt mania among American women.

JB: In the center of the quilt the name "Hattie Burdick"
is prominently appliquéd in orange and red fabrics.

PC: According to family tradition supplied by the dealer
and corroborated through genealogical research, the quilt
was made in New London, Connecticut, by Minnie Burdick, Elvira Mixer, and Annie Adams McKee, possibly
with the help of Hattie Burdick, for whom this quilt top
was made.[4] Since Minnie married Herbert Dwight Childs
in April 1877 and moved to North Adams, Massachusetts,
this suggests the quilt was made before her marriage.

Before we completed additional genealogical research
and learned this, we had conservatively estimated that the
quilt was made between 1870 and 1890, based on an examination of the fabrics used.[5] Supporting our estimated date
are the paisley prints, printed plaids, and printed laces
found in this top, all of which were especially popular
during the last quarter of the nineteenth century. Paisley
prints were inspired by the imported Kashmir shawls so
fashionable earlier in the century. In addition, there are
numerous roller-printed imitations of more complicated
fabrics, including printed plaids, printed laces, and even
some prints meant to imitate ikats, those labor-intensive
fabrics woven from tie-dyed yarns.[6]

JB: This Tile quilt has many pictorial elements, and it
reflects the maker's interest in the craze for all things Asian
that swept America in the nineteenth century. She has cut
from pictorial fabrics images of Arab horsemen, a crane,
a pagoda, and a lotus.

PC: Yes, it makes one wonder whether Minnie and Hattie
attended the Philadelphia Centennial Exposition, where
the arts featured in the Japanese Pavilion captivated millions of Americans. More than 9.5 million Americans
visited the Japanese Pavilion, one of the most popular
attractions at the Centennial Exposition.[7] Were Minnie
and Hattie, who in 1876 would have been about nineteen
and fifteen years of age, respectively, inspired to make this
quilt by something they saw at the exhibition or by news-
paper accounts of the exotic arts on view there?[8]

JB: Because of the similarities among these Tile quilts, I
wonder if *Godey's Lady's Book* or another magazine may
have published instructions for something like this.

17 / OAK REEL

Caroline Ruth (1838–1907)
Marion County, Ohio
Dated 1889
92" × 68"
Cottons
QSPI: 6–9
1997.007.0429
International Quilt Study Center,
Ardis and Robert James Collection

JB: Here is a splendid example of a nineteenth-century red and green appliqué of the type that was most popular when this quilter was a young woman.[1] But Caroline Ruth made hers—or at least finished it—in 1889 at fifty-one years of age, appliquéing both the date and her initials on the quilt.

CD: The six large squares are the Oak Reel pattern, a fairly standard pattern for floral appliqué. But the maker's ingenuity is displayed in her fanciful border.[2]

JB: A conventional meandering vine is enlivened by some four dozen animals and objects set on either side of it.

CD: Some of the "leaves" on the trailing vine transform into platforms on which cows, roosters, horses, and geese are standing. One of the most wonderful of these images is the upright bear, at the bottom left, who carries a walking stick made from a branch.

PC: Caroline Ruth was unconcerned about the relative scale of these animals. In the upper right, for example, the fly is larger than the goat, while the elephant is smaller than either! At both upper corners are pipes; elsewhere we see a boot, axe, anchor, hammer, and pail.

JH: Both in appliqué quilts and in Crazy quilts, we often see family themes presented: history and memorabilia. An anchor, for instance, can signify a family member who served in the navy. In effect, these quilts become albums of family history. The use of folksy-looking animal and sentimental imagery occurs again in the red-embroidered quilts made mostly at the turn of the twentieth century.

PC: We now know that the maker, Caroline Seiter Ruth, was born on June 9, 1838, in Marion County, Ohio, where she remained all her life.[3]

JB: The motifs of paired birds whose beaks meet and paired birds who hold a heart between their beaks were common folk art motifs in painting and carving done by German immigrants.

CD: Ruth is much better with her quilting than with her appliqué stitches. She sometimes fudges the tiny appliqué details, embroidering over them to hide a poor seam.

JB: To return to my initial comment, it's possible that as an older woman, Ruth returned to unfinished appliqué work she had started in her youth. All quilters are familiar with this phenomenon; we know of many women in the twentieth century who started a pattern when it was popular, in the 1930s, for example, and didn't finish it until the 1980s.[4]

18 / MY CRAZY DREAM

Mary M. Hernandred Ricard (1838–1915)
Boston and Haverhill, Massachusetts
Dated 1877–1912
74" × 68 1/2"
Silks
Unquilted top
1997.007.0541
International Quilt Study Center,
Ardis and Robert James Collection

JB: By the 1870s, classic patchwork quilts (e.g., plates 2 and 4) were out of fashion in many urban, middle-class homes, although they continued to be popular in rural areas. A new fad seized America's women, inspired by the international displays at the 1876 Centennial Exposition in Philadelphia. The fine English embroidery on display there impressed many viewers. Soon afterwards, classes in crewelwork and embroidery were being offered in major cities, and popular magazines featured articles on the latest stitches. The Japanese aesthetic, displayed in the decorative objects of the Japanese Pavilion, came as a revelation. From these diverse influences the American quiltmaker devised a new kind of modern quilt and called it the Crazy quilt.[1]

It's popularly thought that the name "Crazy quilt" refers to its somewhat lunatic visual extravagance. While this interpretation is not wrong, the name may have come from the word "crazed," as applied to the allover crazing in some Japanese ceramics where the glaze is cracked into an irregular pattern. Some contemporary accounts even refer to this type of textile as Japanese patchwork.

PC: Crazy quilts were seldom functional bedcovers; more often they were used as smaller, ornamental throws, draped over a sofa or screen in the parlor, or atop a plain bed coverlet as a decorative accent. And they were most often fashioned out of fine silk taffetas, satins, brocades, and velvets. The extravagant use of silk was a result of new developments in trade and manufacturing, which made this formerly costly material more affordable.

JB: In the center of her quilt, the artist embroidered an odd scene in which a giant peacock and a small elephant share the landscape with a house, human figures, and a dog. The sky is composed of light blue silks with embroidered clouds. An embroidered rainbow arcs over the scene, separating it from the wild patchwork of the rest of the coverlet. The prominent central house is a later version of the houses often appliquéd on Baltimore Album quilts or other pictorial quilts (see, for example, plate 12).

PC: Mary Hernandred Ricard proudly stitched an image of herself onto her creation. The image, transferred to a white silk fabric, may have been produced by a photogravure or a photolithograph process from one of her cabinet cards (photographs on cardstock for exchange with family members and friends). She started the quilt when she was about thirty-eight and completed it at about seventy-four years of age, just a few years before her death in 1915.[2]

JB: Sometimes, individual squares of crazed patchwork overlaid with embroidery were organized into a grid. But here, the maker took pains to conceal the fact that her masterpiece is composed of individual blocks fitted together: she overlapped the silks and the embroidery stitches to make an asymmetrical mosaic over the entire picture plane.

CD: There are virtually no patches that have not been embellished. Mrs. Ricard embroidered Japanese-style fans in each corner. In the lower left fan she embroidered her name, M. M. H. Ricard, and the quilt's title, *My Crazy Dream*. In the lower right fan she recorded the information "Boston, 1877–Haverhill, 1912."

JH: Such visually packed Crazy quilts, late-Victorian albums of popular taste, kitsch, and family mementos, reached a zenith in the mid-1880s, when exotic imported designs were transfiguring all of Western decorative art. All the world's images were copied in highly elaborated objects meant for middle-class consumption; the world of manufactured art goods was upon us. The Crazy quilt was a prime example of this globalization of taste.

JB: When M. M. Hernandred Ricard began this quilt in Boston in 1877, she surely never imagined that it would take her thirty-five years to complete. She began just as the Crazy quilt mania was taking hold in America's cities. In 1912, when she finally "finished" the top—finished being a relative term, for she put a final date on it, although there are still basting stitches in the outer border, and it lacks a backing—the Crazy quilt fad was over.[3] But many families handed these exceptional coverlets down through the generations as evidence of the fine artistry of their female ancestors.

19 / WOOL CRAZY QUILT

Maker unknown
Probably Lancaster County, Pennsylvania
Dated February 17, 1891
74" × 71 ½"
Wools and a few cottons
QSPI: 8
1997.007.0107
International Quilt Study Center,
Ardis and Robert James Collection

JB: All Crazy quilts are "wild by design," but this one is especially so. While most of the wool serge and gabardine fabrics are uniform in their values and quite drab, the intensive use of red and two colors of blue wool embroidery along the seam lines and across much of the quilt electrifies it. In many places, lines of herringbone stitch in red and blue appear side by side, adding to a bold effect of nervous energy. The sixty-four crazy blocks, each approximately six-and-a-half-inches square, are surrounded by wonderful borders. There the artist plays with shifting diagonal lines, giving the quilt an extra dimension of dynamism. I think of these wool Crazy quilts as more of a vernacular tradition; many of them show signs of wear, which most of the fine silk Crazy parlor throws do not. Though sharing many characteristics with silk Crazy quilts, they were intended as utility quilts—albeit ones on which much attention was lavished. I see them as a different class of objects.

JH: Crazy quilts had a compositional development from the earliest ones, which were randomly patterned, overall organic compositions with visually necessary borders, to the later ones, which were often worked, as in this case, in the block style. It was a logical thing to do, to tame the irregularity of the style by forcing it into a square format, yet to retain its wonderful randomness and possibilities for improvisation. Sometimes the block format gave it sufficient containment for the makers to feel comfortable eliminating borders. I tend to like the later ones better; they often look, as do some of the blocks in this quilt, like aerial photographs. This is a masterpiece of the genre: sophisticated colors, wonderful, inventive drawing, and a tough border that pops the lively center out.

PC: It's both inspired by the Victorian high style of the 1880s and a reaction to it. This artist wanted to make a quilt in the popular style, but decided to use wool (with a few pieces of cotton) instead of silk, for both her fabric pieces and her embroidery yarns. The acquisition notes indicate that this quilt comes from Lancaster County, Pennsylvania. Pennsylvania, especially the Philadelphia area, was an important center for wool processing and spinning throughout the nineteenth century. In fact, the Germantown borough of Philadelphia became associated with soft woolen three- or four-ply yarns like the ones used for the embroidery in this quilt.

JH: Eastern Pennsylvania was a hotbed of creative quiltmaking. Its mixture of cultural traditions—Amish, Mennonite, Quaker, English, German—and its tradition of fine handwork, produced an incredible variety of quilt styles and innovative aesthetics, ranging from the austerity and classicism of the great Amish quilts to the vibrant and "modernist" color choices of the other Pennsylvania Dutch.

JB: There was great cross-cultural pollination in the textile arts of eastern Pennsylvania, and, as Patricia Herr has shown, a rich and varied tradition was the result.[1]

PC: This quilt is dated by an embroidered inscription: February 17, 1891. As we studied the quilt more carefully, we noticed that the thread used for the embroidered date is a cotton embroidery floss instead of a wool yarn like those used for the embroidery throughout the rest of the quilt. In addition, the embroidered date is the only example of chain stitch anywhere on the quilt. All initials and leaf outlines in the rest of the quilt were done in an outline embroidery stitch. While the maker could reasonably have chosen to use a cotton thread rather than wool because finer cotton embroidery floss would be easier to work into an inscription, the difference nevertheless stands out.

JH: Since the inscription contains a specific date, but is in a different yarn and embroidery stitch from that used in the rest of the quilt, I wonder if the inscription is commemorative in nature and was a later addition. Was it, instead of the date the quilt was finished, the date the quilt was given to someone who wished to memorialize it after the fact? Or was it the birth date of someone to whom it was given later? I consider some such scenario more likely than a fraudulent addition to enhance value. It is, in any case, in its color choices and wonderful drawing, a breakthrough piece, one that reworks a style in a unique way.

20 / GOD'S NIGHT TIME SKY

Harriet Miller Carpenter (1831–1915)
Lancaster County, Pennsylvania
Dated 1892
94 ½" × 85"
Cottons
QSPI: 8
1997.007.0264
International Quilt Study Center,
Ardis and Robert James Collection

JH: This quilter approached her work as if it were a canvas for painting rather than a setting for repetitive pattern. She's ambitious: trying to put the cosmos on her canvas.

PC: And in this case, it wasn't just Harriet Carpenter. She lived with her husband Uriah at Pine Holl Farm near Lancaster, Pennsylvania. According to family tradition, Uriah designed the quilts and Harriet stitched them.

JB: When I first saw this quilt I was astonished by its bold conception and design. I assumed it must be a unique object, but in fact "grandma Carpenter," as she calls herself in the embroidered inscription, made at least twenty unusual quilts, which she embellished in oversize calligraphy for her grandchildren. Some are singular design fields like this one; others are somewhat more conventional in their composition, made of pieced blocks.[1] This is one of her earliest, made for her oldest grandchild Elsie C. Hess (1882–1929). She was evidently pleased with this inventive pattern, since she used it again in 1896 on a quilt for another granddaughter.[2]

PC: Patricia Herr has called Harriet Carpenter, who was Mennonite, "undoubtedly the most innovative Lancaster County quiltmaker yet known."[3]

JH: Pennsylvania quiltmakers in general were very innovative in that they brought their often strong color sense directly to their quilts; that's one of the ways you can spot nineteenth-century Pennsylvania quilts from across a room: few others combined bright colors, or particular combinations of colors, the way they did. We don't see it in painting until the twentieth century.

JB: She has used blue quilting thread on the blue field, and orange quilting thread on her chrome orange border, where she has stitched a sinuous vine with grape leaves and bunches of grapes. The tiny stars on the quilt are all embroidered, as is the Milky Way, while the larger stars are appliquéd. The initials in the center are beautifully embroidered, with a double outline, and filled in with the same sorts of little stitches she used to compose the Milky Way. They look like the illuminated letters on medieval manuscripts. Of course the German immigrants to Pennsylvania had the tradition of *fraktur,* elaborate calligraphy and decorative painting on documents that recorded births, deaths, marriages, and prayers.

JH: Yes, that kind of drawing and conception (fanciful, often asymmetrical; bold, strong colors) had been part of the Pennsylvania folk art tradition since the eighteenth century. You can see it in this quilt in the moon and the shooting star above it, and the composition that draws so many disparate elements, including a visually difficult calligraphic center, into a coherent, lively, and successful composition. Of course, we don't know for sure what Harriet and Uriah Carpenter's actual influences were, but this quilt and their others fall into that group of eccentric, unique pictorial quilts whose makers were often motivated by a felt need to preserve history, to pass on family and cultural information through symbolic and stylized representation.

JB: Some of the Carpenter map quilts were said to have been made for didactic purposes—to teach the grandson his counties and states.[4] Perhaps the maps of the heavens were meant to be astronomy lessons for the granddaughters. On the 1896 quilt, the planets are named; here they appear simply as the larger stars.

JH: We forget what the night sky looked like to nineteenth-century Americans, especially those who lived in the country. It was a brilliant, commanding presence, something we've lost with modern light pollution. Celestial events such as meteor showers were important, often given spiritual significance. We should keep that in mind when we see quiltmakers such as Harriet Carpenter or Harriet Powers, for example (fig. 12), visually recording celestial events.

Made and presented to

E E H

by grandma Carpenter.

1892.

21 / POSTAGE STAMP STAR

Maker unknown
Probably Bowmansville, Lancaster County, Pennsylvania
1880–1900
79" × 77 ½"
Cottons
QSPI: 8
1997.007.0133
International Quilt Study Center,
Ardis and Robert James Collection

JB: People unthinkingly call something like this a scrap quilt, but it only takes a few moments of scrutiny to realize that this quiltmaker planned her work with precision and had sufficient quantities of many different fabrics to allow her to execute the design fully.

PC: Yes, her design was completely intentional. Notice how in the red border framing the star, she alternates a darker Turkey red calico with a lighter double-pink print. The next row alternates white and chrome orange squares, with the darker orange square set next to the lighter pink of the previous row.

JB: The variety of dark brown prints that form the background to the star are repeated in precisely the same pattern of alternation in all four corners. The way she's done this makes me wonder if late-nineteenth-century quiltmakers who were using sewing machines might have figured out for themselves some of our late-twentieth-century labor-saving tricks, such as sewing long strips of different fabrics together and then cutting them into strips of small squares which can be sewn to other strips of small squares.

The maker has also carefully played her solids against her prints. She focuses a lot of clear strong colors in the middle, as well as in the outer border where the solid red and green form a zigzag, enclosing the star by leading the eye around it.

PC: Notice too how she strategically uses solids to outline the large central star. By alternating solid blue and blue-green squares to form a dark outline, she clearly sets the star apart from the background and makes the star almost shimmer along the edges.

JB: This artist understood the effects of even small accents of strong colors: wedged into the "elbow" of each of the four corners of the star is one small square of red polka-dot fabric, which gives a piquant little accent.

There are 4,225 "postage-stamp" pieces in this quilt, each a finished one-and-a-quarter-inch square, and this quiltmaker has placed every one with deliberation as to its optical effect. Though the effect of her mosaic style can only be appreciated by standing back from the quilt, it's only by examining it close-up that we can appreciate the extent of her talent and her labor.

PC: According to Patricia Herr, the star variation of the Postage Stamp pattern is "a classic pattern which does not require close inspection to be identified as a Lancaster County [Pennsylvania] quilt." Herr notes that this variation was made almost exclusively by Mennonite women living in and near the town of Bowmansville in Brecknock Township. In fact, she reports, "It is so closely identified with the area that dealers and collectors often refer to it as the Bowmansville Star."[1]

JH: This has always been a favorite pattern of mine, both aesthetically and intellectually. I saw my first one in a collection in Pennsylvania in the 1970s, and included it in *The Pieced Quilt*.[2] I was then lucky enough to find one myself, so I've been able to study it for some decades. The idea of making the central star from squares rather than diamonds (the more common building shape for such quilts, and harder to work with than squares) was typical of the simplifying of work methods so integral to the visual success of American pieced quilts. "Squaring it up" created a tile-like, Moorish quality during a generation when such exotic design ideas had become part of American visual culture.

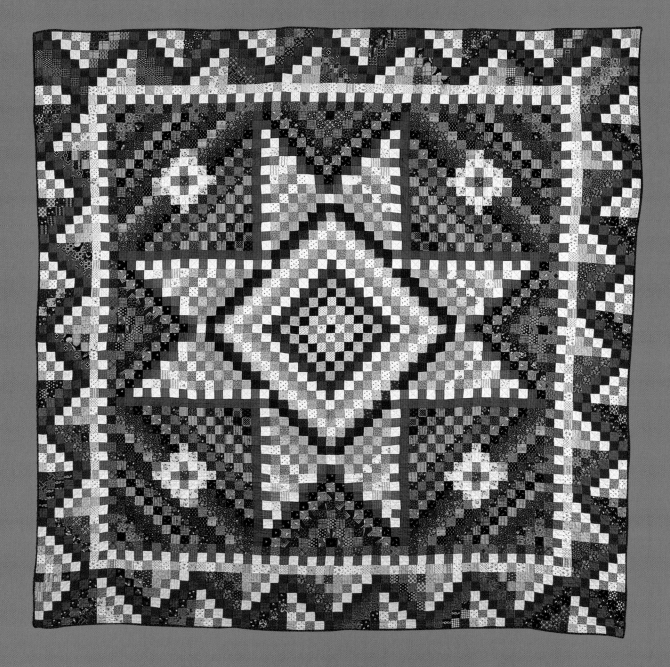

22 / LOG CABIN, CHIMNEY AND CORNERSTONE VARIATION

Maker unknown
Probably Ohio
1880–1900
74" × 69"
Wools and cottons
Tied
1997.007.0561
International Quilt Study Center,
Ardis and Robert James Collection

JB: The chief characteristic of Log Cabin quilts as a group is the optical variety made possible through the ingenious use of materials of different patterns or colors, and the myriad possibilities of block arrangement.

JH: Like some other block quilts, the Log Cabin design is formed by the linkage of adjoining blocks to form large overall designs covering the surface of the quilt. The basic visual structure of the diagonally divided Log Cabin block (normally half dark and half light) allows a group of blocks to be placed to form many distinctive patterns, such as Barn Raising (fig. 14), Streak of Lightning, Straight Furrow, Courthouse Steps (plate 14), and Pineapple (plates 11, 23, 24). This one, in which the fabrics were carefully placed to form a cross set off by a diamond shape, is an unusual configuration.

CD: This variant is called Chimney and Cornerstone. The maker has joined 288 blocks, each four-and-a-half-inches square. These are set sixteen squares by eighteen squares. Each square is composed of thirteen pieces—a red center and twelve pieces added around it, all pieced on a foundation. So this quilt has 3,744 pieces of fabric! Many of the fabrics are wool, but the printed plaid, the one that is red, butterscotch, and white, is cotton. Conse-

quently, the quilt is approximately half wool and half cotton.

JB: The maker uses this red and butterscotch cotton plaid, set against a blue-green and white striped wool and cotton fabric, to particularly fine optical effect. When you stand back from the quilt, the red/yellow diamonds stand out. If you squint, the large red/yellow diamonds with dark crosses in their centers and the smaller red/yellow crosses seem to float over the darker surface of the quilt; hence the name Chimneys and Cornerstones.

CD: In constructing each individual block, the maker often chose the darkest purple, green, or black fabrics as the two outermost strips. This causes the large crosses, as well as the secondary pattern of squares, to appear on the quilt.

JH: The particular genius of the block style—easily manipulated repetitive designs formed within squares—was that it enabled people with no formal training in the visual arts to create extremely powerful and beautiful works of art that were as admired in their day as they are in our own.

It's important to acknowledge that the maker of this powerful quilt, like the designers and makers of most of the other quilts illustrated in this book, clearly visualized her design as a finished work, as a whole, in the manner of any creator of a two-dimensional graphic work.

JB: In my essay in this volume, I address the issue of designs only visible from a distance (pp. 24–25). When looking at quilts in museums, people love to say, "But of course they weren't made to be seen on walls!" Yet it's clear that in most cases of well-designed quilts, the maker did indeed stand back from it, just as we do in a museum setting, in order to ascertain that her bold allover pattern worked—as this one does so brilliantly.

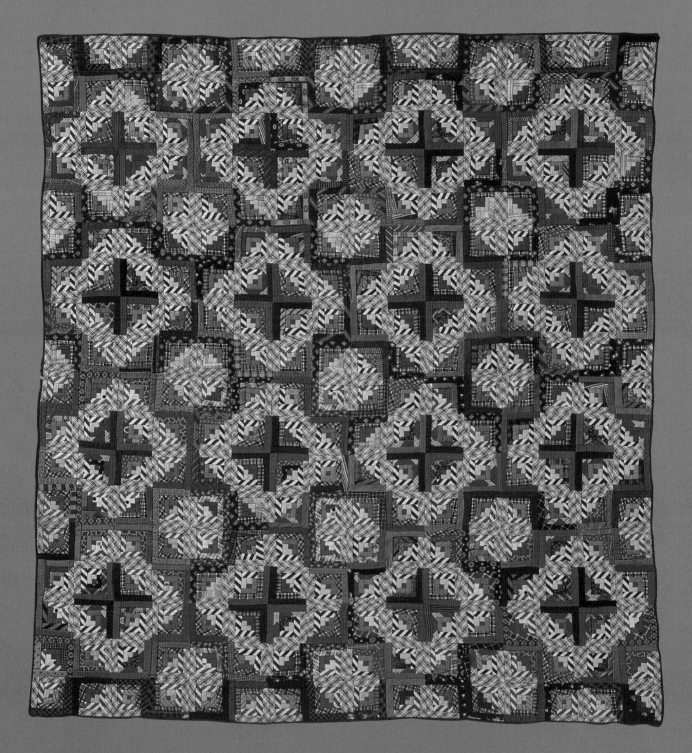

23 / LOG CABIN, PINEAPPLE VARIATION

Maker unknown
Possibly Lancaster County, Pennsylvania
1880–1900
82" × 82"
Wools
QSPI: 8–9
1997.007.0691
International Quilt Study Center,
Ardis and Robert James Collection

JH: These optically active Log Cabin quilts from the late nineteenth century, the end results of generations of visual experimentation, are for me a high point of quilt aesthetics. Pieced quiltmakers had figured out how to make their grids advance and recede on the surface, an almost three-dimensional effect. Here, the grid system anchored with red diamonds seems to overlay a grid beneath; it reminds me of Moorish window treatments.

CD: This Log Cabin quilt is arranged in the Pineapple variation and contains fourteen fabrics of different colors—mainly wool gabardines. The maker set a solid red triangle in each corner of her Pineapple blocks, creating a grid of diamonds superimposed over the individual squares. Strong sashing in glowing complementary colors of red and green define the Pineapple blocks and seem to emphasize a swirling motion created through the interplay of colors and forms.

JH: The great Pineapple Log Cabin patterns, at their most optical, as here, look like buzz saw blades working. I've always thought that the new engines of the nineteenth century, with their fast-moving parts, their flywheels, the circular buzz saws, might have inspired some of these designs.

PC: The origin of the Log Cabin pattern is often attributed to American quiltmakers; however, Janet Rae presents persuasive evidence that it's a pattern of the British Isles that dates back to at least the early nineteenth century and possibly to the mid-eighteenth century. She provides examples of extant British quilts from the first half of the nineteenth century that feature the Log Cabin pattern. Rae states that the pattern was called the Roof pattern on the Isle of Man and Loghouse quilting in Canada.[1]

JB: Yes, for example, *The Dictionary of Needlework,* published in London in 1882, interchangeably uses the terms American Patchwork, Canadian Patchwork, and Loghouse Quilting for the pattern we know as Log Cabin.[2] They advise making it out of three-quarter-inch ribbon rather than fabric strips, which suggests that the British were taking a pattern that was a staple of American quilting practice and turning it to more ornamental ends, as was common during the age of the Crazy quilt and the parlor throw.

CD: An unusual feature of this Log Cabin is that it's hand-quilted from the back in a grid fashion with rows about one and three-quarter inches apart. The quilting stitches, however, do not go through to the front. They appear to go through the backing and foundation fabric only. There is no batting. The quilt's outer border is embellished with a machine-stitched grid of red thread. At first glance, it looks like machine-quilting; however, the stitching does not go through all three layers of the quilt. Instead, the stitching appears to be purely decorative. This seems to be an appropriate finish for a quilt made more for show than for use.

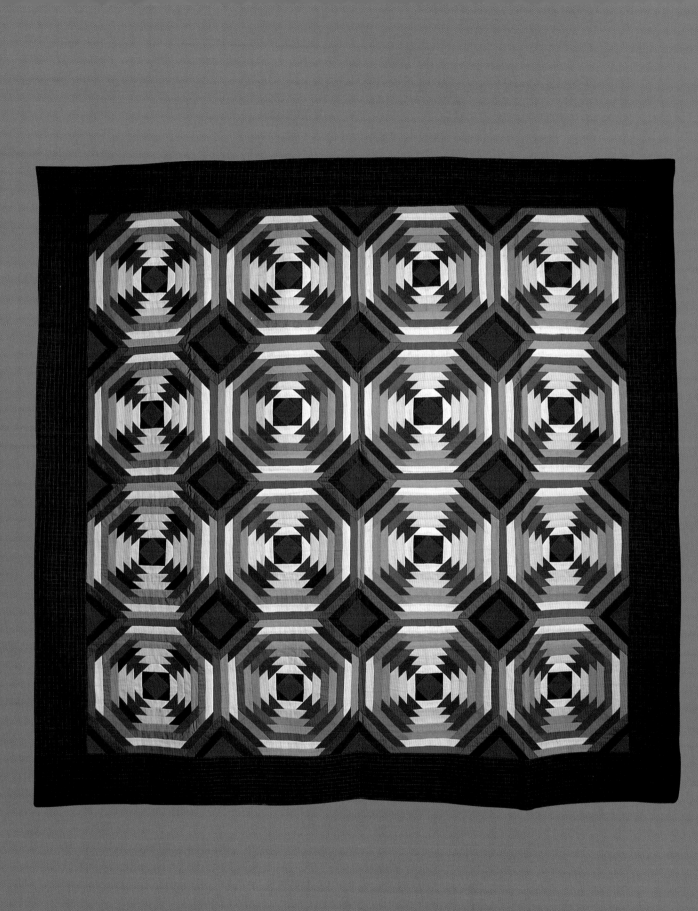

24 / LOG CABIN, PINEAPPLE VARIATION

Maker Unknown
Probably Pennsylvania
1880–1900
70" × 68 ½"
Wools and wool/cotton mixtures
QSPI: 5–6
1997.007.0923
International Quilt Study Center,
Ardis and Robert James Collection

JB: The Pineapple variation of the Log Cabin is especially effective, I think, in suggesting motion. As the fabric strips or logs rotate, four of one color are set around the central hearth, and then four of a different color are set at a forty-five degree angle to the prior set. Sometimes this alternation of just two colors makes up the entire block, resulting in something that looks like serrated windmill blades or pinwheels in motion around a fixed center. We see this in the blue, purple, and black squares that run diagonally from lower left to upper right in the middle of the quilt.

JH: The variable use of light and dark colors and the diverse fabrics within some blocks make the design advance and recede in a lively way. Some of the shapes look like fan blades or windmill blades, as Janet said. Others look like targets.

PC: This is a true scrap quilt, with a lot of variation in the individual blocks. The result is dynamic movement and visual interest.

JB: Note that the maker has tried to place her blocks so that one heathery striped background fabric occurs in most of the inner sixteen blocks, but clearly she ran a little short. Similarly, the outermost row of squares, six on a side, is composed principally of a different background fabric.

PC: The fabrics are an interesting selection of wool and wool/cotton combinations in solids (gabardines, bengalines, and fancy dobbies), prints (several different delaines), as well as plaids and stripes. Testing the border fabric revealed it to be fiber-dyed wool in one direction and a brown cotton yarn in the other. The wool yarn, a blend of different shades of brown and beige fibers (possibly natural colors of the wool fleece), produces a rich, heathery look. The backing is a beautiful cotton paisley print, while the binding is a bias-cut red and blue wool tartan plaid.

CD: Oddly, the decorative machine-quilting in the border—in a cable design—does not go all the way through to the back. The blocks themselves are hand quilted around the edge of the blocks, in the ditch. This decorative use of machine stitching is the same technique as found in plate 23. Could it be a way of stabilizing a foundation fabric added to the border to make it consistent with the rest of the foundation-pieced blocks? Or was this simply a means of showing that she owned a sewing machine?

JH: This block uses Log Cabin–style construction, strips radiating from a central square. What I particularly like about this quilt is the irregularity of the blocks, so different from the normally tight control we see in most Log Cabin–style quilts. The maker gave the blocks so much variation that at first glance it looks more like a pieced album quilt. It was an innovative way to use a standard block, which could have created a visual disaster. But her wonderful color choices, block positioning, and compositional sense made a great painting. It just sings.

25 / ROBBING PETER TO PAY PAUL

Maker unknown
Possibly Pennsylvania
1880–1900
80" × 70"
Wools and wool/cotton mixtures
QSPI: 5
Private Collection of Ardis and Robert James

JB: There are so many wonderfully evocative names for quilt patterns. Some refer to events in American history—Whig Rose and Burgoyne Surrounded, for example. Others refer to biblical sources or inspirational books—Rose of Sharon and Delectable Mountains. Robbing Peter to Pay Paul has an odd derivation. Apparently it comes from an event in British history, when the sixteenth-century king Edward VI ordered St. Peter's church in Westminster to sell some of its land in order to pay for the repair of St. Paul's in London.[1] This pattern is most often composed of just two colors, in which case the "robbing" refers to the alternation of colors.[2]

JH: More specifically, some of the pieces the quilter cuts from one color of fabric are "robbed" to form the design in a square of another color.

CD: In a two-color Robbing Peter to Pay Paul, the circles predominate.[3] In this multicolor version, the circle form recedes somewhat because the maker didn't match up the colors to form a circle. So the viewer is more aware of the individual blocks and the concave squares within them.

PC: The maker of this quilt was a fine colorist. Using both dusty and chalky colors—no pure hues—she has created a sense of visual movement. From a distance, the effect is of the alternation of solid colors, but in fact some of the woolen fabrics are not solids. There's a dark brown pinstripe, a dobby weave, a pin check suiting, and some fancy twills.

JB: The artist achieved a fine balance of repetition and syncopation. The color placement is not random: the diagonal rows of magenta, brown, navy, red, light blue, and butterscotch concave forms move methodically from lower right to upper left in series, across the surface of the quilt. For the most part, the more somber colors are reserved for the perimeter.

CD: A variety of white, black, red, and aqua quilting threads are used, and the quilting stitches are a mere five per inch.

JB: While the hand-quilting isn't noteworthy in terms of technique, it suits the pieced pattern. The curved lines of quilting stitches echo the pieced curves, while the inside of the concave squares are quilted in a diamond grid. This quilter is better at design and color than she is at the needlework itself. Though the corners meet clumsily, and the quilting stitches are unremarkable, this is a work of great graphic power.

JH: It gains some of its visual power from the lack of borders: the maker carried a large-scale design to the edges of the quilt in all directions, creating a very painterly canvas. This is an unusual treatment.

26 / THOUSAND PYRAMIDS VARIATION

Maker unknown
Possibly Michigan
1880–1900
82" × 64"
Cottons
QSPI: 6–7
1997.007.0079
International Quilt Study Center,
Ardis and Robert James Collection

JB: Using very simple means—strips of pieced calico triangles alternating with strips of solid green fabric—the artist has achieved a dramatic visual effect. She has varied the sizes of the green bands to give her design the maximal visual interest: the central bar is five inches wide, the next ones four inches, and the outermost ones three and a half inches.

CD: The use of triangles cut from double-pink calicoes carries a pleasing, slightly irregular rhythm: they occur every fourth, fifth, or sixth triangle, sometimes pointing right, sometimes pointing left.

JB: The choice of the dark pink calico to frame the design field was an excellent one, too. It adds a real visual jolt.

PC: The maker hand-quilted her work with six to seven stitches to the inch in an allover chevron design. Unfortunately the coarse muslin backing shrank considerably, causing the front to pucker when it was washed. So the ripple effect that we see was surely not intentional, and also not the result of poor workmanship.

CD: Bar or strip quilts, with narrow widths of fabric set in vertical or horizontal lines, have been made in many variations throughout the history of American quiltmaking. Early examples from the first quarter of the nineteenth century often used the bars as a showcase for beautiful, expensive fabrics (see plate 1).

PC: Quilts made during the second half of the century, after sewing machines became widely distributed, took advantage of the machine's ability to sew long straight seams for binding edges and attaching borders easily and quickly, tasks that needleworkers did not care for.[1]

CD: During the last quarter of the nineteenth century, Amish quiltmakers, particularly those of Lancaster County, Pennsylvania, sometimes used strip elements in their quilts, the wide fabric panels becoming a canvas for their extraordinary quilting.[2] In the twentieth century, African American quiltmakers in the South also incorporated the strip style into their quilts, although the strips are typically composed of narrow fabric pieces (see plates 36, 44).

JH: Such simple but powerful visual effects, in this case a field of bars that seems to hover over a pieced field, are one of the glories of American quiltmaking.

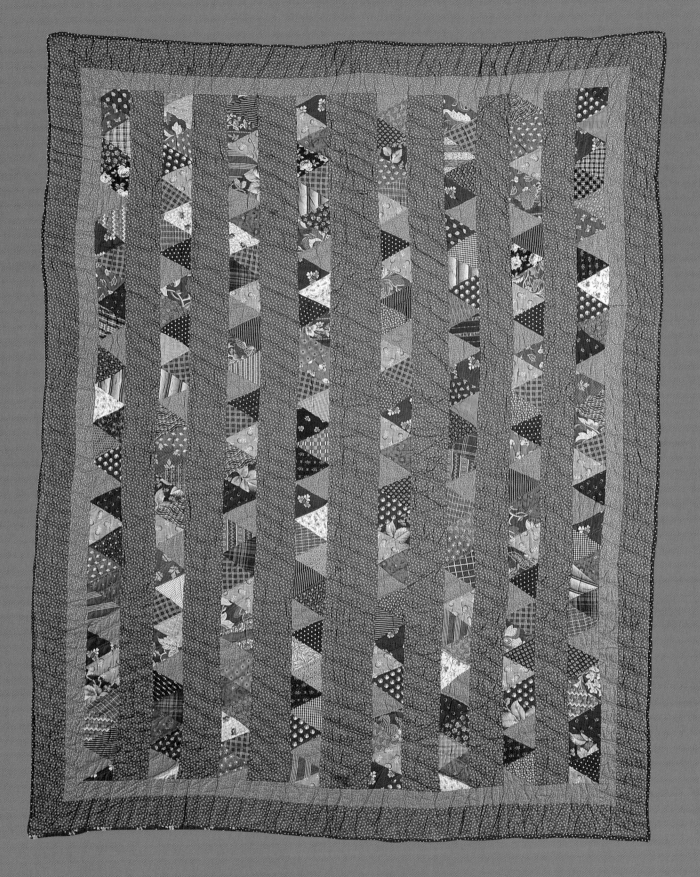

27 / FOUR PATCH VARIATION

Unknown Amish maker
Ohio, probably Holmes County
1890–1900
88 $\frac{1}{2}$" × 74"
Cottons
QSPI: 9–10
Private Collection of Ardis and Robert James

JH: I always have a visceral reaction to great Amish quilts such as this, just as I do to other "perfect" art objects in which form, color, emotion, and intent are seamlessly welded. The control, austerity, and limited design vocabulary of Lancaster Amish quilts lose ground in the Midwest, where many more pieced designs, borrowed from non-Amish neighbors, appear in their quilts. But just as Lancaster Amish quilts are immediately recognizable, so too are those of the Midwestern Amish, because of the ways they interpreted those received designs. They retain the framed center format and solid color materials seen in Pennsylvania. But they set within it repetitive block designs in vibrant colors. The use of black, or in this case, navy blue, for the background, is a characteristic of Ohio Amish quilting. It's a brilliant design concept that produces jewel-like effects, reminiscent of stained glass windows.

Ohio Amish quilters most often use shiny cottons rather than wools, and employ a broader color palette than that of the Amish of Lancaster County, Pennsylvania. They also routinely choose a wide outer border and a thin inner border to enclose a field of pieced blocks, and then complete their quilts with a narrow binding in a contrasting color.

PC: Ricky Clark points out that the center field of alternating pieced and plain blocks is usually "set on point to create a dynamic design."[1] This quilt has all the hallmarks of the Ohio Amish style, corroborating dealer information that it was Amish-made in Holmes County. Ohio has the world's largest community of Old Order Amish. The Germanic sectarian (Amish, Mennonite, Brethren, and Zoarites) quilt style "is especially prevalent in Wayne, Holmes, Stark, and Tuscarawas counties of Ohio."[2]

JH: Here, the artist has chosen red to enclose her design field, and she has introduced subtle color asymmetries in her pieced blocks.

PC: She selected a wide range of somber, muddy colors: magenta, navy blue, black, butterscotch, and blue cotton muslins for her pieced Four Patch blocks. The light grays are chambrays.

CD: Note that the blocks in the outer corners match, and the two blocks in the middle match, but in some of the Nine Patches, the squares advance visually, and in others the Four Patch blocks are emphasized. This Four Patch within a Nine Patch appears to be a variant of the pattern that Barbara Brackman calls "Thrifty."[3]

JB: The woman who made this was a remarkable needlewoman. The hand-quilting demonstrates impeccable workmanship, with nine to ten stitches per inch. Yet one can only appreciate the dazzling hand-quilting by examining the muslin back—it's almost impossible to see on the front.

PC: She marked her feathered plume and rosette quilting pattern for the border and the plain squares, but it looks like she eyeballed the grid design with which she filled the pieced blocks. The size of the grid varies from three-eights of an inch to half an inch.

JB: This quilt exemplifies so much that is noteworthy about an Amish aesthetic. It's a curious mixture of lushness and austerity. The remarkable quilting stitches are hidden from view. The color asymmetry is controlled but enlivens the surface in a manner that manages to be both gay and somber. While we have a long way to go in terms of understanding what this aesthetic may have meant to the makers of Amish quilts, the quilts themselves have captivated the imaginations of collectors and scholars around the world.

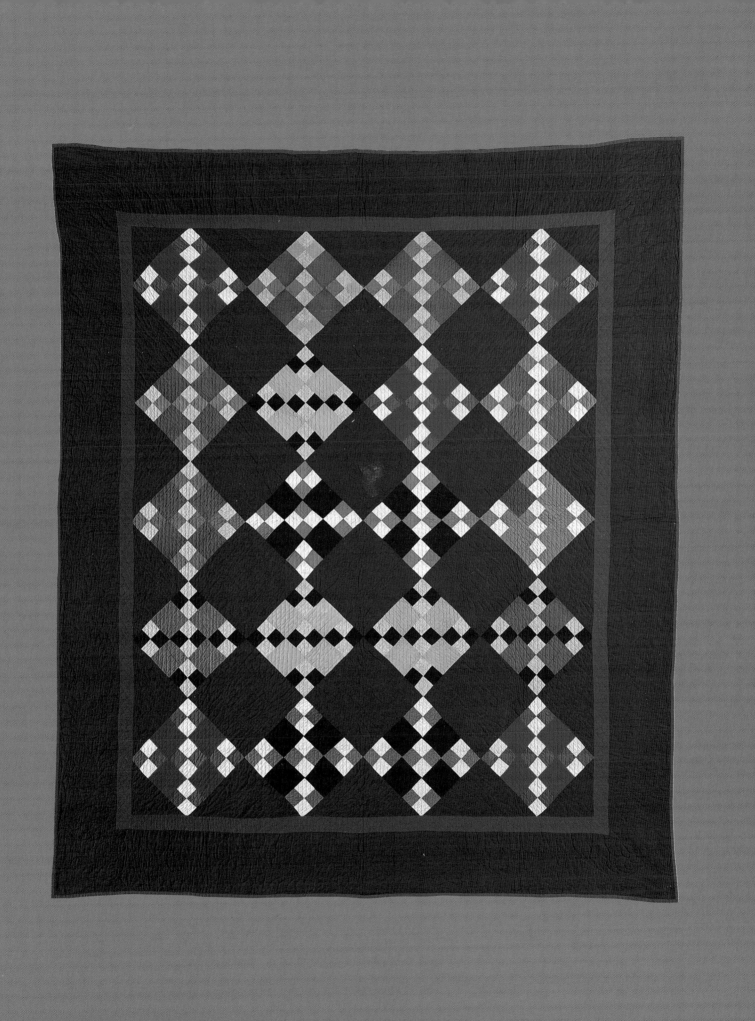

28 / CRAZY STARS

Amy Bucher (1870–1952)
Lebanon County, Pennsylvania
1890–1910
85" × 81"
Cottons
QSPI: 9
1997.007.0658
International Quilt Study Center,
Ardis and Robert James Collection

JB: When Robert Bishop published this quilt in 1975, he wrote, "before making this quilt, Miss Bucher had already made two Star of Bethlehem quilts on red backgrounds. She used the scraps from those projects to make this brilliant example of the quilter's art."[1] Amy Bucher, however, discovered the difficulty of piecing a variety of different sized pieces into larger stars—in some areas, she simply created fabric tucks and stitched them down to make the star's arms fit together. It's rare to see Lone Star or Star of Bethlehem quilts in which the different arms of the stars are made up not only of different fabrics, but also of different sized pieces.

PC: If the provenance of this quilt were unknown, a casual viewer might have suggested that it's African American. This should caution us about speculative cultural attributions based on superficial visual qualities.

JB: The art historian Robert Hobbs calls this tendency "the morphological fallacy"—mistaking visual similarities for historical relationships.[2] This quilt certainly shares some features with Nora Ezell's Star Puzzle (plate 46), including the way the stars are composed of arms made with different fabrics. Both also feature a rather carefree insertion of scraps of many different colors, and blocks made up of offbeat combinations.

Of course an inspection of the exceedingly fine hand-quilting stitches (nine per inch, in diagonal rows one and one-quarter inches apart) would belie a rural Southern African American attribution. Almost all of the twentieth-century African American quilts we've analyzed in the IQSC collection have three to six hand-quilting stitches per inch.[3]

PC: In addition, Amy Bucher chose and executed quilting designs that enhanced each area. For example, she used outline quilting in the stars. African American quiltmakers of the rural South almost always used an allover quilting design, usually fan quilting, with no regard to the pieced pattern.

Amy Bucher pieced her top primarily from cotton muslin solids. She incorporated a few calicoes and printed plaids, but very few. It would have been difficult to estimate a date of origin for this quilt, were it not for the few pieces of calico and printed plaids used in the top. Pieced quilts made entirely from solids are very difficult, if not impossible, to date. The colors of the calicoes and the printed plaids suggest that it was made between 1880 and 1900. Since she would have been only ten years old in 1880, we believe that she made the quilt between 1890 and 1910. Amy Bucher was still unmarried and living with her parents in 1900.[4]

JH: This looks like a Lancaster Amish quilt gone wild. That is, it has the overall format of a classic Amish quilt, with a framed interior, solid-color border and corner blocks, and the use of single-color materials, but there the resemblance ends. The corner blocks are rectangles rather than squares, so they don't meet on point with the border strips. And that interior variety and chaotic energy would never have emerged from an Amish household. I would guess that the maker of this quilt was Mennonite. Whatever her intent, she produced a wonderful play on a number of traditional Pennsylvania design traditions.

29 / BOW TIE

Maker unknown
Possibly Indiana
1890–1910
88" × 76 ½"
Cottons
QSPI: 4–8
1997.007.0029
International Quilt Study Center,
Ardis and Robert James Collection

JH: The Bow Tie pattern can be easily manipulated to create optically active quilts. Here, the ingenious use of white parts to produce a hovering visual field is typical of the kinds of optical effects that skilled designers can create with such simple pieced patterns.

PC: This quilt is typical of turn-of-the-century scrap quilts. But for a scrap quilt, this one is very well planned. The red diagonal rows are offset and strategically placed at just the right locations to provide movement without being predictable. The lone red bow tie at the top right corner provides just the element to punctuate the piece.

JB: And she has added a matching red one, in mirror image, at the top left, too. Not only the red bow ties, but also the pink and beige ones, lend a strong diagonal movement to the work. This may be one of the few true scrap quilts in the book. Whether making something out of completely new yardage or using leftovers from dressmaking, the talented designer is able to achieve the desired optical effects. I know from my own quiltmaking that having to "make do" sometimes causes happy accidents, sending the work in a new direction.

CD: This work is both hand pieced and hand quilted. The quilting stitches vary considerably from four to eight stitches per inch, which makes me think that more than one person was involved in the quilting. The top is com-posed of a variety of ginghams, both printed imitations and yarn-dyed versions, as well as a number of other checks and stripes. There are also some striking red and black prints, characteristic of the period.

PC: The white rounded squares are not solid cottons; instead, they're made from a tiny red polka-dot print that adds subtle visual texture when viewed at close range. When viewed at a distance, the white octagonal squares appear to float on the surface. They recede in a blink of the eye, and the strong diagonals created by the bow ties emerge. The maker created quite an optical effect with the simplest of means.

CD: The pattern now commonly known as Bow Tie was called Necktie during the late nineteenth century. It was published in a catalogue by the Ladies' Art Company of St. Louis, Missouri, founded in 1889.[1] The Necktie pattern was probably in print by 1895. A pattern printed in 1897 that combined four Necktie blocks into an arrangement like the one used in this quilt was called Magic Circle.[2]

The pattern became more widely known as Bow Tie in the 1930s, when it was published under that name by Aunt Martha's Studio, a company based in Kansas City, Missouri, that was still active in the 1990s. Two other mail-order companies that published pattern books in the 1930s, Grandmother Clark and Grandma Dexter, called the pattern Colonial Bow Tie.[3]

JB: In its optics, this quilt reminds me of Mary Maxtion's Broken Stove Eye quilt (plate 39). Modern quilters have experimented with the playful, op-art effects of Bow Tie, too. Judy Speezak's version looks like dark blue octagons floating on a sea of different colored squares, but it's this same Bow Tie pattern.[4] Ohio Amish quilters have often made very restrained, two-color versions of Bow Tie, sometimes with just a few playful, subtle modifications of the design.[5] Like many quilt patterns, it has room for endless inventiveness.

30 / CONCENTRIC SQUARES

Maker unknown
Probably United States
1890–1910
42" × 41 1/2"
Cottons
QSPI: 6
1997.007.0705
International Quilt Study Center,
Ardis and Robert James Collection

JB: Optically, red and white are really effective together, giving a crisp bold look. This quilter accentuated the optical effect that she was seeking by diminishing the width of her strips as she moved toward the center. The outermost red strips are one and one-half inches wide, and shrink to one and one-quarter inches near the center. The white strips, in contrast, even the outermost ones, are never wider than one and one-quarter inches.

PC: So she understood perfectly the optical effects of what she was doing!

This is completely machine pieced, as we would expect. It's hand quilted in a diamond grid, with six quilting stitches per inch. With its small size and square format, I wonder if it was a table cover. It's hard to imagine it being used as a child's quilt.

JB: Some astonishing red and white geometric pieced quilts date from the 1850s, but it's more common to see them from the last decade of the nineteenth century and the first two decades of the twentieth century, like this one.[1]

PC: The combination of red and white has remained a classic color scheme for quilts since the 1850s. Whereas the red cottons used in mid-nineteenth-century red and white quilts were often printed, after 1875 the reds were more often solids like the ones used in this quilt. "Towards the end of the century, the [red and white] color scheme was almost a standard for a number of pieced patterns like the Schoolhouse, Drunkard's Path, Ocean Wave and Sawtooth," according to Barbara Brackman.[2] The fastness of Turkey red cottons may explain the popularity of the color scheme—Turkey red didn't fade or bleed out onto surrounding white areas.[3]

JH: Around midcentury and for some decades afterwards, we see many appliqué quilts made in just green and red on a white ground. They were playing with that large white field as a canvas for their best work—those difficult, curvilinear forms (see plates 8, 9, 17). So I see these red and white quilts as a natural outgrowth of that color experimentation. In the Whitney show, we exhibited one early-twentieth-century quilt very similar to this one, except the red bars have sawtooth edges.[4] It supported our developing ideas about the aesthetics of American quilts: it was so startlingly similar in visual results to the effects some contemporary New York painters were looking for, that it encouraged us to continue to look beyond the received wisdom about quilts and see them as an early expression of modernity.

31 / AMISH CRIB QUILT

Maker unknown
Probably Haven, Kansas
1920–30
38" × 28"
Cottons
QSPI: 6–7
2000.007.0046
International Quilt Study Center,
Sara Miller Collection

PC: Haven, Kansas, where this striking quilt is believed to have been made, is a thriving Old Order Amish community dating back to the early 1880s. According to Eve Granick, "The women who came to the Haven and Hutchinson areas were often newly married and they brought with them their quilts from home and the strong customs of Indiana quiltmaking." In fact, a quilt remarkably similar in design and size made in Indiana, circa 1900–20, is included in Granick's excellent book *The Amish Quilt*.[1]

JB: The irregularities in construction and the hand-quilting stitches of only six to seven per inch make one suspect this quilt was made by a child. Young Amish girls usually learned by piecing doll quilts, whereas teenagers usually pieced their first full-size quilts.[2]

PC: Typical of Midwestern Amish, this quilt is mainly cotton. It includes a beautiful black cotton sateen, as well as a poor quality blue muslin. The depression forced many quiltmakers to resort to lower quality materials.

JB: In the collection of Amish crib quilts that Sara Miller assembled over the years, there are a number of quilts that have this offbeat quality; they seem to bend the rules more than most Midwestern Amish quilts do. Bettina Havig has pointed out that because they were made for children—and some may have been made *by* children—they demonstrate a bit more flexibility than the typical fine Amish quilt.[3] For example, there is even more asymmetry and color experimentation than we see in a typical Midwestern Amish quilt (plate 33).

JH: Children's quilts from all regions are rare. In many small quilts (baby, crib, doll) we often see a loosening of both work method and aesthetics. Perhaps women felt, on the one hand, that their handiwork would be under less scrutiny and criticism, and on the other, that they could express more playfulness in their designs.

In cultural milieus where traditional designs were valued and emulated, as they were among the Amish, such free interpretations (in this case of a traditional Log Cabin design) are particularly striking. To many contemporary observers, the "modernism" of a quilt like this little gem is always a surprise and delight.

JB: Elsewhere in our dialogues (plates 28 and 44) we've talked about the problem of attributing all quilts with offbeat color usage and design asymmetry to an African American source. I believe that a number of these Midwestern Amish baby quilts or children's doll quilts could easily be misattributed in this fashion if they were to come on the market with no provenance, since they do display many of the traits that some people have claimed are the hallmarks of a distinctly African American style: asymmetry, uncommon color usage, large stitches, and improvisational patterning.

32 / SCHOOLHOUSE

Maker unknown
Possibly Tennessee
1925–45
85" × 74"
Wools and a wool/acetate mixture
QSPI: 5–6
1997.007.0156
International Quilt Study Center,
Ardis and Robert James Collection

JB: Domestic architecture has always figured prominently in popular arts of North America, from eighteenth- and nineteenth-century embroidered samplers depicting individual recognizable houses, to nineteenth-century folk paintings, to quilts like this one.[1] In contrast to Lucinda Honstain's painstakingly appliquéd portrait of her own fine home (plate 12), this quilt depicts a more modest American house type.

JH: There are very few abstractions of architecture in American quilts, this being the one most commonly found. One would think that architecture, with mostly straight lines, and other man-made objects would have furnished many images for quiltmakers. Instead, images from nature, most with more difficult curved lines, were the primary source of abstracted images.

CD: The pattern is usually called Schoolhouse, but it seems to be a generic home made of planks or logs, with a pitched roof and two chimneys—an easy design to strip-piece. Each block is fourteen and a quarter by fourteen inches. The houses themselves are hand pieced, although the sashing is pieced by both hand and machine.

PC: The pattern dates from the late nineteenth century, when it was called nostalgic names such as Log Cabin and Old Kentucky Home. However, it's been named Schoolhouse at least since 1929, when Ruth Finley called the pattern Little Red Schoolhouse in her classic book *Old Patchwork Quilts and the Women Who Made Them.*[2]

JB: The pattern evidently was a popular one—by 1898 the Ladies' Art Company of St. Louis had several variations of it in the patterns they sold for ten cents. Those patterns all have upright pieces for the walls of the house, rather than the horizontal logs this maker favored.

PC: She's cleverly used a beige, rust, and brown striped wool fabric for the logs on the houses, and another striped wool fabric for some of the roofs. Elsewhere the quilt top is composed mainly of wool solids—serges and gabardines. The golden tan fabric used in so many of the roofs and gables was made of wool and acetate—all wool in one direction and acetate/wool yarns in the other. Since acetate was not commercially produced in the United States until 1924, we know this quilt was made after that date.

JB: Slight variations in color placement on this quilt give it a great sense of syncopated rhythm. For example, most of the windows are the same color blue as the background, but two are fuchsia. Most of the chimneys are red, but a couple are salmon-colored, echoing the sashing squares.

PC: She's also varied the sashing. Horizontally, the sashing is beige, providing a ground line for the houses to stand on. Because the vertical sashings are blue, they don't read as sashings at all, but as part of the background of the houses. Using five to six stitches per inch, the quilting emphasizes the gables and the lines in the roofs, reminiscent of the seams in a tin roof.

JB: This is another example of a maker who has only mediocre needlework skills, but her superior sense of graphic design and color carry the work. The Schoolhouse pattern is such a pleasing one in all its many manifestations. Is it because we like the combination of geometric piecework and recognizable imagery? Bold two-color designs are common, as are whimsical uses of scrap calicoes. An African American quilter in the last quarter of the nineteenth century devised a completely original use of the design. She alternated the pieced Log Cabin pattern, set on point, with about a hundred small original houses, each slightly different, and genre scenes of people.[3] Quilters today continue to enjoy this pattern, too.

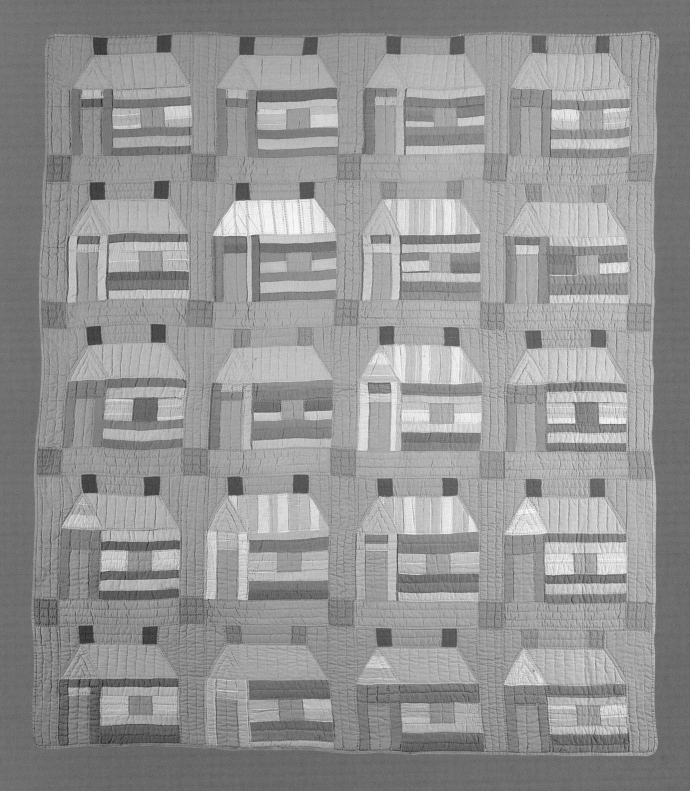

33 / DIAMOND IN THE SQUARE

Amish maker unknown
Probably Lancaster County, Pennsylvania
1925–45
81 1/2" × 80 1/2"
Wools, acetate/rayon mixture, rayon
QSPI: 9–10
1997.007.0627
International Quilt Study Center,
Ardis and Robert James Collection

JH: During the classic period of Lancaster County Amish quiltmaking (the late nineteenth century to World War II), quilters normally employed a very limited range of large-sectioned pieced patterns, few of which by that time were being used in quilt design by their non-Amish neighbors. I've always believed the Diamond in the Square pattern to be a conservative retention of the overall design format of earlier high-style English and American quilts, a simplified schematic of the central medallion type. The Amish would have seen such quilts among their non-Amish neighbors. That powerful, balanced design—the central diamond with multiple borders and often square block corners that we see in late-eighteenth- and early-nineteenth-century English and American quilts—was perfect for the color-saturated, nonpatterned wools the Amish used in their quilts. The colors, too, I believe, date to choices of non-Amish folk of an earlier era. The Amish's particular genius was in adopting that design but giving it a profound twist, constructing very large, unbroken, single-color areas of juxtaposed, contrasting colors. The quilts often read like the work of modern painters, such as Josef Albers and others, who explored color-field painting. Amish quilts are instantly recognizable and absolutely unique in American art. As a body of work, they remain one of the highlights of American art.

PC: At first glance, this quilt appears to be made of all wool fabrics, but microscopic examination revealed that its wide binding is not wool at all; it's a plain weave fabric made entirely of rayon yarns. Another fabric, a crepe, consists of light green rayon yarns in one direction and beige acetate yarns in the other. Since acetate was not commercially produced in the United States until 1924, we know this quilt was made sometime after that date. An additional clue to its date is the backing. The maker used an inexpensive purple calico with orange floral sprigs and bunches of white daisies with leaves in the green shade so typical of the 1930s and 1940s. It looks like the feedsack prints of the era.

JH: For their classic quilts, the Lancaster Amish preferred very fine wools, at first one called henrietta, and later, when that was no longer available, what their suppliers called wool batiste. When rayon first appeared, and particularly after fine wools became unavailable during World War II, they tried it in their quilts, but it was not as satisfactory. It didn't have the look or feel of the fine wools the Amish prized, and the colors were different. I think the unavailability of the wools was one factor that ultimately stopped their production of the classic-style quilts.

CD: The quilting designs are stitched in a dark thread that really stands out against the lighter colors of the quilt—only a supremely confident quilter would draw attention to her stitches this way! Each fabric segment is quilted with a different pattern: in the rose-colored corners, detailed pineapples are crowned with broad leaves. Feathered plumes extend outward from the pineapple in a graceful arc. The plume is repeated in the outer border in a series of S-shaped curls. In the thin sashing, a quartet of pumpkin seeds is set within a linear pattern. The center square holds a simple grid framed by a feathered plume circle.

JB: While one might not think of this quilt as "wild" in the way we've defined it for some of the other selections in this book, its ingenuity is found in the paring down of the classic building blocks of quilt architecture—the square and the diamond. The idea of radical simplicity—the Zen of quilts—is what we're calling attention to in our selection of this classic Amish Diamond in the Square. Just as Shaker architecture and furniture, for example, represent a paring down of structure to its lean essentials, so too does the Amish quilt represent the elegant essence of the American quilt.

34 / DOGWOOD BLOSSOM

Maker unknown
Probably Midwest
1930–40
84" × 68 ½"
Cottons
QSPI: 8–9
1997.007.0851
International Quilt Study Center,
Ardis and Robert James Collection

CD: An unusual pattern: with that one-quarter sunburst, it's reminiscent of Pickle Dish.

JB: But how different the effect is when the artist uses two solid fabrics, rather than the typical assorted calicoes: the bold red against beige is striking. And the construction technique makes what looks like a Sixteen Patch, although it's just the meeting point of four different Four Patches.

CD: The straight seams are mostly machine pieced, but the triangles in the curved quarter-circles are done by hand. Often the edges of the triangles get cut off when she sews her pieces together. She's not really an expert needlewoman, though she's chosen an ambitious pattern!

JB: Yet she does have a great sense of design. Ardis James called this quilt "a marvel of contrast and composition."[1]

PC: We have very little information about this quilt's origin. According to the dealer, it was probably made in the Great Plains region.[2] Quilts made of solids are always difficult to date. Two-color quilts, however, especially in solid reds and white, were popular during the first quarter of the twentieth century. *Cappers Weekly* published this pattern in 1928 and called it Dogwood Blossom,[3] so it seems likely that this quilt was made during the 1930s. It's made of very poor quality muslins, which may indicate that the maker and her family were affected by the Great Depression.

JB: This is one of several curved-seam patterns that became popular in the early twentieth century, along with Double Wedding Ring and Dresden Plate. But they seldom equal, either in technique or in visual effect, the great curved-seam patterns of the nineteenth century, such as New York Beauty (plate 6).

JH: Such complicated, intricate, small-piece designs seem to be characteristic of the early twentieth century, when quilt patterns appeared as regular features in newspapers and magazines. These were widely adopted and had a significant impact on quilt design, as did kit quilts with their preset designs.

35 / CRAZY NECKTIES

Maker unknown
Possibly Anderson, Indiana
1930–50
69 ½" × 89"
Silks, acetates, and/or rayons
Tied
Private Collection of Ardis and Robert James

JB: The maker of this quilt was obviously very familiar with the silk Crazy quilt fad of the end of the nineteenth century (plate 18). Here she modernizes the style, using some three dozen men's ties in silk, acetate, and rayon. Most of them are stylish prints of the 1930s and 1940s. The composition centers on a big sunburst or medallion made of thirty-two ties. She has pieced the center of the medallion from several portions of silk with printing that could be joined to showcase the initials "SK."

PC: "SK" could be the artist, or it could be the person whose ties are immortalized here. The maker has maintained the necktie shape; she wants us to know that these are ties, not just scraps used for her own purpose. The widest portions of the ties are used in the central sunburst, while the narrower ends form the half circles in each of the corners. She has embroidered the edges of the ties in a variety of decorative stitches: blanket stitch, feather stitch, double-feather, chained feather, and herringbone among them.

JB: The ties themselves are wildly patterned, but when the maker had to fill in around the edges of the ties with taffeta and other plainer materials, she took the opportunity to embellish those sections with figurative embroidery, just as nineteenth-century Crazy quilters did.

CD: She used the kinds of embroidery stamping patterns meant for tea towels and available in inexpensive kits. There are scenes of bear cubs, kittens, and rabbits, in addition to the floral designs with their French knots.

JH: So this is also an update of the late-nineteenth-century tradition of embroidering sentimental subjects on the Crazy quilt.

JB: More recent quilters have produced necktie quilts, too. African American quiltmaker Nora Ezell did a series of tie quilts starting in 1984. In *Gambler's Dream,* she envisioned the ties as overlapping playing cards and appliquéd suits and numbers on them. Ezell bought ties at flea markets for her quilts.[1]

PC: Ardis James speculated that the maker had access to a necktie factory because one tie design is found in three colorways on the quilt.[2] While this quiltmaker could certainly have gotten her ties from any number of sources, Crazy Neckties seems intensely personal. I envision this as a repository of one man's ties, which evoked many memories for the family members who viewed the finished quilt. Could they be Grandpa's ties? Or those of a family member who died in World War II? Middle-class men of that era had as many as three dozen ties. What better use of them than to make a memory quilt!

JH: I've heard many quiltmakers say, "Some day I'll make a quilt from my husband's old ties." Yet not many have done so. The notion is to use their given shapes, but those are difficult to work into a quilt format. Also, as here, the result is bound to be pretty wild, not to everyone's taste. This one, however, is particularly successful, achieving a surprising unity by ignoring (as she had to) any question of consistent patterning. Its exuberance wins the day.

36 / LOG CABIN, COURTHOUSE STEPS VARIATION

Top made by Wini Austin (twentieth century; dates unknown)
Quilted by Roberta Jemison in 1997
Holt, Alabama
1930–50
78" × 56"
Cottons
QSPI: 4
2000.004.0011
International Quilt Study Center,
Robert and Helen Cargo Collection

JB: In her original take on the Courthouse Steps variation of Log Cabin, African American quilter Wini Austin was working very differently from the nineteenth-century maker of the quilt in plate 14. She seems to have visualized her pattern as a series of bold vertical stripes.

CD: This strip-pieced variant illustrates a design sensibility that some quilt researchers believe may reflect a tradition of West African textiles: the use of vertical strips reminiscent of weaving done on narrow strip-looms. The offbeat placement of the Log Cabin blocks is another element that scholars consider similar to African textiles.[1] Narrow strips of woven textiles are stitched edge to edge with deliberate offsetting of pattern. It creates a sense of zigzagging motion within the structured design.

JB: It certainly is true that many twentieth-century African American quilts from the rural South subscribe to an aesthetic that Maude Wahlman has described as consisting of large shapes, strong contrasting colors, and asymmetrical pattern variation.[2] But increasingly, scholars who are well educated in the entire history of American quilts, and in the range of quilts made by African American women across the country, are endeavoring to remind us that not only did African American women make many different kinds of quilts, some of them indistinguishable from quilts by women of other ethnicities, but that many other women have made unusual asymmetrical quilts too.[3] (See the dialogues accompanying plates 44 and 45.)

CD: John Picton, a British scholar of African textiles, is wary of sweeping visual generalizations about African American quilts. He notes, "'Africa' certainly figures in the building of new identities growing out of and indeed challenging the experience of vulnerability and displacement . . . [but] [t]here is no basis for a theory of genetic transmission of design preference."[4]

He suggests that the similarities may simply be a common way of "stretching" traditional Euro-American patterns—perhaps as a subtle rebellion against the dominant culture. Economic status may also influence the technique and structure of a quilt—strip-piecing, particularly, makes use of remnants and is a simple way of enlarging a quilt's dimensions.

Certainly, the African American quilts in the IQSC collection that were found in the rural South have a unique look. The asymmetrical placement of pattern, the bold sense of color, and the spontaneity of the quilt's aesthetic are uncommon in traditional American quilts.

JB: I don't think it's as uncommon as some would have us believe. In our dialogue on the Anna Williams quilt (plate 44), we discussed some of the offbeat designs made by Scots-Irish quilters in the rural South. Midwestern Amish quilts sometimes demonstrate asymmetrical color patterning (plate 27) or design (plate 31). Samuel Steinberger, a Jewish tailor in New York City at the end of the nineteenth century, made a Courthouse Steps quilt that Wini Austin and other Southern black quilters might appreciate in terms of its bold improvisational use of color.[5] I think the most we can say is that African American quilters seem to engage in these improvisational design practices more often than other quilters.

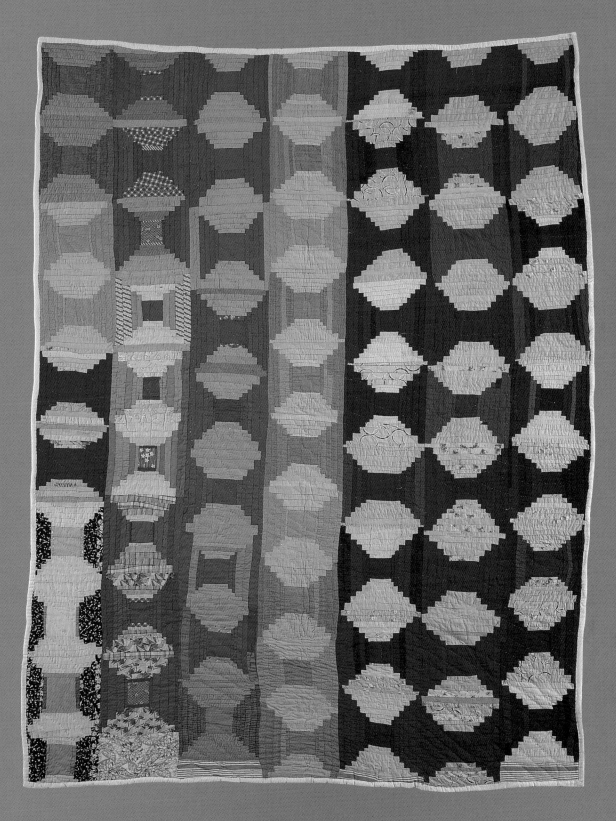

37 / P QUILT

Lureca Outland (1904–)
Greene County, Alabama
1970–80
93" × 82"
Cottons, cotton/polyester blends, polyesters
QSPI: 5
2000.004.0105
International Quilt Study Center,
Robert and Helen Cargo Collection

CD: The Cargo Collection has three alphabet quilts—it seems to be a pattern that was well liked by Alabama quilters; in fact, we have a second P Quilt made by Outland.[1] We asked Robert Cargo if the letter *P*, so often used, has significance, but he was not aware of any.

JH: Evoking the power of letters and words through art is ancient in the cultures of the world. "In the beginning was the word. . . ." These *P*s remind me of the single great illuminated letters that began important religious texts in the West. Meaning and power can be extracted from the evocation of a single letter, and so can mystery: What did this mean to Outland? Was it the first letter of the name of a husband, son, sister, or parent? Did it stand for a text sacred to her, or to her family? Of course, it could be that she simply liked the shape of this letter; some modern artists have evoked the power of letters in a similar way in their work.

PC: There was a tradition of creating alphabet quilts among white quilters in the 1930s. I wonder if those quiltmakers were influenced by eighteenth- and nineteenth-century samplers. Certainly we know that during the Colonial Revival period women derived patterns from earlier quilts, so it would make sense that they looked at samplers. Most samplers included the alphabet stitched in horizontal rows.

CD: Yes, and the format of the pattern, making use of squares, rectangles, and triangles, is similar to the format a woman would use when cross-stitching the alphabet on a sampler: you create curved forms with angled stitches, just like the letter *P*'s rounded shape is created through the use of a straight edge of a triangle.

JB: There are also wonderful nineteenth-century examples of pieced quilts composed entirely of written messages. While these are not likely to have been models for the alphabet quilts done in the rural South in the twentieth century, they do suggest a long heritage of writing in needlework, from eighteenth-century samplers to nineteenth- and twentieth-century quilts.[2] And of course we mustn't forget the well-known red, white, and blue Freedom Quilt made in 1980 by African American quilter Jessie Telfair of Parrot, Georgia, in which the word "freedom" is spelled out six times in block letters like this *P*.[3]

PC: Alphabet patterns were published in a catalogue of the Ladies' Art Company as early as 1906.[4] In 1922, a catalogue advertised the patterns, sold with a color diagram for fifteen cents each or twelve for a dollar. The simple color card without a pattern sold for five cents each or thirty-five cards for a dollar.[5]

CD: The vivid colors of this quilt, however, make it unique. The lime green used for one *P* simply jumps out at the viewer. The maker balanced the strong fabric well: it's used in the lower left corner and as a border at the top and bottom of the quilt. Contrasting magenta squares set in the soft gray sashing fabric are also striking, as is the hot pink backing fabric. A number of other quilts in our collection made by Lureca Outland also feature bright colors—she must enjoy working with vivid hues.

JB: In an interview with Maude Wahlman, Lureca Outland said, "I did not make fancy quilts until after I joined a senior citizen's group with Mary Maxtion. Sometimes she quilts with me. The members usually piece their own blocks. I like red."[6]

CD: Both Lureca Outland and Mary Maxtion (plates 37, 38, 39, and 45), who are sisters-in-law, are members of an Alabama chapter of the Retired Senior Volunteer Program (RSVP Club), whose members made three of the quilts in the IQSC collection. The club's mission is to provide opportunities for persons fifty-five or older to volunteer within their communities. The RSVP Club provides a setting for women to piece and quilt together.[7]

38 / PIG PEN STARS

Mary Maxtion (1924–)
Boligee, Alabama
1980–90
92" × 81"
Cotton/polyester blends and cottons
QSPI: 5
2000.004.0075
International Quilt Study Center,
Robert and Helen Cargo Collection

JB: Though made a century apart by quilters of different ethnicities in different parts of the country, this quilt and the one in plate 30 demonstrate that quilters have always understood how to make forms advance and recede in space: they do it not only by bold color choices, but by varying the width of their strips. Mary Maxtion placed two-inch-wide strips at the perimeters of this quilt, diminishing them to one and three-quarter inches and then one and one-half inches near the center.

PC: The Cargo Collection at the International Quilt Study Center has a fine, representative sample of quilts by Mary Maxtion (see also plates 39 and 45). All are graphically bold designs like this one. Many use a red, white, and blue color scheme and variants of an American flag design. Here, the butterscotch-colored border is a particularly

unusual and effective addition. Maxtion hand-pieced this quilt and hand-quilted it with five stitches per inch.

CD: Pig Pen seems to be a regional name. Robert Cargo explained that the Pig Pen pattern name can be interpreted literally—that the enclosed shape is similar to the shape of a pigpen. However, he also notes that the makers sometimes refer to the bars in the center of the quilt as pigs. He considers it a fairly common pattern among the black quiltmakers of the rural South, perhaps a variation of Log Cabin.[1]

JB: This quilt is far more regular in its patterning than many in the Cargo Collection. The only asymmetrical elements are the borders and the third red frame from the center, which lacks a strip on the right side. But it takes a while to see that subtle irregularity. So this quilt doesn't so easily fit the stereotypical African American aesthetic.

JH: Abstracting patriotic symbolism (red, white, and blue; stars, the flag form) to create her quilts is a specialty of Mary Maxtion (and, apparently, some other Southern African American quiltmakers.)[2] For an American viewer, the immediate patriotic implications in her work complicate our understanding of her quilts. Was she making a patriotic statement? Or did she simply use the elements to create a strong visual work?

39 / BROKEN STOVE EYE

Mary Maxtion (1924–)
Boligee, Alabama
1980–90
91" × 71"
Cottons, cotton/polyester blends, polyesters
QSPI: 4
2000.004.0088
International Quilt Study Center,
Robert and Helen Cargo Collection

JB: The seemingly random color pattern is wonderful: the range of pinks, white, and yellows, paired with the blues and blue-blacks, and the many slight irregularities in the piecing send one's eye all over the surface. In that respect, it's somewhat reminiscent of plate 29, in which the white lozenges seem to float over an irregular surface. I would call this pattern a version of Robbing Peter to Pay Paul. What does "Broken Stove Eye" mean?

PC: In the South, people often call the electric burners on a stove the "eyes" of the stove. With her checkerboard arrangement of darks and lights in this pattern, she creates the effect of a broken circle.

JB: I've always liked the way that some quilt names reflect the poetry of women's domestic existence—Baby's Blocks, Tea Cups, Dresden Plate, and so forth. Stove Eye makes a nice regional addition to this group.

PC: The maker has used a number of different blues, including denims and polyester double-knits, as well as some black fabrics. It's machine pieced and hand quilted with four quilting stitches per inch, done in a pattern of irregular diagonal lines.

JB: Like some of the other quilts we've discussed, the work of rural African American quilters from the South reflects an interest in design and pattern over fineness of technique. They aren't the only ones to experiment in this fashion, of course. Just as in plates 25, 28, and 31, it's the visual play that's most important, not the adherence to a standard of needlework that dictates a certain number of quilting stitches to the inch, or the careful joining of seams.

JH: One thing I find particularly interesting about such African American quilts is that materials don't seem to be "sacred" in the same sense I've observed for many white quiltmakers. That is, there is not the same premium put on conferring dignity through symmetry and balance of color and pattern. Rather, aesthetic dignity appears to be gained through a deliberate, successful blending of disparate elements. Even where symmetry, for instance, might be achieved, it does not appear to be an overriding concern or need. There are elements of both daring and innovation (in the sense of originality) and adherence to some understood aesthetic conventions. I think of the extraordinary abstractions of the human form that some African artists created at the same time Western artists were striving for realism. The latter gave us versions of reality that were ultimately not very satisfying. The former produced powerful new ways of perceiving and understanding the human form and the human condition.

JB: While works like this Stove Eye, and some of the other quilts from the Cargo Collection, are clearly made from scraps of diverse types of materials with different textures and weights, the overall effect is far more than just "making do." Economic deprivation and artistic talent merge into something quite remarkable. One senses that the creation of such work is part of the aesthetic challenge that these women have set for themselves. In this regard, I find them to be closely allied visually with the African American tradition, also prevalent in the rural South, of yard art, or "yard shows" as they are sometimes called, in which the castoffs of daily life are composed into mixed-media installations of great wit and artistry.[1]

40 / NUMBER 41

Pamela Studstill (1954–)
Pipe Creek, Texas
1984
63 ½" × 65 ½"
Cottons
QSPI: 8
1997.007.1029
International Quilt Study Center,
Ardis and Robert James Collection

JB: The more one studies the coloration and patterning on this quilt, the more one appreciates the subtle choices that the artist has made to achieve her desired effect. Pamela Studstill's characteristic mode of working is to use a range of solid-color fabrics that she hand-paints with acrylics. Dots, stripes, and squiggles enliven the surface of the fabric, which she then cuts up and pieces, combined here with solid-colored cloth centers.

CD: She once remarked, "I've always been interested in the color theories of the Impressionists and the fact that when you put two small bits of color side by side the eye mixes them. By painting on my fabrics, I achieve a greater range of color and pattern than would be possible by using just solid-colored fabrics."[1] The ground color of the painted fabric varies from butterscotch to maroon and dark salmon, overpainted with tints of green, pink, yellow, and orange.

JB: She sewed these around plain blue central squares of several different sizes and shades.

CD: Note how the darker and smaller blue squares are concentrated in the lower half of the quilt. Some tiny, dark purplish blue squares are used very sparingly at the bottom, for example. In the top half of the quilt, the blue blocks are both larger and lighter colored, giving the impression that they're floating.

To further complicate the surface, she creates a diagonal pattern within the pattern through complex piecing in gradations of green to blue. These suggest tree branches overlaid on the surface. Note the dark ones hanging down from the upper border.

PC: This gives the effect of a landscape in which the painted lines read as topographical marks. In addition, evocative sky blue squares appear to float across the surface.

JB: Perhaps living in the hill country of Texas has influenced her palette and sense of abstract landscape forms. Studstill has a B.F.A. in painting from the University of Texas at San Antonio. Like Nancy Crow, Caryl Bryer Fallert, Michael James (fig. 1, plate 48), and other studio quilters whose work is the result of rigorous planning and decision making, she takes her individually constructed blocks and pins them on the wall, meticulously arranging them until their subtle gradations of color and pattern look just right.

Note how she has achieved a frame for her pieced landscape by the careful color choices in the outermost row of blocks. It's a very clearly demarcated color shift at the bottom, and then becomes much more subtle at the sides. At the top and sides, the dark "tree branch" effect that Carolyn mentioned unites the border with the interior.

Because the overall effect is so complex and dynamic, it takes a while to appreciate that she is working in a classic repeating block-pattern tradition beloved by quilters since the early nineteenth century. Each of her blue-centered pieced blocks is four inches in size, and the quilt measures twenty-two by twenty-one blocks.

PC: The artist's mother, Bettie Studstill, quilts her daughter's works,[2] here using eight stitches per inch. Pamela Studstill doesn't name her quilts, just embroiders a number on either the back or the front.

JB: So although we want to interpret them as landscapes, she presents a more neutral formal composition, allowing her viewers to read into them what they will.

JH: I don't see specific natural references in Studstill's work. But undoubtedly she establishes those expectations by creating ground and horizon lines through shading (darker at the bottom and lighter at the top) and giving her quilts frames as if they were landscape paintings. While that's interesting, I think more important is her basic technique, a sort of pointillism in cloth, in which the movement, blending, and massing of colors inherent in the juxtaposition of small pieces of different hues is further enhanced by her painted additions, discussed above. Her works are, both figuratively and literally, among the most painterly of modern studio quilts.

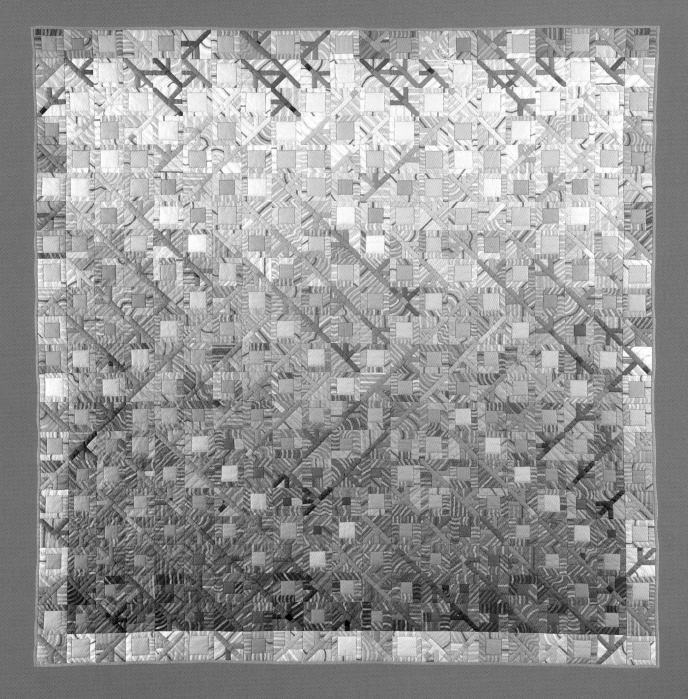

41 / MANHATTAN HEAT WAVE

Elizabeth (Betsy) Cave (1924–)
Mansfield, Ohio
1987
66 ¹/₂" × 82"
Cottons
QSPI: 7
1997.007.1094
International Quilt Study Center,
Ardis and Robert James Collection

JB: I would surmise just from looking at this contemporary quilt that its maker has training in studio art, wouldn't you, Michael?

MJ: Yes, perhaps in graphic art. It has a marvelous graphic quality—a crisp use of positive and negative space, light and dark contrasts, warm and cool values. To me it looks like a game board. The narrow black points in the white field on the two sides evoke a Parcheesi or backgammon board.

PC: Elizabeth Cave has a B.A. in painting. She taught art in the public school system until her retirement, when she returned to her studio full time. She's been active in the studio quilt movement in Ohio since the early 1980s.

JB: I can see the game board quality that Michael refers to, but I think it's equally likely that this artist has looked at a lot of historic quilts and is updating some traditional patterns. I see a simplification of a New York Beauty here (see plate 6).

PC: In which case, the white borders with the narrow black triangles play off the idea of the narrow triangles in the sashing of New York Beauty. Here, however, the maker created an unexpected blade-shape instead of the expected elongated triangles.

JB: Its bisected circle or target pattern also bears an uncanny resemblance to a quilt prominently featured in Jonathan Holstein's influential exhibit *Abstract Design in American Quilts,* which opened at the Whitney Museum in New York in 1971 and traveled for several years. Even if Cave didn't see the show, nearly every quilter in the 1970s and 1980s owned Holstein's book *The Pieced Quilt.* In that book there is a full-page color plate of a bright cheddar orange quilt composed of nine bisected circles, with sashing in between.[1] Both in that quilt and in this one, the quilting stitches follow the circular forms, giving an outwardly rippling effect to the design.

PC: Almost all the fabric is unpatterned, except for a few subtle patterns in the tiny squares at the center of each circle. I see a deliberate use of complementary colors: orange/blue and red/green pairings, for example, in which the shades are matched in their intensity.

JB: But this complementary pairing is not the first thing your eye notices, because they're off shades. But they are Amish colors—the deep solids that Amish quilters favored.

MJ: I also see Nancy Crow's influence at work here, which would be logical for a studio quilter working in Ohio in the 1980s.

JB: Note that the sashing is not striped fabric but carefully pieced strips of beige and blue alternating with slightly narrower strips of black and white.

MJ: The lattice effect provided by the sashing creates an overlaid grid. It's a visual push-pull, in which you read the grid as on top of the circles.

JB: To me this quilt is Mondrian's *Broadway Boogie-Woogie* meets Amish quilts! The artist said she was evoking the hot sun on Manhattan sidewalks during a summer trip to New York.[2]

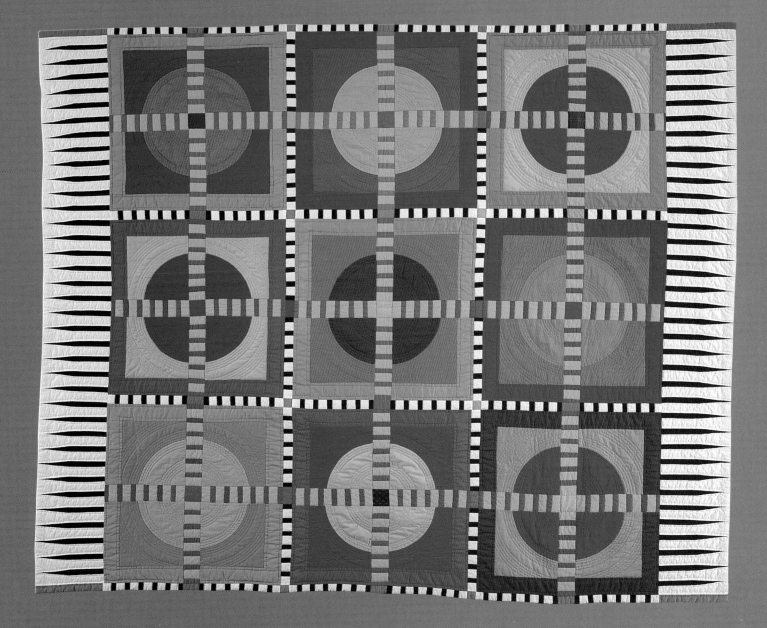

42 / FIREWORKS

Terrie Hancock Mangat (1948–)
Cincinnati, Ohio
1989
109" × 87"
Cottons and various synthetics
QSPI: 9–10
2000.005.0001
Gift of Janis Wetsman

JB: Since the 1980s, Terrie Hancock Mangat has been well known for her award-winning and often-published pictorial quilts, several of which belong to the International Quilt Study Center.[1] They really are multimedia collages, encompassing everything from buttons, beads, ribbons, and other embellishments to old quilt and tablecloth fragments, ethnographic textiles, and electric blankets. This recent piece is extraordinarily large for an art quilt, overwhelming one's visual field the way a fireworks display fills the night sky.

CD: One of the things I've learned to recognize in Mangat's quilts, contrary to my first impression of chaotic disorder, is the organization of the quilt's space. The geometric piecing in the background, with large dark areas bisected by thin strips of color, creates a sense of the night sky—deep and endless, filled with light, shapes, and distant planets. The bright colors interspersed among the dark depths reflect the streams of light radiating from the exploding fireworks.

The many stars also add depth. Bright stars of cream-colored fabric appear to float closer to the viewer than the yellow and orange stars. It's as if the deeper one moves into space, the deeper the color of the individual stars. The falling streams of light from each exploding star are created with fabric paint—some accented by silver sequins dropped into the paint—and with washes of glitter seemingly sprinkled along the trailing ribbons of color.

We discovered when we photographed this quilt that the trailing light from the center white stars was painted with a glow-in-the-dark paint that's embellished with beads that also glow when the lights are off. The shining color fades gradually, disappearing into the background in the same way fireworks slowly fade into the darkness.

JB: The six-pointed stars embroidered in red and gold satin stitch cascading from the upper left to the lower right are fragments of women's blouses, or *huipiles,* from a remote Maya village in the Guatemalan highlands called San Mateo Ixtatán.[2] Here they're appropriated as part of the fireworks display. Hancock has said that her travels in the Third World have influenced her sense of color and surface pattern.[3]

I find it fascinating that at the end of the twentieth century, Latin American and African textiles with their ikats, resist-dyes, and hot color combinations have been so influential in terms of quilt design. From hand-loomed Maya textiles from Guatemala, to Kuna reverse-appliqué *molas* from Panama, to Kuba cut-pile raffias—all have become part of the visual vocabulary of the modern quilter. It's the late-twentieth-century equivalent of the late-nineteenth-century enthusiasm for Asian fabrics, styles, and aesthetics that gave rise to the Crazy quilt (see plate 18).

PC: Another correspondence between late-nineteenth- and late-twentieth-century taste that we see exemplified in this quilt and Crazy quilts is the love of lavish embellishment: embroidery, sequins, buttons, photographic images, and other add-ons. The current taste for such visual extravagance may be a reaction to austere twentieth-century modern design, while the late-Victorian Crazy quilt was a constituent part of the Victorian era of excess. So while these two century's-end impulses may look similar, they clearly are responses to different social conditions.

JB: This artist's earlier quilts were often humorous, with figural imagery as a focus of the design. While this quilt is still clearly pictorial, its extravagant surface patterning becomes almost abstract—its gestural effect is like a Jackson Pollock painting. Mangat studied pottery and printmaking at college before turning to quiltmaking. Like many other successful studio quilters, she brings a whole world of visual influences to bear in her work.

JH: Mangat's jammed surfaces mirror a trait in modern art of adding emotive three-dimensional elements to paintings and sculpture. Most often the intent has been intellectual and emotional in a general sense; Mangat's purpose seems to remain personal, historical, and narrative. While it's clear her surface embellishments must be painstakingly accomplished, through them she has managed to bring a kind of "action painting" drama to this surface.

43 / SQUARE WITHIN A SQUARE

Janie Avant (twentieth century; dates unknown)
Brewton, Alabama
1990s
96 ½" × 94 ½"
Cottons and cotton/polyester blends
QSPI: 3–4
2000.004.0012
International Quilt Study Center,
Robert and Helen Cargo Collection

PC: Janie Avant constructed this simple-looking pattern—squares within squares—with a great deal of precision. The center of each square is a Four Patch block. The Four Patch is framed with strips of fabric that have been mitered at each corner: stitched together on a diagonal. Most quilters use a much simpler construction technique when framing a square.

CD: Note how the maker used only three fabrics in the inner squares of her pattern: a light blue pinwheel print, a black and white printed plaid, and a solid navy blue. In the lower left corner, she varied slightly and included all three in one block. Though she used a number of different fabrics in the outer squares, she didn't incorporate the three inner fabrics in any of the outer squares. Yet she wasn't concerned if the same blocks were placed side by side or in sets of three. This is similar to the "planned random" use of fabric in plate 11, where the quiltmaker uses fabric randomly, yet carefully considers particular elements of her planned layout.

JH: Often quiltmakers try to bring visual unity to square blocks of different colors by using centers of the same color. Avant, however, went the other way, alternating the center colors of disparate blocks in no particular pattern. Just as Victorians were said to have had a distaste for leaving any space undecorated, so Avant and other African American quilters whose work is represented in the IQSC collection seem unconcerned with conventional symmetry, and more interested in visual syncopation.

JB: This quilt reminds me of two others that have been published, neither of which is African American. An unknown Illinois artist at the beginning of the twentieth century made a quilt of blue and white calicoes that moves with the same sort of visual rhythm. Although she was working on a much smaller scale—with more than five times the number of squares than in Avant's quilt—that quiltmaker was also playing with optical movement. The other is a Mennonite quilt in which the optical movement is produced through the play of dark and light in concentric squares of different colors.[1] These three works could stand together as American needlewomen's versions of Josef Albers's celebrated series of modern paintings called *Homage to the Square.*[2]

PC: In the past, many people considered the improvisational style and lack of precision in pieced-work as an indication of African American origin. However, Cuesta Benberry points out that African American quilts range from finely sewn, cut-out chintz appliquéd quilts of the mid-nineteenth century to Crazy quilts.[3] The only way to be sure is to have documentation about the quiltmaker. We have such documentation for all the quilts in the Cargo Collection.

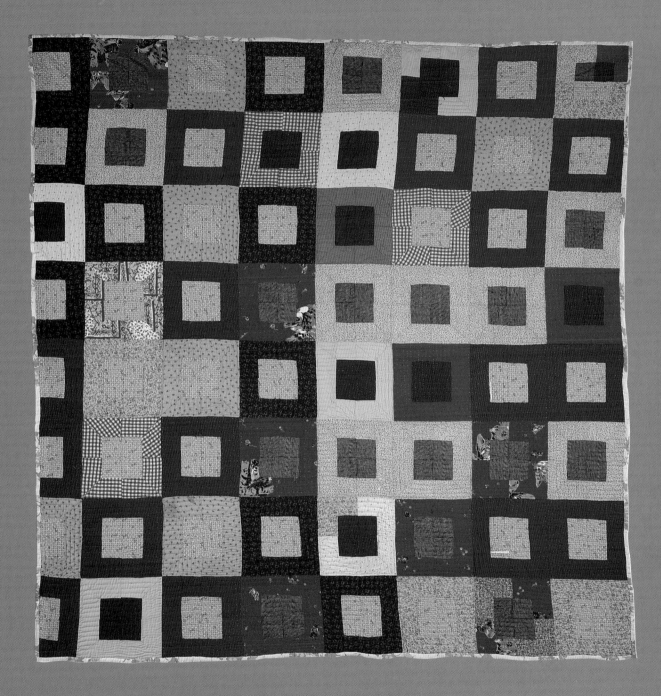

44 / LIX: LOG CABIN

Anna Williams (1927–)
Baton Rouge, Louisiana
1993
77" × 65"
Cottons and cotton/polyester blends
QSPI: 4–6
1997.007.1104
International Quilt Study Center,
Ardis and Robert James Collection

JB: Anna Williams is an African American quilter whose work came to the attention of the studio quilt world when, in the late 1980s, the woman for whom she works as a domestic (Katherine Watts, herself a quilter) saw one of Williams's extraordinary quilts. Contemporary artist Nancy Crow arranged an exhibition of Williams's work at the Quilt/Surface Design Symposium in Columbus, Ohio, in 1990. Since then, Williams has had other exhibitions, most notably at the Museum of the American Quilter's Society in Paducah in 1995. Her work has been widely published and has influenced a number of studio quilters, including Nancy Crow.[1] This Log Cabin is inventive and exuberant—the definition of "wild by design"!

JH: It's my understanding that Williams's source of at least some materials for her quiltmaking was the scraps left from the quiltmaking efforts of Watts and her friends. That idea intrigued me, that Williams was taking the scraps of traditional quiltmaking and using them in transforming ways, in a manner similar to that employed by artists who transform the leftovers and throw-aways of an industrial society into wonderful art.

PC: This is truly an improvisational quilt, made of diverse fabrics joined with little premeditation.

JB: It's astonishing that Williams can work on several such quilts at once, in very close quarters in her bedroom, without the studio quilter's wall on which a work in progress can be tacked up, observed, and its success judged. Looking at this surface up close, one sees only the color dissonances and pattern irregularities.

PC: But from six feet away, the optical properties are amazing. She takes the classic Log Cabin pattern and moves it into another dimension.

JB: In graduate school, when I studied with Robert Farris Thompson, the historian of African and African American art, he would talk about the African American propensity for improvisation by comparing a quilt like this to a jazz riff, while he compared a more rigorously ordered Anglo-American quilt to a John Philip Sousa march. The analogy still seems apt.

PC: Yes, as we're trying to demonstrate in this book, quilters of all sorts engaged in visual experimentation and improvisation. For example, a number of rural quilters in West Virginia of Scots-Irish descent imposed little visual order in their work.[2] Like Anna Williams they appear more absorbed in the process of quiltmaking—the sewing of one piece of fabric to another—than in making overall visual arrangements. They favored spontaneity over calculated designs. In fact, some of the quilts made by rural West Virginia quiltmakers share remarkable visual similarities with those of African American quiltmakers of the rural South.[3] So it can be misleading to ascribe such aesthetic propensities to just one ethnic group.

JB: It's a vernacular tradition that knows no ethnic boundaries, although admittedly it occurs more often in the work of rural African American quilters in the South. In *The Natural History of the Traditional Quilt,* John Forrest and Deborah Blincoe talk about this as a discrepancy between public and private aesthetic values. They suggest that in many instances a woman's so-called "Sunday best" quilts might be regular and symmetrical, while ones she made for everyday domestic use might be freer, more irregular, more daring.[4] Incidentally, we see this not only in historic Anglo-American quilts but in British ones, too.[5]

PC: This appears to be all machine pieced, and quilted with four to six stitches per inch. Williams doesn't quilt her own works; she pieces the tops and Katherine Watts (for whom she has worked for many years and who is now her agent) gives them to others to sandwich and quilt. It is the piecing that most interests her.

JB: Williams has said that she does both machine- and hand-piecing: "I always have my pocketbook with something in it. I'll take that and sew it in the car or wherever I'll be, I'll sew. And then when I am at home, I use the machine."[6]

45 / LOG CABIN

Mary Maxtion (1924–)
Boligee, Alabama
Circa 1994
88" × 73"
Cottons, cotton/polyester blends, polyesters
QSPI: 4–5
2000.004.0080
International Quilt Study Center,
Robert and Helen Cargo Collection

CD: When viewed from a distance, the main focus of this quilt is the bright green squares in the sashing. Those green squares float! But Maxtion hasn't placed the green squares in a consistent rhythmic pattern; the distribution is very irregular.

JB: Thus providing a beautiful example of visual syncopation. The surface is electric with movement, like Anna Williams's quilt (plate 44). Maxtion has used a cacophony of different fabrics in the Log Cabins. The composition is unified by the sashing grid of red and green. The fact that these are complementary colors adds to the visual power of the work. Note that the artist has been very judicious with her use of green elsewhere; there is one block with three green "logs," but very little elsewhere, except in the sashing.

CD: It also reads differently from many Log Cabins because there is no accentuation of the central "hearth" squares, as there usually is in a classic Log Cabin or Pine-apple pattern (see, for example, plates 11, 23, 24). Instead the square is placed in a corner of the block, and the "logs" are added on two sides of the square. The asymmetrical placement of the square makes the blocks appear to recede.

JB: This quilt is a superlative demonstration of the propensity of African American quilters in the rural South to take a classic pattern and visually rearrange it—a trend that scholars have identified in African American music and literature, as well as the visual arts. Henry Louis Gates talks about black vernacular language as a "parallel discursive universe" in which mainstream formal conventions are used, ruptured, and reassembled. Such language, he says, "luxuriates in the chaos of ambiguity that repetition and difference yield."[1] This is precisely what we see in many of the masterworks of African American quilting in the deep South, as identified by Maude Wahlman, Eli Leon, and Roland Freeman.[2]

JH: A problem arises, however, when people tend to assume that any unidentified quilt that does this is, therefore, by an African American quilter, or conversely, that something is not truly African American if it does not fulfill these aesthetic criteria.

JB: And the problem with an exclusive focus on some African textile systems as the primary aesthetic wellspring of an African American quilting tradition is that it ignores the larger cultural context of quiltmaking in North America, where African American quilters have been working for at least two hundred years. And of course they have not been working in isolation from other strands of American culture.

JH: I'm encouraged that we're beginning to discuss the visual attributes of African American quilts both in a national context and in a regional style context (see, for example, the discussion of plates 28, 31, 36, 43, and 44), rather than in an exclusively ethnic context. We know that in Pennsylvania, for instance, quiltmakers of different backgrounds used the very strong colors and color combinations that are a hallmark of some Pennsylvania quilts. These characteristics might have at one time been brought to the aesthetic of Pennsylvania quiltmaking by a particular ethnic or religious group, but the style was adopted by others who found it appealing. Perhaps the same thing was at work here. Anthropologists look at similar traits among different groups and try to determine if they were cases of parallel and independent evolution, or if there were crosscurrents of influence. It is not only interesting but important to apply that same question to quilts.

JB: Actually, I think the issues are more complex and subtle than the rather old-fashioned anthropological paradigms of influence and independent evolution would suggest. We now appreciate much more fully the way that all cultures (and cultural products such as quilts) are dynamic systems that grow, innovate, and appropriate from other systems with which they are inextricably interrelated. And that it is far too essentialist and reductionist to propose a history of quilts, for example, that doesn't allow for complex interrelationships among all aspects of a hybrid and vital American culture.

46 / STAR PUZZLE

Nora Ezell (1917–)
Eutaw, Alabama
1995
96" × 71"
Cotton/polyester blends and cottons
QSPI: 5
2000.004.0029
International Quilt Study Center,
Robert and Helen Cargo Collection

JB: Nora Ezell has been making this pattern, which she calls Star Puzzle, since the 1970s. She often embroiders her name and the date in one corner of the border. This one is dated January 1995.[1]

Ezell is among the best-known contemporary Southern African American quilters. Her work has been in numerous exhibits, and she won an Alabama Folk Heritage Award in 1990 and an NEA National Heritage Fellowship in 1992 in recognition of her artistic achievements. She is very versatile in the range of styles she employs, from traditional patterns like Lone Star, Nine Patch, and Grandmother's Flower Garden to original story quilts, to unique designs based on traditional piecework like this Star Puzzle.[2]

PC: In addition to the bold solids in primary colors that are so effective here, Ezell has used a dynamic mixture of checks, plaid, and ginghams. The quilt is predominantly hand pieced, and is quilted with five stitches per inch.

JB: In her quilting autobiography, she says that she prefers to hand-piece, using a sewing machine only for borders, backings, and bindings. Ezell has said, "I don't try to be perfect, but I have to excel; I never could satisfy myself by doing something simple."[3]

Though each of her Star Puzzles is unique, Ezell typically includes one complete large star and several complete small stars, combined with eighth, quarter, or half stars fit in like puzzle pieces. All are composed of parallelograms or diamonds (hard to work with because they are bias-cut and warp easily).

JH: It's always interesting when artists decide to work in a series, creating a progression of works based on a single idea or design concept. I particularly like her playful manipulations of the classic star pattern, working variations in scale, balance, and composition. She has made good use here of the three-dimensional effects seen in some of the later nineteenth-century large star quilts, using them as isolated incidents that appear unexpectedly in her composition. It is, in a sense, a narrative of design forms, like an artist's sketchbook.

JB: Ezell's bold color and graphic sense give these works a pyrotechnic effect—to me they look like exploding stars or fireworks.

CD: Yes, the quilt makes me think of Terrie Hancock Mangat's *Fireworks* (plate 42). Both women create depth by overlaying different-sized stars, composed of different colors. The dark backgrounds look like the endless depths of the night sky, with large stars that dominate the space and smaller stars that seem to be fading into the distance.

JB: Many contemporary quilters can identify with Nora Ezell's sentiment when she says, "It's the hardest thing in the world for me to put my quilting down. I may work on three or four quilts at the same time. . . . I am never bored."[4]

47 / PAINTED CANYON

Katie Pasquini Masopust (1955–)
Santa Fe, New Mexico
1999
64" × 52"
Cottons, acetates, vinyls
Machine quilted
2000.002.0001
International Quilt Study Center
Gift of Robert and Ardis James
in honor of Dean Emeritus Karen Craig

CD: This work exemplifies the way in which machine-quilting as a tool for creative embellishment can add so much texture and depth to a quilt. It contains a lot of free-motion machine-quilting—heavily packed zigzag stitches in some areas, linear quilting following the narrow fabric strips in other areas. Sometimes the artist emphasizes the patterns within the fabrics themselves by use of machine-quilting.

JB: The imagery is both abstract and representational, although it's very different from that of Pamela Studstill, for example (plate 40), who also combines rigorously geometric abstraction with subtle hints of representation. Masopust is known for a number of different styles of quilts over the years. Her iconography ranges from explorations in three-dimensional space and isometric perspective to representational landscapes.[1] In several recent series, she has been particularly interested in abstract depictions of the dramatic landscape of the desert Southwest, where she has lived for more than a decade. *Painted Canyon* is less directly representational than many of her works, however.

CD: With her skillful layering of colors and textures, it's reminiscent of stratigraphic layers, geological layers of the landscape.

JB: The artist has described the *Canyon Series* as transitional, from her *Fractured Landscapes* into her more recent *Ghost Layers*. Her design process is a complex one, beginning with a photographic expedition into the terrain. Then she superimposes the photograph with geometric drawings and watercolor washes.[2] In *Painted Canyon*, the "ghost layer" is the imposition of two circles and several horizontal and vertical lines. This fractures the landscape, moving the work beyond a mere literal rendition. The geometric layer adds complexity and allows the artist to play with numerous small pieces, color values, and patterns.[3]

PC: She brings together a whole range of unusual colors here, from reds and whites to browns, violets, and yellows. The daring use of the violet and yellow is particularly effective. This complementary color scheme is used far less often than red and green, for example.

CD: She also conjoins a host of fabrics—not only traditional cottons (including assorted prints in the same color families) but even corduroy, shiny lamés, velvets, vinyls, and satins. Like Michael James, who occasionally incorporates satins to add a subtle glow amid commercial cotton prints, Masopust is not afraid to use the full range of commercially available fabrics. The different fibers, textures, and finishes add depth and visual excitement.

JB: This abstract landscape organized around the circles and lines is a pleasing way to contain and organize the wild colors and patterns.

48 / SPIRITUS MUNDI

Michael James (1949–)
Somerset, Massachusetts
2000
55 ½" X 61 ½"
Cottons
Machine quilted
Private Collection of Ardis and Robert James

JB: You've said that when you first looked at quilts as a young artist, you were overwhelmed by what they represented in terms of the "incredible will and perseverance" of their makers.[1] Do you still feel that way?

MJ: No. People say that about my quilts, too, but when it's an art form that you love, the number of hours involved is inconsequential.

JB: Yet it's so often what a viewer comments on: how many hours it must have taken to make it. What do you see as your intellectual or artistic relationship to traditional quilts?

MJ: I've always thought of my quilts as "traditional" in the sense that they are faithful to the form of the quilt. Where they differ is in the construction of the surfaces, and obviously they are a lot less "traditional," though for many years traditional notions of how a quilt surface should be designed—using block repeats, etc.—governed what I did.

JB: What's the relationship of your work of the last few years to that body of work from the 1980s and early 1990s for which you're best known?

MJ: In a work like *Suspended Animation* of 1992 (fig. 1), I was still thinking along formal lines, concerned with issues of the figure/ground relationship. I had worked out how to disentangle myself from the grid that had contained my work for a long time. And I was beginning to work in a more free-form mode.

JB: In *Suspended Animation,* which is quite large scale, it seems that you were exploring issues of dissonance:

all those jagged edges and concave forms were very surprising in a medium that people think of as being about harmony, balance, and prettiness. How do your post–1995 quilts, exemplified by *Spiritus Mundi,* differ in terms of their conception? How do you build them? The verb "build" seems the appropriate one for this newer work.

MJ: I *do* think of the process as building. I'm working with the horizontal and perpendicular relationship of panels. In this one the imagery has to do with the landscape we carry within us, a whole motion-filled system of blood and organs. It's a little internal cosmos of which we're often completely oblivious. I think of the form at the upper left as a heart, a pumping mechanism.

JB: There's a restraint and rigor to the geometry, combined with sensual colors.

MJ: Recently I've been working with painted fabric, which seems to have more capacity to hold emotion—the texture, the color, the way the water pools as the fabric is painted. So these have much more painterly surfaces than most quilts.

Incidentally, *Spiritus Mundi* was the last quilt I completed before moving from New England to Nebraska. It was also my two hundredth quilt.

JB: In their combination of sensuality and rigor, your works remind me of the British artist Andy Goldsworthy.[2] Both of you work in labor-intensive ways. He composes in the materials of nature: leaves, stones, sand, ice, which he meticulously arranges in strikingly geometric patterns.

MJ: What's significant to me about Goldsworthy is that he creates circumstances that allow us to engage with the natural world in a way that's surprising and seductive. If you've seen a Goldsworthy leaf piece, you'll never look at leaves quite the same way again. My work is about investing fabric with meaning beyond the functional and the quotidian. I want people to think twice about fabric, its nature, and the possibilities for expression that it offers. Maybe after seeing one of my quilts they won't think of fabric in quite the same way.

NOTES

Research for my essay, and the discussions about individual quilts that became the catalogue entries in this volume, were conducted during my visits to the International Quilt Study Center (IQSC) during 2001–2002, when I held the IQSC Visiting Faculty Fellowship in Quilt Studies. I am grateful to the University of Nebraska–Lincoln for funding this Fellowship, and particularly grateful to Dr. Patricia Crews for awarding me the first one.

The staff at the International Quilt Study Center (Carolyn Ducey, Curator; Marin Hanson, Assistant Curator; and Janneken Smucker, Graduate Curatorial Assistant) provided warmth and hospitality during my visits to the Center in 2001 and 2002. They also unfolded a lot of quilts. Thank you!

My best friends and colleagues in American Indian Art History, Aldona Jonaitis and Ruth Phillips, took time to offer comments on a draft of my essay, as did my friends and colleagues in American Studies, Bryan Wolf and Angela Miller. All provided penetrating insights that made me think more deeply about these topics in relation to American history and feminist art history. Patricia Crews, Carolyn Ducey, and Jonathan Holstein's assiduous use of the editing pencil kept this neophyte quilt scholar from making too many errors.

My graduate students in the Visual and Cultural Studies Program at the University of Rochester challenge me to think more profoundly about issues of race, gender, and the cultural construction of knowledge. I thank Norman Vorano and Elizabeth Kalbfleish for offering feedback on my essay. Linda Edwards and Liz Czach were tireless research assistants.

My greatest thanks are reserved for Patricia Cox Crews and Jonathan Holstein—friends, colleagues, co-conspirators—who responded enthusiastically when I proposed the topic for this collaborative enterprise in the summer of 2001 after the board meeting of the International Quilt Study Center. Pat and Jon: working with the two of you is as good as it gets. This has been one of the highlights of my professional career.

Janet Catherine Berlo

"Acts of Pride, Desperation, and Necessity"

1. For women's history, see, for example, Elaine Hedges, Pat Ferrero, and Julie Silber, *Hearts and Hands: Women, Quilts, and American Society* (Nashville: Rutledge Hill Press, 1996). For an exemplary instance of quilt history as social and economic history, see Linda Welters and Margaret Ordoñez, eds., *Down by the Old Mill Stream: Quilts in Rhode Island* (Kent, Ohio: Kent State Univ. Press, 2000).

2. Jonathan Holstein, *Abstract Design in American Quilts* (New York: Whitney Museum, 1971), 9–10. See also his *The Pieced Quilt: An American Design Tradition* (New York: Galahad Books, 1973).

3. Patricia Mainardi, "Quilts: The Great American Art," *Feminist Art Journal* 2, no. 1 (1973): 1.

4. Holstein, *The Pieced Quilt*, 9, 115. Twenty years after the pivotal Whitney show, Holstein reprised it in Louisville, Kentucky. The accompanying catalogue, *Abstract Design in American Quilts: A Biography of an Exhibition* (Louisville: Kentucky Quilt Project, 1991) is a fascinating account of the events leading up to the 1971 exhibit and its aftermath. It is noteworthy that, as Holstein describes there, his selection of

more than one hundred possible quilts for inclusion in the exhibit was distilled to a group of sixty-two through a process that included conversations and slide shows with his friends Barnett Newman, Roy Lichtenstein, and Bob Murray—all masters of the modern art world at the time (26–37).

5. Mainardi, "Quilts," 1. This manifesto was republished in *Radical America* 7, no. 1 (1973): 36–68. Excerpts were published in *Ms,* Dec. 1973, 58–62, and *Art News* 73, no. 6 (1974): 30–32. It was later reprinted as a small booklet of the same name (San Pedro, Calif.: Miles and Weir, 1978), as well as in Norma Broude and Mary Garrard, eds., *Feminism and Art History: Questioning the Litany* (New York: Harper and Row, 1982), 330–46.

6. Mainardi, "Quilts," 22.

7. See also Rachel Maines, "Fancywork: The Archaeology of Lives," *Feminist Art Journal* 3, no. 4 (1974–75): 1–3, for a subsequent influential article about women's needlework and feminist art history. For examples of how quilts have become part of feminist scholarly discourse in other areas of American Studies, see Cheryl Torsney and Judy Elsley, *Quilt Culture: Tracing the Pattern* (Columbia: Univ. of Missouri Press, 1994) and Elaine Showalter, "Common Threads," in *Sister's Choice: Tradition and Change in American Women's Writing* (Oxford: Clarendon Press, 1991).

8. In 1965, the Newark Museum had mounted an exhibit entitled *Optical Quilts* highlighting the similarity between paintings and quilts. Another important contribution to quilt history from this era is Patsy and Myron Orlofsky, *Quilts in America* (New York: McGraw-Hill, 1974).

9. It is only in recent years, with the publication of several superb European catalogues, that more people have come to recognize the parallel tradition in European quilt history. See, for example, An Moonen, *Quilts: en Nederlandse traditie/ The Dutch Tradition* (Arnhem, Nederlands: Nederlands Openluchtmuseum, 1992), Dorothy Osler's *Traditional British Quilts* (London: Batsford, 1987) and *North Country Quilts: Legend and Living Tradition* (County Durham: Bowes Museum, 2000), and Janet Rae et al., *Quilt Treasures of Great Britain* (Nashville: Rutledge Hill Press, 1995).

10. I am grateful to my former student Ruth A. Maasen for her research paper "Centennial and Bicentennial Quilts," written for my class "Quilts: A Social and Feminist History," Univ. of Missouri–St. Louis, April 1997. For the MAFA/*Good Housekeeping* quilts, see Erica Wilson, *Erica Wilson's Quilts of America* (Birmingham, Ala.: Oxmoor House, 1979). Examples of local heritage quilts appear on 84–86. See also Jacqueline Atkins, *Shared Threads: Quilting Together Past and Present* (New York: Museum of American Folk Art and Viking Studio Books, 1994), plate 117.

11. Jean Ray Laury, *Quilts and Coverlets: A Contemporary Approach* (New York: Van Nostrand Reinhold, 1970). Laury quilts in the IQSC collection include *Heaven and Earth,* 1985

(1997.007.1030); *Starfire,* 1981 (1997.007.1031); *Light Shower,* 1984 (1997.007.1032); *Doppler Effect #1,* 1984 (1997.007.1033); *Doppler Effect #2,* 1984 (1997.007.1034). One of Laury's quilts was chosen as one of the century's best. See Mary Leman Austin, ed., *The Twentieth Century's Best American Quilts* (Golden, Colo.: Primedia Publications, 1999), 18. In addition to Laury's *Quilts and Coverlets,* other important how-to books from this era include Beth Gutcheon, *The Perfect Patchwork Primer* (New York: David McKay Co., 1973) and Michael James, *The Quiltmaker's Handbook* (Englewood Cliffs, N.J.: Prentice Hall, 1978).

12. Illustrated in Patricia Harris, David Lyon, and Patricia Malarcher, *Michael James: Studio Quilts* (Neuchatel, Switzerland: Éditions Victor Attinger, 1995), 31.

13. It is noteworthy that Lincoln, Nebraska, now home to the International Quilt Study Center and the American Quilt Study Group, has long been in the forefront of interest in quilts. One of the first large-scale symposia, "Fine Art/Folk Art," with speakers such as Jean Ray Laury and Michael James, was held in Lincoln in 1977. More than six hundred people attended. See Carolyn Ducey, "Fine Art, Folk Art: The 1970s Quilt Revival in Nebraska," research paper for course on the history of quilts, Univ. of Nebraska–Lincoln, June 2001.

14. Illustrated in Thalia Gouma-Peterson, *Miriam Schapiro: A Retrospective, 1953–1980* (Wooster, Ohio: College of Wooster, 1980): *Dollhouse,* plate 9; *Anatomy of a Kimono,* plate 1; *Lady Gengi's Maze,* plate 10; *Mary Cassatt and Me,* fig. 32. The phrase "redress the trivialization of women's experience" is from Miriam Schapiro, "Notes from a Conversation on Art, Feminism, and Work," in Sara Ruddick and Pamela Daniels, eds., *Working It Out* (New York: Pantheon Books, 1977), 300.

15. For data on the economic impact of contemporary quiltmaking, see "Quilting in America 1994: A Comprehensive Study of the U.S. Quilting Market" (Golden, Colo.: Leman Publications, 1994) and its update, "Quilting in America 2000."

16. For cultural reasons for the rise of an Arts and Crafts aesthetic in America, see T. J. Jackson Lears, *No Place of Grace: Antimodernism and the Transformation of American Culture, 1880–1920* (New York: Pantheon Books, 1981). On the Colonial Revival, see Alan Axelrod, ed., *The Colonial Revival in America* (New York: W. W. Norton, 1985).

17. See Penny McMorris, *Crazy Quilts* (New York: E. P. Dutton, 1984); Rozsika Parker, *The Subversive Stitch: Embroidery and the Making of the Feminine* (New York: Routledge Press 1989), chap. 7.

18. See Beatrix Rumford, "Uncommon Art of the Common People: A Review of Trends in the Collecting and Exhibiting of American Folk Art," in *Perspectives on American Folk Art,* ed. Ian Quimby and Scott Swank, 13–53 (Winter-

thur, Del.: Winterthur Museum, 1980) and Eugene Metcalf and Claudine Weatherford, "Modernism, Edith Halpert, Holger Cahill, and the Fine Art Meaning of American Folk Art," in *Folk Roots, New Roots: Folklore in American Life,* ed. Jane Becker and Barbara Franco, 141–66 (Lexington, Mass.: Museum of Our National Heritage, 1988).

19. Quoted in Bruce Bustard, *A New Deal for the Arts* (Washington, D.C.: National Archives and Records Administration, 1997), 233. Original source not cited.

20. John Cotton Dana, *American Art—How It Can Be Made to Flourish* (Woodstock, Vt.: Elm Tree Press, 1914), 5, quoted in John Michael Vlach, "Holger Cahill as Folklorist," *Journal of American Folklore* 98, no. 388 (1985): 153. See also E. O. Christensen, *The Index of American Design* (New York: Macmillan Company, 1950). This book contains four hundred plates selected from some twenty-two thousand renderings of American folk art and craft objects done by WPA artists between 1935 and 1941; see chap. 11, "The Linen Closet," 103–19, for a discussion of quilts and other textiles. For brief data on the numerous quilts recorded in the project, see Thomas Woodard and Blanche Greenstein, *Twentieth Century Quilts, 1900–1950* (New York: E. P. Dutton, 1988), 5.

21. I have written further on the topic of America's relationship to folk art in the early twentieth century in an unpublished paper, "Native Art/Folk Art: Loaded Categories/ Parallel Histories," delivered at the symposium "Native Art History and Folk Art History: Critiquing the Paradigms," Fenimore Art Museum, Cooperstown, N.Y., August 7, 1999. For more on the Nadelmans' collection, see Christine Oaklander, "Pioneers in Folk Art Collecting: Elie and Viola Nadelman," *Folk Art* (fall 1992): 48–55.

22. Carrie Hall and Rose Kretsinger, *The Romance of the Patchwork Quilt* (Caldwell, Idaho: Caxton Printers, 1935); quotes are from 13, 28, and 17, respectively.

23. Henry McBride, quoted by Rumford, "Uncommon Art," 37. See Holger Cahill, *American Folk Art: The Art of the Common Man in America, 1750–1900* (New York: Museum of Modern Art, 1932). Cahill's visits to Sweden, and then to the Ogunquit Colony in Maine, ignited his interests in folk art. See Vlach, "Holger Cahill as Folklorist," 148–62, and Metcalf and Weatherford, "Modernism." The indefatigable Holger Cahill curated *American Primitives* in 1930 and *American Folk Sculpture* in 1931, both at the Newark Museum, as well as the 1932 exhibit at MOMA. Pieces from the Abby Aldrich Rockefeller collection dominated the MOMA show. Just three years later, Rockefeller would transfer these to Colonial Williamsburg, with a few items being given to Newark, MOMA, and elsewhere. See Rumford, "Uncommon Art," 42.

24. See, for example, Mary Saltonstall Parker's samplers from the 1920s in Paula Bradstreet Richter, *Painted With Thread: The Art of American Embroidery* (Salem, Mass.: Peabody Essex Museum, 2000), 126–31. For the 1970s, in

addition to Schapiro, "Notes from a Conversation on Art," see Judy Chicago, *The Dinner Party: A Symbol of Our Heritage* (Garden City, N.Y.: Anchor Doubleday, 1979) and *Embroidering Our Heritage: The Dinner Party's Needlework* (Garden City, N.Y.: Anchor Books, 1980).

25. See Barbara Brackman's introduction to the 1992 edition of Ruth E. Finley, *Old Patchwork Quilts and the Women Who Made Them* (1929; reprint, McLean, Va.: EPM Publications, 1992), 12.

26. David Lowenthal, *The Past Is a Foreign Country* (Cambridge: Cambridge Univ. Press, 1985), xvii.

27. Marie Webster, *Quilts: Their Story and How to Make Them* (New York: Doubleday and Page, 1915); Finley, *Old Patchwork Quilts;* and Hall and Kretsinger, *Romance of the Patchwork Quilt.*

28. See Eliza Calvert Hall, *Aunt Jane of Kentucky* (Boston: Little Brown & Co., 1907). Hall's book is listed in the bibliographies of Webster, *Quilts,* and Hall and Kretzinger, *Romance of the Patchwork Quilt,* who quote her on p. 17. Finley's book has no bibliography, but on p. 77 she quotes the same passage I cited above about "how much piecin' a quilt is like livin' a life."

29. In addition to the 1907 book and its reprintings in 1908, 1910, and 1911, two modern editions have been published, one edited by Melody Graulich (Albany: New College and Univ. Press, 1992) and one with a foreword by Bonnie Jean Cox (Lexington: Univ. Press of Kentucky, 1995). Aunt Jane's folksy quilt sayings have also been distilled into a little gift book: E[liza] C[alvert] Hall, *Quilter's Wisdom* (San Francisco: Chronicle Books, 1996). The story in the anthology that focuses on quilts and is the source of most subsequent quotations is "Aunt Jane's Album," (55–82 in the 1995 edition; originally published in *Cosmopolitan,* Feb. 1900, 385–94.

30. Hall, *Aunt Jane* (1995 edition), 73–75.

31. Ibid., 59. The trope of quilt as diary was also dear to feminist writers at the end of the twentieth century, as the quote from Schapiro and Meyer that opens this essay demonstrates.

32. Hall, *Aunt Jane* (1995 edition), 82.

33. One of the few firmly dated pre-revolutionary quilts is a whole-cloth silk quilt with an embroidered inscription, "Drawn by Sarah Smith Stiched [*sic*] by Hannah Callender and Catherine Smith in Testimony of their Friendship 10 mo 5th 1761." See Atkins, *Shared Threads,* fig. 44.

34. Webster, *Quilts,* 65.

35. Finley, *Old Patchwork Quilts,* 33.

36. Hall and Kretsinger, *Romance of the Patchwork Quilt,* 15, 27.

37. See, for example, ibid., 15.

38. Linda Otto Lipsett, *Pieced from Ellen's Quilt: Ellen Spaulding Reed's Letters and Story* (Dayton, Ohio: Halstead and Meadows, 1991), 68. See also 59, 75, 87, 100, and 107.

39. Elaine Hedges, "The Nineteenth Century Diarist and Her Quilts," *Feminist Studies* 8, no. 2 (1982): 297. There is, of course, the occasional textual evidence from the mid-nineteenth century to support the scrap bag story. Sally Experience Brown of Vermont wrote in her diary on Oct. 19, 1833, "Began to piece a bed quilt out of two old calico gowns." Quoted in Lynn Bonfield, "Diaries of New England Quilters before 1860," *Uncoverings* 9 (1988): 186. Linda Welters has documented the recycling of finely quilted silk petticoats into the center of bed quilts after such petticoats went out of fashion in the 1790s, in "A Petticoat Quilt," in Welters and Ordoñez, *Down by the Old Mill Stream*, 197–200. In the same volume, fig. 36, one quilt demonstrates the length to which New England frugality could be taken: it is made entirely from the selvedges of British fabrics, resulting in a collage of style numbers and manufacturer's stamps.

40. This story is undated but clearly took place in the early 1890s, for Della Smith was born in 1877 and married in 1898. See Sara Reimer Farley and Nancy Hornback, "The Quilting Records of Rachel Adella Jewett and Lucyle Jewett," *Uncoverings* 18 (1997): 11.

41. Patricia Cooper and Norma Bradley Buford, *The Quilters: Women and Domestic Art, An Oral History* (Garden City, N.Y.: Anchor Doubleday, 1978), 58.

42. Welters and Ordoñez, *Down by the Old Mill Stream*, figs. 65 and 66, pp. 138–41.

43. Jonathan Holstein, "In Plain Sight: The Aesthetics of Amish Quilts," in *A Quiet Spirit: Amish Quilts from the Collection of Cindy Tietze and Stuart Hodosh*, by Donald Kraybill, Patricia Herr, and Jonathan Holstein (Los Angeles: Fowler Museum of Cultural History, UCLA, 1996), 81.

44. Laurel Thatcher Ulrich, *The Age of Homespun: Objects and Stories in the Creation of an American Myth* (New York: Alfred Knopf, 2001), quotes are from pp. 17 and 29.

45. Virginia Gunn, "From Myth to Maturity: The Evolution of Quilt Scholarship," *Uncoverings* 13 (1993): 198.

46. Cooper and Buford, *The Quilters*. Second edition by Patricia Cooper and Norma Bradley Allen, 1989. Reprinted by Texas Tech Univ. Press, 1999. The stage play by Molly Newman and Barbara Damashek, which premiered at the Denver Center for the Performing Arts in 1982, went to Broadway in 1984 and was nominated for six Tony awards in 1985. It is only a slight exaggeration to say that it has been performed almost continuously somewhere in the United States since that time. It has also been staged abroad at festivals in Edinburgh and Dublin. (This information was provided by the Dramatists' Play Services, New York, February, 2002.)

47. Cooper and Buford, *The Quilters*, 20.

48. See Jacqueline Tobin and Raymond Dobard, *Hidden in Plain View: The Secret Story of Quilts and the Underground Railroad* (New York: Doubleday, 1999) and Nora Ezell, *My Quilts and Me: The Diary of an American Quilter* (Mont-gomery, Ala.: Black Belt Press, 1999). For children, there is Deborah Hopkinson, *Sweet Clara and the Freedom Quilt* (New York: Alfred A. Knopf, 1993).

49. See Barbara Brackman's introduction to Finley, *Old Patchwork Quilts*, 9–12, and Judy Elsley, "Uncovering Eliza Calvert Hall," *Encyclia* 68 (1991): 155–71.

50. Finley, *Old Patchwork Quilts*, 51.

51. Hall and Kretsinger, *Romance of the Patchwork Quilt*, 14.

52. See *Right out of History: The Making of Judy Chicago's Dinner Party*, a film by Johanna Demetrakas, Phoenix Films, New York, 1980.

53. Mainardi, "Quilts," 19.

54. Tobin and Dobard, *Hidden in Plain View*, and Maude Wahlman, *Signs and Symbols: African Images in African American Quilts* (New York: Studio Books in association with the Museum of American Folk Art, 1993).

55. See Robert Farris Thompson, *Flash of the Spirit: African and Afro-American Art and Philosophy* (New York: Random House, 1983) and Wahlman, *Signs and Symbols*.

56. Paul Oliver, *Savannah Syncopators: African Retentions in the Blues* (New York: Stein and Day, 1970) and Henry Louis Gates, *The Signifying Monkey: A Theory of Afro-American Literary Criticism* (New York: Oxford Univ. Press, 1988).

57. Tobin and Dobard, *Hidden in Plain View*, 22–23. Tobin holds an M.A. in Women's Studies, while Dobard, who is himself a quilter of partial African American descent, holds a Ph.D. in twentieth-century European art history. Neither is a scholar of quilts, of African American history in general, or of the Underground Railroad in particular.

58. Ibid., 79, caption to last unnumbered plate before page 51, and 83, respectively.

59. Ibid., 85. See Giles R. Wright, Director of Afro-American History, New Jersey Historical Commission, review posted on the Web site of the Camden County Historical Society, *HistoricCamdenCounty.com*, June 2001. For a diplomatic critique of Tobin and Dobard's methods and assertions by a quilt scholar, see Marsha MacDowell, "Quilts and Their Stories: Revealing a Hidden History," in *Uncoverings* 21 (2000): 155–66.

60. On the relationship of Harriet Powers's work to West and/or Central Africa, see Regenia Perry, *Harriet Powers's Bible Quilts* (New York: Rizzoli Art Series, 1994), 2, 4; Wahlman, *Signs and Symbols*, 89; and Gladys-Marie Fry, *Stitched from the Soul: Slave Quilts from the Ante-Bellum South* (New York: Dutton Studio Books in association with the Museum of American Folk Art, 1990), 85. Critiques of the Afrocentric position have been put forth by Stacy Hollander, "African-American Quilts: Two Perspectives, *Folk Art* (spring 1993): 44–51 (although she says that Harriet Powers's "debt to the appliqué banners of the Fon people of Dahomey is not in question"). See also Jennie Chinn, "African-American Quilt-making Traditions: Some Assumptions Reviewed," in *Kansas*

Quilts and Quilters, ed. Barbara Brackman (Lawrence: Univ. Press of Kansas, 1993), 157–75, as well as a pithy letter from Ricky Clark published in *The Clarion,* summer 1990, 22.

61. For excellent preliminary efforts, see Ricky Clark, *Quilted Gardens: Floral Quilts of the Nineteenth Century* (Nashville: Rutledge Hill Press, 1994), 59–65, and her "Coverlets, Quilts, and Fancy Needlework: Similarities in Folk Design," in *Woven Coverlets: Textiles in the Folk Tradition,* ed. Patricia Cunningham (Bowling Green, Ohio: McFall Center Gallery, Bowling Green Univ., 1984), 26–32.

62. For families of male weavers and female quilters sharing iconographic motifs, see, for example, Ricky Clark, ed., *Quilts in Community: Ohio's Traditions* (Nashville: Rutledge Hill Press, 1991), figs. 31 and 99. For works by women who were both quilters and weavers, see, for example, Karoline Bresenhan and Nancy Puentes, *Lone Stars, Volume I: A Legacy of Texas Quilts, 1836–1936* (Austin: Univ. of Texas Press, 1986), 38–39. Few fully professional female coverlet weavers are known. But see Carol Strickler, *American Woven Coverlets* (Loveland, Colo.: Interweave Press, 1987), 20–21, for information on Sarah LaTourette of Indiana, who at age twenty-seven inherited her father's coverlet weaving business.

63. Janice Tauer Wass, *Weaver's Choice: Patterns in American Coverlets* (Springfield: Illinois State Museums, 1988), 22.

64. Bresenhan and Puentes, *Lone Stars, Volume I,* 39. For a star quilt with a pine tree border, see also Jacqueline Atkins and Phyllis Tepper, *New York Beauties: Quilts from the Empire State* (New York: Dutton Studio Books, 1992), fig. 149.

65. For illustrations of other woven names of maker or buyer, see Mildred Davison and Christa Mayer-Thurman, *Coverlets: A Handbook of the Collection of Woven Coverlets in the Art Institute of Chicago* (Chicago: Art Institute of Chicago, 1973), figs. 42a, 43a, 60a, 64a, 85.

66. Clark, *Quilted Gardens,* 59–61.

67. See, for example, Robert Shaw, *Quilts: A Living Tradition* (New York: Hugh Lauter Levin Associates, 1995) and Roderick Kirakofe, *The American Quilt* (New York: Clarkson Potter, 1993).

68. For whole-cloth quilts, see, for example, Lynne Bassett and Jack Larkin, *Northern Comfort: New England's Early Quilts, 1780–1850* (Nashville: Rutledge Hill Press, 1998), plates 4, 7, 9. For palampores, see, for example, Jeremy Adamson, *Calico and Chintz: Antique Quilts from the Collection of Patricia S. Smith* (Washington, D.C.: Renwick Gallery of the Smithsonian Institution, 1997), plates 1 and 2; John Irwin and Katharine Brett, *Origins of Chintz, with a Catalogue of Indo-European Cotton-Paintings in the Victoria and Albert Museum, London, and the Royal Ontario Museum, Toronto* (London, H.M.S.O., 1970), plates 1–90. These types were also favored in Europe. See Moonen, *Quilts,* plates 1–14, 18. Examples of these in the IQSC collection include whole-cloth quilts, 1997.007.0416, 1997.007.0620, 1997.007.0719; palampore,

1997.007.0606; and cut-out chintz or *broderie perse,* 1997.007.0152, 1997.007.0253, 1997.007.0257, 1997.007.0479, 1997.007.0634, 1997.007.0654.

69. Jennifer Goldsborough, *Lavish Legacies: Baltimore Album and Related Quilts from the Collection of the Maryland Historical Society* (Baltimore: Maryland Historical Society, 1994), 10. See also Jennifer Goldsborough, "An Album of Baltimore Album Quilt Studies," *Uncoverings* 14 (1994): 73–110. Baltimore Album quilts in the IQSC collection include 1997.007.0319 and 1997.007.0320, the latter illustrated in Patricia Cox Crews, ed., *A Flowering of Quilts* (Lincoln: Univ. of Nebraska Press, 2001), plate 7.

70. See Nancy Hornback, "Nineteenth Century Red and Green Appliqué Quilts," *Kansas Quilts and Quilters,* ed. Barbara Brackman (Lawrence: Univ. of Kansas Press, 1993) and Clark, *Quilted Gardens.* Examples of symmetrical repetitive patterns and wilder designs can be found in both of those studies, as well as in Crews, *A Flowering of Quilts.*

71. See, for example, Atkins, *Shared Threads.*

72. See Amelia Peck, *American Quilts and Coverlets in the Metropolitan Museum* (New York: Metropolitan Museum of Art, 1990), plate 1. A dozen years later, she created an even more inventive appliquéd landscape in the central medallion of the quilt she made for a niece. Within a scalloped medallion, she created a village scene with some five dozen people and animals, surrounded by a profusion of flowery vines. This quilt, damaged in a 1970 fire at the Henry Ford Museum in Greenfield, Michigan, is known today through photographs. See ibid., 18.

73. This quilt has often been published, but the best recent color illustrations are in Sandi Fox, *Wrapped in Glory: Figurative Quilts and Bedcovers, 1700–1900* (Los Angeles: L.A. County Museum of Art, 1990), 48–53. Another ambitious early pictorial quilt is Jane Reagan's 1827 Pictorial Medallion, in which scores of human and animal figures are appliquéd into scenes of life in Europe and Canada. See Marilyn Walker, *Ontario's Heritage Quilts* (Toronto: Boston Mills Press, 1992), 88–91.

74. At Elizabeth Mitchell's death in 1857, her daughter Sarah Mitchell Stallcup became custodian of the quilt. In the central graveyard, she sewed down her mother's coffin, to join those of her little brothers. Sarah also had the unhappy task of adding her own husband's and her own baby's coffins to the quilt. Neither these coffins, nor those of spouses or other babies of the next generation, were put in the graveyard itself. Apparently the small graveyard was reserved for the thirteen immediate members of the artist's family, for in addition to the four coffins resting there, hand-stitched outlines indicate where nine others might fit. After 1870, no more coffins were moved and no more cloth strips with penned notations were added. Although the quilt passed down through the Mitchell family for ninety more years, it no longer served as an active family death register, but simply

as a reminder of the woman who had conceived such an unusual use for a quilt. All data on the Mitchell quilt comes from Linda Otto Lipsett, *Elizabeth Roseberry Mitchell's Graveyard Quilt* (Dayton, Ohio: Halstead and Meadows, 1995). Mitchell began an earlier version of this work in 1836, but never finished it. Another quilt that Sandi Fox has convincingly argued is a mourning quilt is the Maria Hanks quilt of 1857. See Fox, *Wrapped in Glory,* 88–91.

75. For an illustration of Betsey Haring's 1859 quilt that depicts furniture, a horse-drawn carriage, and strawberry baskets, see Rita Erickson and Barbara Schaffer, "Characteristics of Signed New Jersey Quilts, 1837–1867," in *On the Cutting Edge,* ed. J. Lasansky (Lewisburg, Pa.: Union County Historical Society, 1994), 79. For other examples, see the Ackerman quilt of 1859 illustrated in Fox, *Wrapped in Glory,* 93, and a quilt in the Museum of American Folk Art illustrated in Cyril Nelson and Carter Houck, *Treasury of American Quilts* (New York: Greenwich House, 1982), plate 7.

76. Illustrated in Maggi McCormick Gordon, *Pictorial Quilting* (New York: Watson-Guptill, 2000).

77. See Eva Grudin, *Stitching Memories: African American Story Quilts* (Williamstown, Mass.: Williams College Museum of Art, 1990), 27–29.

78. For recent research on these organizations, see Mark Carnes, *Secret Ritual and Manhood in Victorian America* (New Haven: Yale Univ. Press, 1989) and Mary Ann Clawson, *Constructing Brotherhood: Class, Gender, and Fraternalism* (Princeton, N.J.: Princeton Univ. Press, 1989), especially chap. 6, "The Rise of the Women's Auxiliary."

79. In addition to the quilt illustrated here, see also IQSC 1997.007.0761, an Odd Fellows album quilt, dated 1850. See also Ellie Sienkiewicz, *Baltimore Beauties and Beyond,* vol. 2 (Lafayette, Calif.: C & T Publishing, 1991), plate 4.26, for an 1852 Baltimore Album quilt with Odd Fellows symbols. See *Important Americana, January 28–30, 1988* (New York: Sotheby's, 1988), no. 1475, a Baltimore Album quilt with Odd Fellows Rebekah Degree iconography, and no. 1481, a Masonic quilt, Edwin Binney and Gail Binney-Winslow, *Homage to Amanda: Two Hundred Years of American Quilts* (Nashville: Rutledge Hill Press, 1984), fig. 14, for an 1854 Baltimore Album quilt with Odd Fellow imagery. An extraordinarily inventive Masonic quilt made by Martha Hewitt in 1855 is illustrated in Marsha MacDowell and Ruth Fitzgerald, *Michigan Quilts: 150 Years of a Textile Tradition* (East Lansing: Michigan State Univ. Museum, 1987), plate 21; another completely original one, made by Sallie Hasson, ca. 1870, is illustrated in Cynthia Rubin, "Southern Exposure: One Curator in Search of an Exhibition," *The Clarion,* spring/summer 1985, 34.

80. IQSC 1997.007.0318, illustrated in Crews, *A Flowering of Quilts,* plate 51.

81. See, for example, Susan Robb's Confederate Quilt in Bets Ramsey and Merikay Waldvogel, *Southern Quilts: Surviving Relics of the Civil War* (Nashville: Rutledge Hill Press, 1998), 20, and the Abraham Lincoln Presentation counterpane, 1865, in Celia Y. Oliver, *Fifty-five Famous Quilts from the Shelburne Museum* (New York: Dover Press, 1990), 18.

82. For genealogical and biographical data, see Melissa Jurgena and Patricia Cox Crews, "The Reconciliation Quilt: Lucinda Ward Honstain's Pictorial Diary of an American Era," *Folk Art* (2003, in press).

83. Sara Dillow, personal communication, Lincoln, Nebraska, December 2001.

84. This is well illustrated in Fox, *Wrapped in Glory,* 104–7. For the relationship of this quilt to one in the IQSC collection, see discussion in note 8 for plate 16. See also Phoebe Cook's "calico community" of nearly one hundred figures on her quilt in Fox's *Wrapped in Glory* 114–17.

85. See McMorris, *Crazy Quilts,* fig. 80. See also her figs. 96 and 99 for other distinctive and autobiographical crazy quilts.

86. See Gerald Ward et al., *American Folk: Folk Art from the Collection of the Museum of Fine Arts, Boston* (Boston: Museum of Fine Arts, 2001), 72–73.

87. See Nancy Slack, "Nineteenth-Century American Women Botanists: Wives, Widows, and Work," in *Uneasy Careers and Intimate Lives: Women in Science, 1789–1979,* ed. Pnina Abir-Am and Dorinda Outram (New Brunswick, N.J.: Rutgers Univ. Press, 1987), 78–103; John Lankford and Rickey Slavings, "Gender and Science: Women in American Astronomy, 1859–1949," *Physics Today,* March 1990, 58–65; and Pamela Mack, "Straying from Their Orbits: Women in Astronomy in America," in *Women of Science,* ed. G. Kass-Simon and P. Farnes (Bloomington: Indiana Univ. Press, 1990) 72–116.

88. See Nelson and Houck, *Treasury of American Quilts,* plate 35. For other quilts with botanical motifs, see Crews, *A Flowering of Quilts.*

89. Illustrated in *What's American about American Quilts* (Washington, D.C.: National Museum of American History, Smithsonian Institution, 1995), appendix, 2.

90. See, for example, Gladys-Marie Fry, "Harriet Powers: Portrait of a Black Quilter," in *Missing Pieces: Georgia Folk Art, 1770–1976,* ed. Anna Wadsworth (Atlanta: Georgia Council for the Arts and Humanities, 1976), 16–23, reprinted as an epilogue in Fry, *Stitched from the Soul,* 84–91; John Michael Vlach, *The Afro-American Tradition in Decorative Arts* (Cleveland, Ohio: Cleveland Museum of Art, 1978), 44–54; Marie Jeanne Adams, "The Harriet Powers Pictorial Quilts," *Black Art: An International Quarterly* 3, no. 4 (1979): 12–28. Perry, *Harriet Powers's Bible Quilts,* provides superlative full-page illustrations of details from both quilts. See also Grudin,

Stitching Memories, 1–6, and Wahlman, *Signs and Symbols,* 64–67.

91. As expressed verbally to the buyer of the Smithsonian quilt, Jennie Smith, quoted in Fry, *Stitched from the Soul,* 86.

92. Although Powers was illiterate, her descriptions were recorded in 1898 by an anonymous writer. These are on file at the Museum of Fine Arts, Boston. Significant excerpts are published in Perry, *Harriet Powers's Bible Quilts.*

93. Adams, "The Harriet Powers Pictorial Quilts," 21.

94. Perry, *Harriet Powers's Bible Quilts,* n.p.

95. Fry, *Stitched From the Soul,* 85. John Michael Vlach follows suit in *Afro-American Tradition in Decorative Arts,* 48–54. He says that "not all appliqué quilts made by Blacks are necessarily tied to African sources" but goes on to compare at length Powers's two quilts to Fon appliqué, asserting that "all of the similarities between her work and that of Fon appliqué sewers cannot be explained by serendipitous accident" (54). He does compare Powers's work with an Anglo-American appliqué quilt, yet in contrast to that one illustration he offers ten illustrations of Fon appliqué from West Africa.

96. Perry, *Harriet Powers's Bible Quilts,* n.p. In a children's book by Mary Lyons, Powers's work is contextualized within its own culture before the link with West Africa is introduced: "Appliqué was quite popular with American women in Harriet's time. . . . Harriet decided on appliqué because she had seen it all her life," *Stitching Stars: The Story Quilts of Harriet Powers* (New York: Aladdin Paperbacks, 1997), 32.

97. Fry, *Stitched From the Soul,* 86.

98. Vlach, in *Afro-American Tradition in Decorative Arts,* 48, points out that in the late eighteenth and early nineteenth centuries, most slaves in Georgia were being imported from the Central African regions of Congo and Angola rather than West Africa. Because West African appliquéd flags are a perishable art form in a tropical climate, there are none known from the eighteenth century. Scholar Suzanne Blier, who has conducted extensive research among the Fon, says that oral history there claims that the appliqué-work tradition began during the seventeenth-century reign of King Agaja, although the first documentation of it is in European illustrations of Fon flags in situ in the 1850s. Moreover, she points out that traditional West African fabric woven on strip looms (which produce strips of fabric less than six inches wide that are then sewn together) could not successfully be cut up to make this sort of appliqué. It relied instead on European cloth and Chinese silk. She suggests that this tradition may ultimately have a European origin, introduced by the Portuguese, who began their explorations in West Africa in the late fifteenth century (personal communication, Professor Suzanne Blier, Department of History of Art and Architecture, Harvard Univ., March 2002). Similarly, the Akan tradition of appliqué banner-making in Ghana is thought to have been an early

European introduction. Silk banners and flags of different European trading companies were common gift items in West Africa. See Doran Ross, *Fighting with Art: Appliquéd Flags of the Fante Asafo* (Los Angeles: UCLA Museum of Cultural History, 1979), 12–14.

99. This section's epigraph, from *Godey's Lady's Book,* Feb. 1860, 163, is quoted in Peck, *American Quilts and Coverlets,* 67.

100. Frances Trollope, *Domestic Manners of the Americans* (1832; reprint, New York: Alfred A. Knopf, 1949), 416.

101. Nancy Cott, *The Bonds of Womanhood: "Woman's Sphere" in New England, 1780–1835* (New Haven: Yale Univ. Press, 1977), 190. See also Carroll Smith-Rosenberg, "The Female World of Love and Ritual," in *Disorderly Conduct: Visions of Gender in Victorian America* (Oxford: Oxford Univ. Press, 1985), 53–76.

102. One of Sarah Bryant's drawings looks like a variant of the Irish Chain pattern. An example of a block-style quilt in this pattern, with the date 1806 hand-quilted into it, is illustrated in Bassett and Larkin, *Northern Comfort,* plate 44.

103. This quilt may have been made in Britain and brought to North America. See Jacqueline Beaudoin-Ross, "An Early Eighteenth Century Pieced Quilt in Montreal," *RACAR: Revue d'art canadienne/Canadian Art Review* 6, no.2 (1979–80): 106–9. The Saltonstall quilt, made of silk, brocade, and velvet pieced triangles, which has been repeatedly published with the family's attribution of 1704, is almost certainly about a century later than that date. See Orlovsky, *Quilts in America,* plate 3, which is often cited for this 1704 date.

104. See Jonathan Holstein, "The American Block Quilt," in *In the Heart of Pennsylvania,* ed. Jeannette Lasansky (Lewisburg, Pa.: Union County Historical Society, 1986), fig. 3.

105. Ibid., fig. 2.

106. See Lucinda Cawley et al., *Saved for the People of Pennsylvania: Quilts from the State Museum of Pennsylvania* (Harrisburg, Pa.: Pennsylvania Historical and Museum Commission, 1997), 11. See also Paula Locklair, *Quilts, Coverlets, and Counterpanes: Bedcoverings from the MESDA and Old Salem Collections* (Winston-Salem, S.C.: Old Salem, 1997), plate 31. It is noteworthy how many more of these very early quilts seem to have names and dates inscribed on them, recalling the eighteenth-century custom of embroidering initials and dates on bed linens (see discussion in catalogue entry for plate 2). Most nineteenth-century quilts have neither name nor date pieced, quilted, or written on them.

107. See IQSC 1997.007.0939. Other fine examples of the Carpenter's Square pattern have been published in Binney and Binney-Winslow, *Homage to Amanda,* fig. 43, and Bresenhan and Puentes, *Lone Stars, Volume I,* 93.

108. Mainardi, "Quilts," 22, was the first. More recent challenges to a supposedly male, art-world appropriation of quilts include Susan Bernick, "A Quilt is an Art Object

When It Stands up Like a Man," in *Quilt Culture: Tracing the Pattern,* ed. Cheryl Torsney and Judy Elsley (Columbia: Univ. of Missouri Press, 1994), 134–50, and Beverly Gordon, "Intimacy and Objects: A Proxemic Analysis of Gender-Based Responses to the Material World," in *The Material Culture of Gender/The Gender of Material Culture,* ed. Katharine Martinez and Kenneth Ames (Winterthur, Del.: Winterthur Museum, 1997), 237–52. Notably, of these authors, only Mainardi is an art historian.

109. Gordon, "Intimacy and Objects," 244. I am grateful to Patricia Crews for calling my attention to this source.

110. Webster, *Quilts,* 146–48. The fictional Aunt Jane, too, has something to say on this topic, opening her story "Aunt Jane's Album" with the scene of a "a bizarre mass of color on the sweet spring landscape, those patchwork quilts, swaying in a long line under the elms and maples." Aunt Jane's niece asks her if she is having a fair all by herself. Hall, *Aunt Jane* (1995 edition), 56. In a more jocular vein, humorist George Washington Harris in 1867 described the display of quilts set up on the day of a quilting party: "All the plow lines an' clothes lines wer staiched tu every post an tree. Quilts purvailed. Durn my gizzard ef two acres roun that ar house warn't jis' one solid quilt, all out a-sunnin, an' tu be seed. They dazzled the eyes, skeered the hosses, giv wimin the heartburn, and perdominated." George Washington Harris, "Mrs. Yardley's Quilting," 1867, reprinted in *"Sut Lovingoods Yarns" and American Literature,* ed. Cleanth Brooks et al. (New York: St. Martin's Press, 1973), 70–71.

111. See Hedges et al., *Hearts and Hands,* 72–81; Beverly Gordon, "Playing at Being Powerless: New England Ladies Fairs, 1830–1930," *Massachusetts Review* 26, no. 4 (spring 1986): 144–66; Barbara Brackman, "Fairs and Expositions: Their Influence on American Quilts," in *Bits and Pieces: Textile Traditions,* ed. Jeanette Lasansky (Lewisburg, Pa.: Union County Historical Society, 1991), 90–99; Virginia Gunn, "Quilts at Nineteenth Century State and County Fairs: An Ohio Study," *Uncoverings* 9 (1998): 105–28; Jane Przybysz, "Quilts, Old Kitchens, and the Social Geography of Gender at Nineteenth Century Sanitary Fairs," in *The Material Culture of Gender/The Gender of Material Culture,* ed. Katharine Martinez and Kenneth Ames (Winterthur, Del.: Winterthur Museum, 1997), 411–41; and Mary Jane Furgason and Patricia Cox Crews, "Prizes from the Plains: Nebraska State Fair Award-Winning Quilts and Quiltmakers," *Uncoverings* 14 (1994): 188–220.

112. See Webster, *Quilts,* 136, and Hall and Kretsinger, *Romance of the Patchwork Quilt,* 17.

113. In the nineteenth century, there were perhaps a handful of entrepreneurial women who designed quilts for others. Best known is Baltimore's Mary Simon, who seems to have produced kit blocks of her own designs for other women to stitch into the renowned Baltimore Album quilts. See Golds-

borough, "An Album of Baltimore Album Quilt Studies," 73–110. Marie Webster's role has been well documented by Cuesta Benberry, "Marie D. Webster: A Major Influence on Quilt Design in the Twentieth Century," *Quilter's Newsletter Magazine,* July–Aug. 1990, 32–35. Webster's patterns have been reissued for a new generation in Rosalind Webster Perry and Marty Frolli, *A Joy Forever: Marie Webster's Quilt Patterns* (Santa Barbara, Calif.: Practical Patchwork, 1992). The finest examples of the kinds of quilts designed by Webster and others can be found in Austin, *The Twentieth Century's Best American Quilts,* 40, 66, 69, 78, 90, 91.

114. Early twentieth-century patterns and kits have been well documented by Anne Copeland and Beverly Dunivent, "Kit Quilts in Perspective," *Uncoverings* 15 (1994): 141–67; Xenia Cord, "Marketing Quilt Kits in the 1920s and 1930s," *Uncoverings* 16 (1995): 139–73; Merikay Waldvogel, "The Origin of Mountain Mist Patterns," *Uncoverings* 16 (1996): 95–105; Louise Townsend, "Kansas City Star Quilt Patterns," *Uncoverings* 5 (1984): 115–25. See also Merikay Waldvogel, *Soft Covers for Hard Times: Quiltmaking and the Great Depression* (Nashville: Rutledge Hill Press, 1990), 2–37.

115. See Jonathan Holstein and Carolyn Ducey, *Masterpiece Quilts from the James Collection* (Tokyo: Nihon Vogue, 1998), 90–92.

116. Merikay Waldvogel and Barbara Brackman, *Patchwork Souvenirs of the 1933 World's Fair* (Nashville: Rutledge Hill Press, 1993), figs. 96, 112, 140.

117. Chappell's quilt is illustrated in Austin, *The Twentieth Century's Best American Quilts,* 85, while Hamilton's (IQSC 1997.007.0843) is illustrated in Shaw, *Quilts,* 90–91.

118. Two of Stenge's quilts are published in Austin, *The Twentieth Century's Best American Quilts,* 94, 95. Both the Art Institute of Chicago and the Illinois State Museum in Springfield have significant collections of her quilts. In 1998, the Illinois State Museum mounted an exhibit of her work entitled *A Cut and Stitch Above: Quilts by Bertha Stenge, 1930s–1950s.*

119. See Jay Johnson and William C. Ketchum, *American Folk Art of the Twentieth Century* (New York: Rizzoli International, 1983), 179–81, and *Selections from the American Folk Art Collection of Mr. and Mrs. Robert P. Marcus, October 14, 1989* (New York: Sotheby's, 1989), nos. 62, 63.

120. See, for example, Marsha MacDowell and C. Curt Dewhurst, *To Honor and Comfort: Native Quilting Traditions* (Santa Fe: Museum of New Mexico Press, 1997), which examines both Native and Hawaiian quilts; for Hawaiian quilts, see Joyce Hammond, *Taifaifai and Quilts of Polynesia* (Honolulu: Univ. of Hawaii Press, 1986) and Reiko Michinaga Brandon, *The Hawaiian Quilt* (Honolulu: Academy of Arts, 1996); for Amish quilts, see Robert Hughes and Julie Silber, *Amish: The Art of the Quilt* (New York: Alfred A. Knopf, 1990) and Kraybill, Herr, and Holstein, *A Quiet Spirit.*

121. Lakota Sioux Kevin Locke, quoted in Christopher Martin, *Native Needlework: Contemporary Indian Textiles from North Dakota* (Fargo: North Dakota Council on the Arts 1988), 7.

122. For examples of Plains star quilts, see MacDowell and Dewhurst, *To Honor and Comfort,* passim. Several authors have noted the formal continuities between the nineteenth-century hides patterned in concentric circles of feathers that Plains women painted, and modern star quilts. See Patricia Albers and Beatrice Medicine, "The Role of Sioux Women in the Production of Ceremonial Objects: The Case of the Star Quilt," in *The Hidden Half: Studies of Indian Women in the Northern Plains,* ed. Patricia Albers and Beatrice Medicine (Lanham, Md.: The Univ. Press of America, 1983).

123. Among the Lakota, they also have a central place in *yuwipi,* a healing ceremony in which the religious practitioner is wrapped and tied in a star quilt as if he were dead. He visits the spirit world and re-emerges to heal the sick. See Marla N. Powers, *Oglala Women: Myth, Ritual, and Reality* (Chicago: Univ. of Chicago Press, 1986), 139, 199–201.

124. Mary Inkanish remembered that as early as the 1880s, quilts lined the Cheyenne Sun Dance lodge. See Alice Marriott and Carol Rachlin, *Dance around the Sun: The Life of Mary Little Bear Inkanish* (New York: Thomas Y. Crowell, 1977), 14.

125. Florence Pulford, *Morning Star Quilts* (Los Altos, Calif.: Leone Publications, 1989), color plates on pages 15, 44, 45, 46, 53, 74.

126. This passage describes the scene of a first meeting of female fiber artists from two different cultures: "On Monday morning, April 3, 1820, the American Board of Missions held its first sewing circle in the Sandwich Islands. The place of meeting was the brig Thaddeus, one hundred and sixty-two days out of Boston, as, almost at her journey's end, she sailed along the western coast of Hawaii after a brief stop at Kawaihae. A group of eleven women were seated on lauhala mats on deck: Kalakua, queen dowager; Namahana, her sister and also widow of Kamehameha I; two wives of chief Kalanimoku, their ample figures wrapped in folds of tapa from waist to below the knees, their brown bosoms and shoulders bare; and seven young New England matrons, wives of the first missionaries to these islands. Lucy Thurston, Lucia Holman, Sybil Bingham, Nancy Ruggles, Mercy Whitney, Jerusha Chamberlain, and Mrs. Elisha Loomis were dressed in the tight-waisted, tight-sleeved garments of the day, their ankles no doubt tucked discreetly beneath their billowing skirts. Mrs Thurston later wrote, 'Kalakua, queen dowager, was directress . . . Mrs. Holman and Mrs. Ruggles were executive officers, to ply the scissors and prepare the work. The four women of rank were furnished with calico patchwork to sew, a new employment to them.'" Stella Jones, *Hawaiian Quilts* (Honolulu: Honolulu Academy of Arts, 1930), 7.

127. Particularly fine examples are illustrated in full-page color plates in Brandon, *Hawaiian Quilt,* pages 47–53, 73, 75, 83, 85. One noteworthy subcategory of Hawaiian quilts conjoins aspects of British, Hawaiian, and American flags, with the Hawaiian coat of arms appliquéd in the central medallion. See ibid., 20–45.

128. Hughes and Silber, *Amish,* 15.

129. Superlative color plates of Amish quilts can be seen in Hughes and Silber, *Amish,* and in Kraybill, Herr, and Holstein, *A Quiet Spirit.*

130. Kraybill, Herr, and Holstein, *A Quiet Spirit,* 86.

131. Patricia Herr, *Quilting Traditions: Pieces from the Past* (Atglen, Pa.: Schiffer Publishing, 2000) illustrates a Joseph's Coat in figs. 198 and 199. Information on the Postage Stamp Star comes from pp. 145–46.

132. See ibid., chap. 7, "Two Mennonite Grandmothers."

133. Gloria Seaman Allen, "Slaves as Textile Artisans: Documentary Evidence for the Chesapeake Region, *Uncoverings* 22 (2001): 1–36, and her "Quiltmaking on Chesapeake Plantations," in *On the Cutting Edge: Textile Collectors, Collections, and Traditions,* ed. Jeanette Lasansky (Lewisburg, Pa.: Union County Historical Society, 1994, 57–69.

134. See for example, Vlach, *Afro-American Tradition in Decorative Arts,* 44–75; Maude Wahlman, "The Art of Afro-American Quiltmaking: Origins, Development, and Significance," Ph.D. diss., Yale Univ., 1980; Wahlman, *Signs and Symbols;* Eli Leon, *Who'd A Thought It: Improvisation in African-American Quiltmaking* (San Francisco: San Francisco Craft and Folk Art Museum, 1987); and Roland Freeman, *Something to Keep You Warm* (Jackson, Miss.: Mississippi Department of Archives and History, 1981).

135. Maude Wahlman, "The Aesthetics of Afro-American Quilts," in Freeman, *Something to Keep You Warm,* 6–8.

136. See Cuesta Benberry, *Always There: The African-American Presence in American Quilts* (Lexington: Kentucky Quilt Project, 1992) and *A Piece of My Soul: Quilts by Black Arkansans* (Fayetteville: Univ. of Arkansas Press, 2000), especially plates 1, 22, 37–39, 44–49, 57, 61; Marsha MacDowell, ed., *African American Quiltmaking in Michigan* (East Lansing: Michigan State Univ. Press, 1997); Chinn, "African-American Quiltmaking Traditions," 157–75; Bets Ramsey, "The Land of Cotton: Quiltmaking by African-American Women in Three Southern States," *Uncoverings* 9 (1988): 9–28.

137. Benberry, *Always There,* 15.

138. As I finish editing this essay, in March of 2002, the Whitney Biennial 2002 has just opened in New York City. Thirty-one years after Jonathan Holstein's breakthrough exhibit at the Whitney, *Abstract Design in American Quilts,* the Whitney Biennial has chosen to feature among its 113 artists the work of "Rosie Lee Tompkins," which is the pseudonym for an African American quilter who chooses to remain anonymous. Born in Arkansas in 1936, she lives in

Richmond, California, and had a solo exhibit at the Berkeley Art Museum in 1997. Her work was also included in Eli Leon's *Who'd A Thought It,* fig. 28, and many of the artist's works are in Leon's collection. In the *New York Times* review of the influential Whitney Biennial, Roberta Smith characterized Tompkins as the "best painter" in the show, "whose patchwork geometries provide some of the show's few spots of color." See Roberta Smith, "Bad News for Art, However You Define It," *New York Times,* Sunday, March 31, 2002, section 2, 33. See also Lawrence Rinder, ed., *Whitney Biennial 2002* (New York: Whitney Museum and Harry N. Abrams, 2002). The Whitney Museum featured an exhibition of work by African American quilters from Gees Bend, Alabama, November 21, 2002–March 2, 2003.

139. Ringgold's quilts in the IQSC collection include 1997.007.1082 and 1997.007.1083.

140. Dan Cameron et al., *Dancing at the Louvre: Faith Ringgold's French Collection and Other Story Quilts* (Berkeley: Univ. of California Press, 1998), 99. Transcription of narrative is on p. 133.

141. It is noteworthy that fourteen of the eighteen artists in the influential exhibit and catalogue *The Art Quilt* hold degrees in diverse areas of studio art. See Penny McMorris and Michael Kile, *The Art Quilt* (Lincolnwood, Ill.: Quilt Digest Press, 1986), 61.

142. For an expert introduction to the rise of the art quilt movement from the 1960s to 1986, see McMorris and Kile, *The Art Quilt;* Robert Shaw's *The Art Quilt* (New York: Hugh Lauter Levin Associates, 1997) masterfully surveys all aspects of the last quarter-century.

143. For the many other fine contributors to this aspect of the contemporary quilt, see Shaw, *The Art Quilt,* chap. 6, "Abstract Quilts," 160–207. See also Caryl Bryer Fallert, *A Spectrum of Quilts, 1983–1995* (Paducah, Ky.: American Quilter's Society, 1996) and Katie Pasquini, *Three-Dimensional Design* (Lafayette, Calif.: C & T Publishing, 1988), plates 8–18.

144. Nancy Crow, *Nancy Crow: Quilts and Influences* (Paducah, Ky.: American Quilter's Society, 1990), 54–55. She also opens the book with a photo essay on historic Ohio quilts that interest her (30–49). I would suggest that each one of these is "wild by design."

145. Ibid., 136–37 for tramp art; 158–69 for Mexican iconography (as well as IQSC 1997.007.1089, *Lady of Guadalupe II*). For African American influences, see Nancy Crow, *Nancy Crow: Improvisational Quilts* (Washington, D.C.: Renwick Gallery and C & T Publishing, 1995).

146. James, *Quiltmaker's Handbook.* This chronology of events is drawn from his artistic biography in Harris, Lyon, and Malarcher, *Michael James: Studio Quilts,* 111–15.

147. Harris, Lyon, and Malarcher, *Michael James: Studio Quilts,* 14.

148. Personal communication, December 2001.

149. Michael James, *Michael James: Art and Inspirations* (Lafayette, Calif.: C & T Publishing, 1998), 57.

150. Ibid., 111. See also Michael James and David Hornung, *Michael James: Iconographies* (Neuchatel, Switzerland: Éditions Victor Attinger, 1999).

151. Other contemporary works in the IQSC collection that explore issues of geometry and abstraction include Jan Myers-Newbury, *Depth of Field, II* (1997.007.1062), illustrated in McMorris and Kile, *The Art Quilt,* plate 19; Pamela Studstill, *Number 41* (plate 40); and Caryl Bryer Fallert (1997.007.1052, 1997.007.1053). See also Pauline Burbidge, *Pink Teapot,* (IQSC 1997.007.1081) and Lucy Wallis, *Circle on Square I,* (IQSC 1997.007.1025), illustrated in Shaw, *The Art Quilt,* 206 and 195, respectively.

152. Chosen as one of the century's best, this quilt demonstrates that May was among the earliest to experiment with breaking out of quiltmaking's formal boundaries. See illustration in Austin, *The Twentieth Century's Best American Quilts,* 96.

153. *It's a Wonderful Life* is illustrated in *Quilt National: Contemporary Designs in Fabric* (Ashville, N.C.: Lark Books, 1995), 37. *Georgia, Frida, Mary and Me* is illustrated in *The New Quilt 2, Dairy Barn: Quilt National* (Newtown, Conn.: Taunton Press, 1993), 75.

154. Jane Burch Cochran's quilt *Southern Devotion* is illustrated in *New Quilt 2, Dairy Barn,* 59. *Paper Plates and Bone China* is in *The Best Contemporary Quilts: Quilt National 2001* (New York: Lark Books, 2001), 101.

155. See, for example, her *Hancock Memorial Quilt* in Stevii Graves, ed., *Visions: Quilts, Layers of Excellence* (San Diego: Quilt San Diego and C & T Publishing, 1994), 46. *Dashboard Saints* (IQSC 1997.007.1093) was chosen one of the century's best quilts. See illustration in Austin, *The Twentieth Century's Best American Quilts,* 31. Other quilts by Mangat are cited in footnote 1 of plate 42.

156. A number of quilters (usually those not trained in studio art) appear to be interested in how closely they can approximate a photograph in their work. While popular with the general public, these quilts strike an art audience as essentially misguided—to be exploring questions that have not been of central interest in the art world since the rise of photography eclipsed painting's attempts at exact representation more than a century ago. They seek to deny rather than explore the nature of their materials, making them beholden to another representational paradigm rather than true to their own. While sometimes works of technical bravura, they are seldom more than curiosities. Among the very best such works, however, are Charlotte Anderson's *Naiad* (1994), Hollis Chatelain's *Sahel* (1997), and Shirley Kelly's *Two Minutes in May* (1995). All of these are illustrated

in Austin, *The Twentieth Century's Best American Quilts,* 63, 83, and 102, respectively.

157. See *The Best Contemporary Quilts: Quilt National 2001,* 78–81.

158. See the dialogue that accompanies plate 42, below. To cite just two recent examples, two quilters in the 2001 Quilt National use Kuba women's raffia-cloth designs from equatorial Africa. See Ann Adams and Anne Woringer in *The Best Contemporary Quilts: Quilt National 2001,* 40 and 76.

159. In art history, a work is said to be "primitivizing" if it consciously seeks to mimic an untutored look of previous historical eras or of folk or ethnic traditions.

160. See Carolyn Mazloomi, *Spirits of the Cloth: Contemporary African American Quilts* (New York: Clarkson Potter, 1998) and Shaw, *Quilts,* 205. For Yvonne Wells, see Shaw, *Quilts,* 202.

161. This is well documented in Carolyn Mazloomi's *Spirits of the Cloth,* especially in the chapter "Visions of Africa," 17–41.

162. In 2001, more than 34,000 people attended the AQS exhibit in Paducah. In 1999, an estimated 50,000 people attended the International Quilt Festival in Houston. The Patchwork and Quilt Expo in Europe had over 18,000 visitors in 2000, while the three-day Quilt '98 in Japan drew an astonishing 104,000 attendees. More than 86,000 people attended International Quilt Week in Yokohama, Japan, in 2000. I am grateful to Janneken Smucker, Graduate Curatorial Assistant at the IQSC for assembling these figures.

163. See, for example, the popular books by British studio quilter Pauline Burbidge, *Quilt Studio* (Lincolnwood, Ill.: Quilt Digest Press, 2000) and British textile designer Kaffe Fassett, *Glorious Patchwork* (New York: Clarkson Potter, 1997). The contemporary Japanese love of working in both historical and contemporary American styles is documented in *123 Japanese Quilt Artists Collection* (Tokyo: Nihon Vogue, 1998). The European art quilt movement is documented in numerous publications, among them, Helene Blum-Spicker, *Europäische Quilt-Triennale 2000* (Heidelberg: Textilmuseum Max Berk, 2000); Jette Clover, *European Art Quilts* (Tilburg, Nederlands: Nederlands Textielmuseum, 1997); and Michele Walker, *The Passionate Quilter* (London: Edbury Press, 1990). Instructions on copying European art quilts for an American audience are to be found in Gul Laporte, *Quilts from Europe: Projects and Inspiration* (Lafayette, Calif.: C & T Publishing, 2000).

PLATE I

1. For examples of whole-cloth chintz, see Asa Wettre, *Old Swedish Quilts* (Loveland, Colo.: Interweave Press, 1995), 11, 97; Peck, *American Quilts and Coverlets,* 112, 115–17, 124; Roderick Kiracofe, *The American Quilt,* 62, 65.

2. For examples of early strip quilts, see Peck, *American Quilts and Coverlets,* plate 39, and Kiracofe, *The American Quilt,* fig. 75. Also, IQSC collection, 1997.007.0427, 1997.007.0480, 1997.007.0486, and 1997.007.0757.

3. Adamson, *Calico and Chintz,* 80.

4. Florence Montgomery, *Printed Textiles: English and American Cottons and Linens, 1700-1850* (New York: Viking Press, 1970), 291.

5. Peck, *American Quilts and Coverlets,* 111.

PLATE 2

1. Margaret Ordoñez, "Technology Reflected," in *Down by the Old Mill Stream: Quilts in Rhode Island,* ed. Linda Welters and Margaret Ordoñez (Kent, Ohio: Kent State Univ. Press, 2000), 137.

2. Genealogical research completed by Melissa Jurgena, IQSC Graduate Research Fellow. According to dealer information, this quilt was from Berks County, Pennsylvania. Berks County and Bucks County adjoin one another, and Sarah Headley's descendants lived in both Bucks and Berks Counties. So it's likely that the dealer acquired the quilt in Berks County from a descendant, but Sarah Headley lived in Bucks County all her life.

PLATE 3

1. For a discussion of the prevalence of star patterns in quilts registered in the statewide quilt documentation projects of Indiana, Nebraska, New Jersey, New York, and Tennessee see Patricia Cox Crews and Wendelin Rich, "Nebraska Quilts, 1870–1989: Perspectives on Traditions and Change," *Great Plains Research* 5 (fall 1995): 218–20.

2. See, for example, Binney and Binney-Winslow, *Homage to Amanda,* plate 8; Peck, *American Quilts and Coverlets,* plate 7; Shaw, *Quilts,* 195; Shelly Zegart, *American Quilt Collections, Antique Quilt Masterpieces* (Tokyo: Nihon Vogue, 1996), 113; Patricia Cox Crews and Ronald Naugle, *Nebraska Quilts and Quiltmakers* (Lincoln: Univ. of Nebraska Press, 1991), plate 2. For another example in the IQSC collection, see Crews, *A Flowering of Quilts,* 29.

3. Jenny Yearous, "Stitches in Time: The Development of Sewing Threads in the Nineteenth Century and Beyond," in *Uncoverings* 19 (1998): 98.

PLATE 5

1. Another quilt with separately bound blocks in the IQSC James Collection is a Civil War era Nine Patch, 1997.007.0569. A similar example is published in Shaw, *Quilts,* 58.

2. See, for example, Mimi Dietrich, *Quilts from the Smithsonian* (Bothell, Wash.: That Patchwork Place, 1995), 34; Bres-

enhan and Puentes, *Lone Stars, Volume I,* 97; Binney and Binney-Winslow, *Homage to Amanda,* plate 11; Indiana Quilt Registry Project, *Quilts of Indiana* (Bloomington: Indiana University Press, 1991), 39.

PLATE 6

1. Merikay Waldvogel, "The Mountain Mist Historical Quilt Collection," in *Mountain Mist Blue Book of Quilts* (n.p.: Stearns Technical Textiles Company, 1996), 35.

2. See, for example, Bresenhan and Puentes, *Lone Stars, Volume I,* 62–63, 109.

PLATE 7

1. Clark, *Quilted Gardens,* 39, and plates 35–38. For a quilt that depicts the one large drooping blossom of the amaranth plant, see Indiana Quilt Registry Project, *Quilts of Indiana,* 19.

2. Clark, *Quilts in Community,* 23, 26.

3. The following are examples of classic red and green floral appliqué quilts in the IQSC collection: 1997.007.0075, 1997.007.0539, 1997.007.0686, and 1997.007.0908. For a blue and white Princess Feather in the IQSC collection, see 1997.007.0646. For a slave-made Princess Feather said to date before 1850, see Lisa Turner Oshins, *Quilt Collections: A Directory for the United States and Canada* (Washington, D.C.: Acropolis Books, 1987), unnumbered color plate.

4. This quilt was purchased from Sandra Mitchell, who supplied the quiltmaker's name and location. Genealogical records located by Melissa Jurgena, IQSC Research Fellow, show that the Gingrich family settled in Pennsylvania during the mid to late 1700s. Based on census records of the 1850s, there are four women named M. (all Mary) Gingrich who were old enough to have made a quilt by 1854 , the date inscribed on this quilt (all would have been at least in their teens). The Gingrich family was of Swiss and German descent.

5. See, for example, boldly colored Princess Feather quilts in Herr, *Quilting Traditions,* 106–8.

6. Personal communication, January 2002, from scholar Ruth Phillips, who is conducting research on Native arts made in response to the visit of the Prince of Wales to North America in 1860.

PLATE 9

1. Hornback, "Nineteenth-Century Red and Green Appliqué Quilts," 81–82.

2. Ulrich, *The Age of Homespun,* especially chap. 9 and figs. on pp. 334–37. For other examples of these embroidered and stenciled blankets, see Binney and Binney-Winslow, *Homage to Amanda,* figs. 4–6, and color illustration of a handspun

wool embroidered blanket dated 1848 in an advertisement in *The Clarion,* winter 1990, 27.

3. Susan Curtis, "Blessed Be God for Flowers," in *A Flowering of Quilts,* ed. Patricia Cox Crews (Lincoln: Univ. of Nebraska Press, 2001), 22.

4. See examples in Crews, *A Flowering of Quilts,* plates 9, 11, 14–16, 25, 27, 29, 30.

5. Rachel Maines, "Paradigms of Scarcity and Abundance: The Quilt as an Artifact of the Industrial Revolution," in *In the Heart of Pennsylvania,* ed. Jeanette Lasansky (Lewisburg, Pa.: Union County Historical Society, 1986), 80.

6. Virginia Gunn, personal communication, June 2000.

PLATE 10

1. See, for example, Jeannette Lasansky, *Pieced By Mother* (Lewisburg, Pa.: Union County Historical Society, 1987), figs. 8–11. See also Atkins and Tepper, *New York Beauties,* figs. 72, 72a.

PLATE 12

1. Jurgena and Crews, "The Reconciliation Quilt."

2. Previous publications include "The Winter Art Show," *American Heritage Magazine,* Feb.–Mar. 1992, 60; *Sotheby's Art at Auction: The Art Market Review, 1991–92* (New York: Rizzoli International Publications, 1992), 197; Amy Tyler, "Quilts: Piecing the Market Back Together," *Antique Monthly,* June 1993, 28–31; Robert Bishop and Jacqueline Atkins, *Folk Art in American Life* (New York: Viking Studio Books, 1995), 142; Lori Gray, "Textiles with Tales to Tell," *Traditional Home,* Sept. 1997, 134–39; Gordon, *Pictorial Quilting,* 10–11.

PLATE 13

1. Preston J. Blanchard, *Revised Odd-Fellowship Illustrated. The Complete Revised Ritual* (Chicago: Ezra Cook, Publisher, 1893), 125–31. Another album quilt in the IQSC collection, 1997.007.0761, dated 1850, depicts many of the same symbols.

2. This quilt was purchased at Sotheby's. They supplied the information attributing the quilt to Charlotte Gardner of New York or New Jersey and told the Jameses that according to family tradition, the quilt was made for Charlotte Gardner's dowry in 1886. Genealogical research is currently underway to corroborate this information.

3. See, for example, an Odd Fellows quilt illustrated in Lilian B. Carlisle, *Pieced Work and Appliqué Quilts at the Shelburne Museum,* Museum Pamphlet #2 (Shelburne, Vt.: Shelburne Museum, 1957), 90–91.

4. See numbers 1766–1768 in the catalogue *Important Americana, January 24–30, 1995* (New York: Sotheby's, 1995).

PLATE 14

1. Other fine quilts in the Courthouse Steps pattern in the IQSC collection include 1997.007.0439 and 1997.007.0928, both illustrated in Holstein and Ducey, *Masterpiece Quilts from the James Collection*, 86, 87.

2. Maines, "Paradigms of Scarcity and Abundance," 87.

3. Herbert R. Mauersberger, ed., *Matthews' Textile Fibers*, 5th ed. (New York: John Wiley, 1947), 725.

PLATE 15

1. James Liles, "Dyes in American Quilts Made Prior to 1930, with Special Emphasis on Cotton and Linen," *Uncoverings* 5 (1984): 29–40.

2. Crews and Rich, "Nebraska Quilts," 218–19.

3. Clark, *Quilts in Community*, 35.

4. Barbara Brackman, *Clues in the Calico: A Guide to Identifying and Dating Antique Quilts* (McLean, Va.: EPM Publications, 1989), 94.

PLATE 16

1. Edith Montgomery's quilt, said to be from Oregon, circa 1870, is illustrated in Zegart, *American Quilt Collections*, 37.

2. For other examples, see Nelson and Houck, *Treasury of American Quilts*, fig. 89, said to have been made in Pennsylvania circa 1900; Michael Kile, "The Collector: On the Road," *Quilt Digest* 4 (1986): 85, said to have been made in New England, circa 1875–1900; and McMorris, *Crazy Quilts*, 41, with Masonic symbols. One in the New England Quilt Museum is given the name Boston Pavement and said to have been made in Boston ca. 1895. See Jennifer Gilbert, *The New England Quilt Museum Quilts* (Lafayette, Calif.: C & T Publishing, 1999), 88.

3. See Carol Shankel, ed. *Quilts from the Shelburne Museum* (Tokyo: Kokusai Art, 1996), 104–5. Shelburne's Tile quilt, called Streets of Boston, was made by Martha and Augusta Kimberly of Nepaug, Connecticut, as a wedding present for their older sister Ellen May.

4. To corroborate dealer (Sandra Mitchell) information, IQSC curator Carolyn Ducey and IQSC Graduate Research Fellow Melissa Jurgena located census records and other genealogical records showing that a Hattie Burdick lived in New London, Connecticut, during the period when this quilt was likely made, and that she had a sister named Minnie. We have not yet been able to determine what relation the other women might have had to Hattie.

5. Marin Hanson, *Reflections of the Exotic East in American Quilts* (Lincoln: International Quilt Study Center and the Lentz Center for Asian Culture, Univ. of Nebraska, 2001), 19.

6. Susan Meller and Joost Elffers. *Textile Designs: Two Hundred Years of European and American Patterns* (New York: Harry N. Abrams, 1991), 282.

7. McMorris, *Crazy Quilts*, 12.

8. Another Burdick quilt survives in the Shelburne Museum, a pictorial album coverlet made by members of a Burdick-Childs family from North Adams, Massachusetts. It's well known, having been published many times (see Shaw, *Quilts*, 71). Both that quilt and the one at IQSC exhibit superb appliqué work and even contain a number of the same calicoes. Based on our genealogical research, and the discovery that Minnie Burdick married a Childs and moved to North Adams, we now believe that Hattie Burdick and her sister Minnie Burdick Childs were also the makers of the quilt owned by the Shelburne Museum.

PLATE 17

1. See Clark, *Quilted Gardens*, plates 29 and 30, for examples with appliquéd dates of 1854 and 1856.

2. A related quilt with a similar border made by Paulina Herdrich (who we believe was Caroline's aunt) also resides in the IQSC collections. See Crews, *A Flowering of Quilts*, 46.

3. Genealogical research completed by Carolyn Ducey, IQSC Curator, shows that Caroline's mother was Mary (Maria) Magdelena Schwaderer, born in 1816 in Marbach Backnung, Wuerttemburg, Germany. She married Johannes (John) Seiter on November 30, 1837, in Marion County, Ohio. Mary died young, in 1852, a few months after the birth of her seventh child, leaving her daughter Caroline, age fourteen, as the oldest female in the household. Caroline married Charles C. P. Ruth on April 18, 1858, and gave birth to ten children.

4. See, for example, Crews and Naugle, *Nebraska Quilts and Quiltmakers*, 62–63, 108–9; and Atkins and Tepper, *New York Beauties*, 130.

PLATE 18

1. See McMorris, *Crazy Quilts*, and Virginia Gunn, "Crazy Quilts and Outline Quilts: Popular Responses to the Decorative Art/Art Needlework Movement, 1876–1893," *Uncoverings* 5 (1984): 131–52.

2. Only "M. Hernandred Ricard" appears below the silk photo on the quilt, but census records show that her first name was Mary and that she was born January 17, 1838, in Vermont. Around 1860, she married Hubert Ricard, born September 1835 in Canada. According to her obituary in the *Haverhill Gazette*, she died April 2, 1915, at seventy-seven years of age.

3. According to Barbara Brackman, *Clues in the Calico*,

140, many Crazy quilts were never backed. She speculates that this happened because the yards of silk satin or velvet required for the "perfect backing" proved too expensive for many women to afford. This explanation, however, does not seem plausible for a woman who could afford to have a photogravure of herself on silk produced for the quilt. The unfinished quilt delights the eye, but also baffles the viewer who notes this incongruity.

PLATE 19

1. See Herr, *Quilting Traditions.*

PLATE 20

1. See Herr, *Quilting Traditions,* 71–81, for a fuller discussion of Carpenter's work and other quilts with visual similarities.

2. Ibid., fig. 108.

3. Ibid., 71.

4. Ibid., 72, and figs. 104 and 105.

PLATE 21

1. Herr, *Quilting Traditions,* 145, 146.

2. Holstein, *The Pieced Quilt,* plate 13.

PLATE 23

1. Janet Rae, *The Quilts of the British Isles* (London: E. P. Dutton, 1987), 63–68.

2. Sophia Caulfield and Blanche Saward, *The Dictionary of Needlework* (1882; facsimile, New York: Arno Press, 1972), 379–80.

PLATE 25

1. Dorothy Bond, *Blest Be the Quilts that Bind* (Eugene, Oreg.: Eugene Printers, 1992), n.p., block no. 57.

2. See, for example, Karoline Bresenhan and Nancy Puentes, *Lone Stars, Volume II: A Legacy of Texas Quilts, 1936–1986* (Austin: Univ. of Texas Press, 1990), 50.

3. See, for example, other two-color Robbing Peter to Pay Paul quilts in the IQSC collections: 1997.007.0106 and 1997.007.0925.

PLATE 26

1. Rachel Maines, "The Tools of the Workbasket," in *Bits and Pieces: Textile Traditions,* ed. Jeannette Lasansky (Lewisburg, Pa.: Union County Historical Society, 1991), 117.

2. For examples of Amish strip or bar quilts, see Kraybill, Herr, and Holstein, *A Quiet Spirit,* 116, 128–33; for examples

from the IQSC Collection, see 1997.007.0270, 1997.007.0442, and 1997.007.0463.

PLATE 27

1. Clark, *Quilts in Community,* 31–32.

2. Ibid., 31, 35.

3. Barbara Brackman, *Encyclopedia of Pieced Quilt Patterns* (Paducah, Ky.: American Quilter's Society, 1993), no. 1602, 204.

PLATE 28

1. Robert Bishop, *New Discoveries in American Quilts,* (New York: E. P. Dutton, 1975), 39.

2. See conversation among Maude Wahlman, Theophus Smith, Robert Hobbs, William Arnett, and Paul Arnett, "The Hidden Charms of the Deep South," in *Souls Grown Deep: African-American Vernacular Art of the South,* vol. 1 (Atlanta: Tinwood Books, 2000), 68.

3. Of course, there are many examples of fine workmanship by African American needlewomen in the nineteenth century. See, for example, Benberry, *Always There,* 83, 85. Yet the definition of an "African American style" used by many people is based on twentieth-century works principally from the rural South.

4. Genealogical research completed by Melissa Jurgena, IQSC Graduate Research Fellow. Amy Bucher's father was a bishop in the German Baptist Church.

PLATE 29

1. Wilene Smith, "Quilt History in Old Periodicals: A New Interpretation," *Uncoverings* 11 (1990): 188–213. See appendix A, "The Ladies' Art Inventory of Quilt Patterns as Documented by Company Advertising," 204. It isn't known when their first catalogue was published, but an 1895 ad in the magazine *Good Literature* mentions 272 patterns available. Each pattern was numbered chronologically as it was published.

2. Brackman, *Encyclopedia of Pieced Quilt Patterns,* 188, 314. Necktie was no. 119; Magic Circle was no. 384.

3. Ibid., 314.

4. See Shaw, *Quilts,* 135.

5. See Kraybill, Herr, and Holstein, *A Quiet Spirit,* 198–99. Another Bow Tie quilt in the IQSC collection in which black octagons rather than white seem to float, is 1997.007.0269. It is believed to be Ohio Amish.

PLATE 30

1. For a quilt from the 1850s, see Zegart, *American Quilt Collections,* 51. For early-twentieth-century red and

white geometric quilts, see Shaw, *Quilts,* 86; Woodard and Greenstein, *Twentieth Century Quilts,* fig. 122; and IQSC 1997.007.0602.

2. Brackman, *Clues in the Calico,* 157.

3. For an excellent description of the Turkey red process, see Martin Bide, "Secrets of the Printer's Palette," in *Down by the Old Mill Stream: Quilts in Rhode Island,* ed. Linda Welters and Margaret Ordoñez (Kent, Ohio: Kent State Univ. Press, 2000), 106–7.

4. Holstein, *The Pieced Quilt,* plate 86.

PLATE 31

1. Eve W. Granick, *The Amish Quilt* (Intercourse, Pa.: Good Books, 1989), 143, 156.

2. Ibid., 155.

3. Bettina Havig, *Amish Kinder Comforts: Quilts from the Sara Miller Collection* (Paducah, Ky.: American Quilter's Society, 1996).

PLATE 32

1. See, for example, Ward, *American Folk;* Richter, *Painted with Thread;* and Deborah Harding and Laura Fisher, *Home Sweet Home: The House in American Folk Art* (New York: Rizzoli International, 2001).

2. Brackman, *Clues in the Calico,* 170.

3. See Harding and Fisher, *Home Sweet Home,* 44–49. The African American Log Cabin is illustrated on p. 44.

PLATE 34

1. Notes on IQSC 1997.007.0851 compiled by the collector, Ardis James.

2. John Sauls, e-mail communication, December 3, 2000, with Linda Wruck, Univ. of Nebraska–Lincoln graduate student enrolled in TXCD 876 Artifact Analysis, for an unpublished research paper concerning this quilt.

3. Brackman, *Encyclopedia of Pieced Quilt Patterns,* 275.

PLATE 35

1. IQSC 2000.004.0025, illustrated in Ezell, *My Quilts and Me,* 138. The necktie quilt became a national fad in the 1990s. See Shirley Botsford, *Daddy's Ties* (Radnor, Pa.: Chilton Books, 1994) and Janet Elwin, *Traditional Quilts from Neckties* (Paducah, Ky.: American Quilter's Society, 1996).

2. Ardis James and Penny McMorris, *Quilts in the James Collection* (Tokyo: Kokusai Art, 1990), 84.

PLATE 36

1. For examples of African American strip quilts, see Wahlman, *Signs and Symbols,* 34, 37. Also see IQSC Robert and Helen Cargo Collection 2000.004.0048, 2000.004.0079, 2000.004.0131, 2000.004.0150. Strippy quilts have been made by artists of various ethnicities throughout the nineteenth and twentieth centuries. For a discussion of early European and American examples, see plate 1 dialogue. For discussion of post–Civil War era American strip quilts, see plate 26 dialogue.

2. Wahlman, *Signs and Symbols,* 25–59.

3. Benberry, *Always There;* MacDowell, *African American Quiltmaking in Michigan.*

4. John Picton, "Africa and African American Quilts," *Quilters' Review* 26, winter 1998, 2–3.

5. Bishop, *New Discoveries,* plate 93.

PLATE 37

1. Second P quilt by Lureca Outland, 2000.004.0104. Other alphabet quilts in the IQSC Cargo Collection include 2000.004.0002 by an unknown maker, 2000.004.0083 by Mary Maxtion, and in the IQSC James Collection 1997.007.0324 and 1997.007.0392.

2. See, for example, Nancy Butler's Tombstone Quilt of 1842 in the Smithsonian, illustrated in Carter Houck, *The Quilt Encyclopedia Illustrated* (New York: Harry N. Abrams, 1991), 108; Maria Cadman Hubbard's Pieties Quilt of 1848, which looks more like a sampler than any other quilt known, illustrated in Bishop, *New Discoveries,* plate 33, see also plates 34 and 35; Deborah Wildman's 1833 Sampler Quilt in the Fenimore Art Museum, illustrated in *Heritage: Magazine of the New York State Historical Association* 12, no. 4 (summer 1996): 20. See also Carleton Safford and Robert Bishop, *America's Quilts and Coverlets* (New York: E. P. Dutton, 1980), plates 198, 199.

3. The Freedom Quilt is illustrated in Shaw, *Quilts,* 14.

4. Smith, "Quilt History in Old Periodicals," 188–213. See appendix A, "The Ladies' Art Inventory of Quilt Patterns as Documented by Company Advertising," 204.

5. Ladies' Art Company, *Quilt Patterns: Patchwork and Applique* (1928; reprint, Wichita, Kans.: Vanderkellen Galleries, 1996), 21.

6. Wahlman, *Signs and Symbols,* 8, and color plates 63, 64.

7. Other quilts in the IQSC Cargo Collection made by Alabama RSVP Clubs include 2000.004.0110, 2000.004.0111, 2000.004.0112, and 2000.004.0113.

PLATE 38

1. Robert Cargo, taped interview with Carolyn Ducey, February 23, 2001.

2. Patriotic quilts from the Cargo Collection include 2000.004.0070, 2000.004.0071, 2000.004.0072, 2000.004.0073, 2000.004.0074, and 2000.004.0075 by Mary Maxtion; 2000.004.0103 by Lureca Outland; and 2000.004.0113 by the RSVP Club.

PLATE 39

1. Much has been written on the tradition of African American yard art in the last few years. See, for example, William Arnett and Paul Arnett, eds., *Souls Grown Deep: African American Vernacular Art of the South*, 2 vols. (Atlanta: Tinwood Books, 2000–2001), especially the sections on Lonnie Holley.

PLATE 40

1. Penny McMorris, *The Art Quilt* (San Francisco: Quilt Digest Press, 1986), 64.

2. Betsa Marsh, "With Brush and Needle," *Creative Ideas for Living*, July–Aug. 1988, 14–15.

PLATE 41

1. See Holstein, *The Pieced Quilt*, plate 31.

2. Ardis James file description for 1997.007.1094.

PLATE 42

1. Her *Memory Jars* (1984, Private Collection of Ardis and Robert James) and *Dashboard Saints* (1985, IQSC 1997.007.1093) are both illustrated in Shaw, *Quilts*, 283 and 301, respectively. See also Austin, *The Twentieth Century's Best American Quilts*, 31.

2. See, for example, Ann Rowe, *A Century of Change in Guatemalan Textiles* (New York: Center for Inter-American Relations, 1981), 144–47.

3. Betsa Marsh, "Storytelling, Stitch by Stitch," *Creative Ideas for Living*, May 1987, 12–13.

PLATE 43

1. The first, IQSC 1997.007.0181, is published in Holstein and Ducey, *Masterpiece Quilts*, 92. The second is published in Shaw, *Quilts*, 87.

2. Josef Albers, *Homage to the Square* (Zurich: Kaser Presse, 1965).

3. Benberry, *Always There*, 15–16.

PLATE 44

1. See, for example, Shaw, *The Art Quilt*, 89; *Anna Williams: Her Quilts and Their Influences* (Paducah, Ky.: Museum of the American Quilter's Society, 1995); Katherine Watts and Elizabeth Walker, "Joyful Improvisations: The Quiltmaking of Anna Williams," *American Quilter*, winter 1997, 36–40; for Nancy Crow, see Crow, *Nancy Crow: Quilts and Influences*, and Penny McMorris, *Nancy Crow: Work in Transition* (Paducah, Ky.: American Quilter's Society, 1992).

2. See Fawn Valentine, *West Virginia Quilts and Quiltmakers* (Athens: Ohio Univ. Press, 2000), 88–93.

3. For examples, see Valentine, *West Virginia Quilts and Quiltmakers*, 147, 151.

4. John Forrest and Deborah Blincoe, *The Natural History of the Traditional Quilt* (Austin: Univ. of Texas Press, 1995), 185.

5. For diverse examples of offbeat quilts, see Holstein, *The Pieced Quilt*, plate 27; Zegart, *American Quilt Collections*, 111; Barbara Brackman, "Out of Control: Quilts That Break the Rules," *Quilt Digest* 3 (1985): figs. 1, 3, 6; Rae, *Quilts of the British Isles*, 45; Dorothy Osler, *North Country Quilts: Legend and Living Tradition* (County Durham: Bowes Museum, 2000), fig. 45.

6. Interview with Anna Williams by Shelley Keis Wells, April 17, 1998, unpublished transcript in the files of the International Quilt Study Center.

PLATE 45

1. Gates, *The Signifying Monkey*, xvii, 45.

2. See, for example, Maude Wahlman, *Ten Afro-American Quilters* (Oxford: Center for Southern Culture, Univ. of Mississippi, 1983); Wahlman, *Signs and Symbols*; Leon, *Who'd a Thought It*; Freeman, *Something to Keep You Warm*.

PLATE 46

1. See Ezell, *My Quilts and Me*, 168–69. A quilt similar to this one is held by the Museum of American Folk Art in New York and is dated August 1977 in embroidery thread on the border (1991.13.1).

2. See Ezell, *My Quilts and Me*, passim, and especially 22, 27, 37, 66, 74, 87, 138.

3. Ibid., 53, 61.

4. Nora Ezell, quoted in Wahlman, *Signs and Symbols*, 5.

PLATE 47

1. See Katie Pasquini, *Mandala* (Eureka, Calif.: Sudz Publishing, 1983); Pasquini, *Three Dimensional Design*, especially plates 8–18; Katie Pasquini Masopust, *Fractured Landscape Quilts* (Lafayette, Calif.: C & T Publishing, 1996); Katie Pasquini Masopust, *Ghost Layers and Color Washes* (Lafayette, Calif.: C & T Publishing, 2000).

2. In *Ghost Layers*, Masopust uses this very quilt to describe her process of design; see pp. 30–31, 51–55.

3. For a description of this process, see Masopust, *Fractured Landscape Quilts*, chap. 3.

PLATE 48

1. Michael James, "Getting Our Bearings: Quilt Art at Century's End," *American Quilter*, fall 1992, 52.

2. See, for example, Andy Goldsworthy, *A Collaboration With Nature* (New York: Harry N. Abrams, 1990).

BIBLIOGRAPHY

ADAMS, MARIE JEANNE. "The Harriet Powers Pictorial Quilts." *Black Art: An International Quarterly* 3, no. 4 (1979): 12–28.

ADAMSON, JEREMY. *Calico and Chintz: Antique Quilts from the Collection of Patricia S. Smith.* Washington, D.C.: Renwick Gallery of the Smithsonian Institution, 1997.

ALBERS, JOSEF. *Homage to the Square.* Zurich: Kaser Presse, 1965.

ALBERS, PATRICIA, AND BEATRICE MEDICINE. "The Role of Sioux Women in the Production of Ceremonial Objects: The Case of the Star Quilt." In *The Hidden Half: Studies of Indian Women in the Northern Plains,* edited by Patricia Albers and Beatrice Medicine, 135–43. Lanham, Maryland: University Press of America, 1983.

ALLEN, GLORIA SEAMAN. "Quiltmaking on Chesapeake Plantations." In *On the Cutting Edge: Textile Collectors, Collections, and Traditions,* edited by Jeanette Lasansky, 57–69. Lewisburg, Pennsylvania: Union County Historical Society, 1994.

———. "Slaves as Textile Artisans: Documentary Evidence for the Chesapeake Region." *Uncoverings* 22 (2001): 1–36.

ANNA WILLIAMS: HER QUILTS AND THEIR INFLUENCES. Paducah, Kentucky: Museum of the American Quilter's Society, 1995.

ANNETTE [HARRIET FARLEY OR REBECCA THOMPSON, PSEUD.]. "The Patchwork Quilt." *The Lowell Offering* 5 (1845): 201–3. Reprinted in *The Lowell Offering: Writings by New England Mill Women, 1840–1845,* edited by Benita Eisler, 150–54. New York: Harper and Row, 1977.

ARNETT, WILLIAM, AND PAUL ARNETT, EDS. *Souls Grown Deep: African American Vernacular Art of the South.* 2 vols. Atlanta: Tinwood Books, 2000–2001.

ATKINS, JACQUELINE. *Shared Threads: Quilting Together Past and Present.* New York: Museum of American Folk Art and Viking Studio Books, 1994.

ATKINS, JACQUELINE, AND PHYLLIS TEPPER. *New York Beauties: Quilts from the Empire State.* New York: Dutton Studio Books, 1992.

AUSTIN, MARY LEMAN, ED. *The Twentieth Century's Best American Quilts.* Golden, Colorado: Primedia Publications, 1999.

AXELROD, ALAN, ED. *The Colonial Revival in America.* New York: W. W. Norton, 1985.

BASSETT, LYNNE, AND JACK LARKIN. *Northern Comfort: New England's Early Quilts, 1780–1850.* Nashville: Rutledge Hill Press, 1998.

BEAUDOIN-ROSS, JACQUELINE. "An Early Eighteenth Century Pieced Quilt in Montreal." *RACAR: Revue d'art canadienne/Canadian Art Review* 6, no. 2 (1979–80): 106–9.

BENBERRY, CUESTA. "Marie D. Webster: A Major Influence on Quilt Design in the Twentieth Century." *Quilter's Newsletter Magazine,* July–August 1990, 32–35.

———. *Always There: The African-American Presence in American Quilts.* Lexington: Kentucky Quilt Project, 1992.

———. *A Piece of My Soul: Quilts by Black Arkansans.* Fayetteville: University of Arkansas Press, 2000.

BERLO, JANET C. "Native Art/Folk Art: Loaded Categories/ Parallel Histories." Paper delivered at the symposium "Native Art History and Folk Art History: Critiquing the Paradigms," Fenimore Art Museum, Cooperstown, New York, August 7, 1999.

BERNICK, SUSAN. "A Quilt Is an Art Object When It Stands up Like a Man." In *Quilt Culture: Tracing the Pattern,* ed. Cheryl Torsney and Judy Elsley, 134–50. Columbia: University of Missouri Press, 1994.

THE BEST CONTEMPORARY QUILTS: QUILT NATIONAL 2001. New York: Lark Books, 2001.

BIDE, MARTIN. "Secrets of the Printer's Palette." In *Down by the Old Mill Stream: Quilts in Rhode Island,* edited by Linda Welters and Margaret Ordoñez, 106–7. Kent, Ohio: Kent State University Press, 2000.

BINNEY, EDWIN, AND GAIL BINNEY-WINSLOW. *Homage to Amanda: Two Hundred Years of American Quilts.* Nashville: Rutledge Hill Press, 1984.

BISHOP, ROBERT. *New Discoveries in American Quilts.* New York: E. P. Dutton, 1975.

BISHOP, ROBERT, AND JACQUELINE ATKINS. *Folk Art in American Life.* New York: Viking Studio Books, 1995.

BLANCHARD, PRESTON J. *Revised Odd-Fellowship Illustrated. The Complete Revised Ritual.* Chicago: Ezra Cook, Publisher, 1893.

BLUM-SPICKER, HELENE. *Europäische Quilt-Triennale 2000.* Heidelberg: Textilmuseum Max Berk, 2000.

BOND, DOROTHY. *Blest Be the Quilts that Bind.* Eugene, Oregon: Eugene Printers, 1992.

BONFIELD, LYNN. "Diaries of New England Quilters before 1860." *Uncoverings* 9 (1988): 171–97.

BOTSFORD, SHIRLEY. *Daddy's Ties.* Radnor, Pennsylvania: Chilton Books, 1994.

BRACKMAN, BARBARA. "Out of Control: Quilts That Break the Rules." *Quilt Digest* 3 (1985): 68–77.

———. *Clues in the Calico: A Guide to Identifying and Dating Antique Quilts.* McLean, Virginia: EPM Publications, 1989.

———. "Fairs and Expositions: Their Influence on American Quilts." In *Bits and Pieces: Textile Traditions,* edited by Jeannette Lasansky, 90–99. Lewisburg, Pennsylvania: Union County Historical Society, 1991.

———. *Encyclopedia of Pieced Quilt Patterns.* Paducah, Kentucky: American Quilter's Society, 1993.

BRANDON, REIKO MICHINAGA. *The Hawaiian Quilt.* Honolulu: Academy of Arts, 1996.

BRESENHAN, KAROLINE, AND NANCY PUENTES. *Lone Stars, Volume I: A Legacy of Texas Quilts, 1836–1936.* Austin: University of Texas Press, 1986.

———. *Lone Stars, Volume II: A Legacy of Texas Quilts, 1936–1986.* Austin: University of Texas Press, 1990.

BURBIDGE, PAULINE. *Quilt Studio.* Lincolnwood, Illinois: Quilt Digest Press, 2000.

BUSTARD, BRUCE. *A New Deal for the Arts.* Washington, D.C.: National Archives and Records Administration, 1997.

CAHILL, HOLGER. *American Folk Art: The Art of the Common Man in America, 1750–1900.* New York: Museum of Modern Art, 1932.

CAMERON, DAN, ET AL. *Dancing at the Louvre: Faith Ringgold's French Collection and Other Story Quilts.* Berkeley: University of California Press, 1998.

CARLISLE, LILIAN. *Pieced Work and Appliqué Quilts at the Shelburne Museum.* Museum Pamphlet #2. Shelburne, Vermont: Shelburne Museum, 1957.

CARNES, MARK. *Secret Ritual and Manhood in Victorian America.* New Haven: Yale University Press, 1989.

CAULFIELD, SOPHIA, AND BLANCHE SAWARD. *The Dictionary of Needlework.* 1882. Facsimile edition, New York: Arno Press, 1972.

CAWLEY, LUCINDA, ET AL. *Saved for the People of Pennsylvania: Quilts from the State Museum of Pennsylvania.* Harrisburg, Pennsylvania: Pennsylvania Historical and Museum Commission, 1997.

CHICAGO, JUDY. *The Dinner Party: A Symbol of Our Heritage.* Garden City, New York: Anchor Doubleday, 1979.

———. *Embroidering Our Heritage: The Dinner Party's Needlework.* Garden City, New York: Anchor Books, 1980.

CHINN, JENNIE. "African-American Quiltmaking Traditions: Some Assumptions Reviewed." In *Kansas Quilts and Quilters,* ed. Barbara Brackman, 157–75. Lawrence: University Press of Kansas, 1993.

CHRISTENSEN, E. O. *The Index of American Design.* New York: Macmillan Company, 1950.

CLARK, RICKY. "Coverlets, Quilts, and Fancy Needlework: Similarities in Folk Design." In *Woven Coverlets: Textiles in the Folk Tradition,* edited by Patricia Cunningham, 26–32. Bowling Green, Ohio: McFall Center Gallery, Bowling Green University, 1984.

———. Letter to the editor. *The Clarion,* summer 1990, 22.

———. *Quilted Gardens: Floral Quilts of the Nineteenth Century.* Nashville: Rutledge Hill Press, 1994.

CLARK, RICKY, ED. *Quilts in Community: Ohio's Traditions.* Nashville: Rutledge Hill Press, 1991.

CLAWSON, MARY ANN. *Constructing Brotherhood: Class, Gender, and Fraternalism.* Princeton, New Jersey: Princeton University Press, 1989.

CLOVER, JETTE. *European Art Quilts.* Tilburg, Nederlands: Nederlands Textielmuseum, 1997.

COOPER, PATRICIA, AND NORMA BRADLEY BUFORD. *The Quilters: Women and Domestic Art, An Oral History.* Garden City, New York: Anchor Doubleday, 1978. Second edition by Patricia Cooper and Norma Bradley Allen, 1989. Reprint, Lubbock: Texas Tech University Press, 1999.

COPELAND, ANNE, AND BEVERLY DUNIVENT. "Kit Quilts in Perspective." *Uncoverings* 15 (1994): 141–67.

CORD, XENIA. "Marketing Quilt Kits in the 1920s and 1930s." *Uncoverings* 16 (1995): 139–73.

COTT, NANCY. *The Bonds of Womanhood: "Woman's Sphere" in New England, 1780–1835.* New Haven: Yale University Press, 1977.

CREWS, PATRICIA COX, ED. *A Flowering of Quilts.* Lincoln: University of Nebraska Press, 2001.

CREWS, PATRICIA COX, AND RONALD NAUGLE. *Nebraska*

Quilts and Quiltmakers. Lincoln: University of Nebraska Press, 1991.

CREWS, PATRICIA COX, AND WENDELIN RICH. "Nebraska Quilts, 1870–1989: Perspectives on Traditions and Change." *Great Plains Research* 5 (fall 1995): 218–20.

CROW, NANCY. *Nancy Crow: Quilts and Influences.* Paducah, Kentucky: American Quilter's Society, 1990.

———. *Nancy Crow: Improvisational Quilts.* Washington, D.C.: Renwick Gallery and C & T Publishing, 1995.

CURTIS, SUSAN. "Blessed Be God for Flowers." In *A Flowering of Quilts,* edited by Patricia Cox Crews, 11–23. Lincoln: University of Nebraska Press, 2001.

DANA, JOHN COTTON. *American Art—How It Can Be Made to Flourish.* Woodstock, Vermont: Elm Tree Press, 1914.

DAVISON, MILDRED, AND CHRISTA MAYER-THURMAN. *Coverlets: A Handbook of the Collection of Woven Coverlets in the Art Institute of Chicago.* Chicago: Art Institute of Chicago, 1973.

DIETRICH, MIMI. *Quilts from the Smithsonian.* Bothell, Washington: That Patchwork Place, 1995.

DUCEY, CAROLYN. "Fine Art, Folk Art: The 1970s Quilt Revival in Nebraska." Research paper for course on the history of quilts, University of Nebraska–Lincoln, June 2001.

ELSLEY, JUDY. "Uncovering Eliza Calvert Hall." *Encyclia* 68 (1991): 155–71.

ELWIN, JANET. *Traditional Quilts from Neckties.* Paducah, Kentucky: American Quilter's Society, 1996.

ERICKSON, RITA, AND BARBARA SCHAFFER. "Characteristics of Signed New Jersey Quilts, 1837–1867." In *On the Cutting Edge,* edited by J. Lasansky, 71–83. Lewisburg, Pennsylvania: Union County Historical Society, 1994.

EZELL, NORA. *My Quilts and Me: The Diary of an American Quilter.* Montgomery, Alabama: Black Belt Press, 1999.

FALLERT, CARYL BRYER. *A Spectrum of Quilts, 1983–1995.* Paducah, Kentucky: American Quilter's Society, 1996.

FARLEY, SARA REIMER, AND NANCY HORNBACK. "The Quilting Records of Rachel Adella Jewett and Lucyle Jewett." *Uncoverings* 18 (1997): 7–40.

FASSETT, KAFFE. *Glorious Patchwork.* New York: Clarkson Potter, 1997.

FINLEY, RUTH E. *Old Patchwork Quilts and the Women Who Made Them.* 1929. Reprint, McLean, Virginia: EPM Publications, 1992.

FORREST, JOHN, AND DEBORAH BLINCOE. *The Natural History of the Traditional Quilt.* Austin: University of Texas Press, 1995.

FOX, SANDI. *Wrapped in Glory: Figurative Quilts and Bedcovers, 1700–1900.* Los Angeles: L.A. County Museum of Art, 1990.

FREEMAN, ROLAND. *Something to Keep You Warm.* Jackson: Mississippi Department of Archives and History, 1981.

FRY, GLADYS-MARIE. "Harriet Powers: Portrait of a Black Quilter." In *Missing Pieces: Georgia Folk Art, 1770–1976,* edited by Anna Wadsworth, 16–23. Atlanta: Georgia Council for the Arts and Humanities, 1976.

———. *Stitched from the Soul: Slave Quilts from the Ante-Bellum South.* New York: Dutton Studio Books in association with the Museum of American Folk Art, 1990.

FURGASON, MARY JANE, AND PATRICIA COX CREWS. "Prizes from the Plains: Nebraska State Fair Award-Winning Quilts and Quiltmakers." *Uncoverings* 14 (1993): 188–220.

GATES, HENRY LOUIS. *The Signifying Monkey: A Theory of Afro-American Literary Criticism.* New York: Oxford University Press, 1988.

GILBERT, JENNIFER. *The New England Quilt Museum Quilts.* Lafayette, California: C & T Publishing, 1999.

GOLDSBOROUGH, JENNIFER. *Lavish Legacies: Baltimore Album and Related Quilts from the Collection of the Maryland Historical Society.* Baltimore: Maryland Historical Society, 1994.

———. "An Album of Baltimore Album Quilt Studies." *Uncoverings* 15 (1994): 73–110.

GOLDSWORTHY, ANDY. *A Collaboration with Nature.* New York: Harry N. Abrams, 1990.

GORDON, BEVERLY. "Playing at Being Powerless: New England Ladies Fairs, 1830–1930." *Massachusetts Review* 26, no. 4 (spring 1986): 144–66.

———. "Intimacy and Objects: A Proxemic Analysis of Gender-Based Responses to the Material World." In *The Material Culture of Gender/The Gender of Material Culture,* edited by Katharine Martinez and Kenneth Ames, 237–52. Winterthur, Delaware: Winterthur Museum, 1997.

GORDON, MAGGI MCCORMICK. *Pictorial Quilting.* New York: Watson-Guptill, 2000.

GOUMA-PETERSON, THALIA. *Miriam Schapiro: A Retrospective, 1953–1980.* Wooster, Ohio: College of Wooster, 1980.

GRANICK, EVE W. *The Amish Quilt.* Intercourse, Pennsylvania: Good Books, 1989.

GRAVES, STEVII, ED. *Visions: Quilts, Layers of Excellence.* San Diego: Quilt San Diego and C & T Publishing, 1994.

GRAY, LORI. "Textiles with Tales to Tell." *Traditional Home,* September 1997, 134–39.

GRUDIN, EVA. *Stitching Memories: African American Story Quilts.* Williamstown, Massachusetts: Williams College Museum of Art, 1990.

GUNN, VIRGINIA. "Crazy Quilts and Outline Quilts: Popular Responses to the Decorative Art/Art Needlework Movement, 1876–1893." *Uncoverings* 5 (1984): 131–52.

———. "Quilts at Nineteenth Century State and County Fairs: An Ohio Study." *Uncoverings* 9 (1988): 105–28.

———. "From Myth to Maturity: The Evolution of Quilt Scholarship." *Uncoverings* 13 (1992): 192–205.

GUTCHEON, BETH. *The Perfect Patchwork Primer.* New York: David McKay Co., 1973.

HALL, CARRIE, AND ROSE KRETSINGER. *The Romance of the Patchwork Quilt.* Caldwell, Idaho: Caxton Printers, 1935.

HALL, ELIZA CALVERT. "Aunt Jane's Album." *Cosmopolitan,* Feb. 1900, 385–94.

———. *Aunt Jane of Kentucky.* Boston: Little Brown & Co., 1907.

———. *Aunt Jane of Kentucky.* Edited by Melody Graulich. Albany: New College and University Press, 1992.

———. *Aunt Jane of Kentucky.* Foreword by Bonnie Jean Cox. Lexington: University Press of Kentucky, 1995.

———. *Quilter's Wisdom.* San Francisco: Chronicle Books, 1996.

HAMMOND, JOYCE. *Taifaifai and Quilts of Polynesia.* Honolulu: University of Hawaii Press, 1986.

HANSON, MARIN. *Reflections of the Exotic East in American Quilts.* Lincoln: International Quilt Study Center and the Lentz Center for Asian Culture, University of Nebraska, 2001.

HARDING, DEBORAH, AND LAURA FISHER. *Home Sweet Home: The House in American Folk Art.* New York: Rizzoli International, 2001.

HARRIS, GEORGE WASHINGTON. "Mrs. Yardley's Quilting." 1867. Reprint, in *"Sut Lovingoods Yarns" and American Literature,* edited by Cleanth Brooks et al., 70–71. New York: St. Martin's Press, 1973.

HARRIS, PATRICIA, DAVID LYON, AND PATRICIA MALARCHER. *Michael James: Studio Quilts.* Neuchatel, Switzerland: Éditions Victor Attinger, 1995.

HAVIG, BETTINA. *Amish Kinder Comforts: Quilts from the Sara Miller Collection.* Paducah, Kentucky: American Quilter's Society, 1996.

HEDGES, ELAINE. "The Nineteenth Century Diarist and Her Quilts." *Feminist Studies* 8, no. 2 (1982): 293–99.

HEDGES, ELAINE, PAT FERRERO, AND JULIE SILBER. *Hearts and Hands: Women, Quilts, and American Society.* Nashville: Rutledge Hill Press, 1996.

HERR, PATRICIA. *Quilting Traditions: Pieces from the Past.* Atglen, Pennsylvania: Schiffer Publishing, 2000.

HOLLANDER, STACY. "African-American Quilts: Two Perspectives." *Folk Art* (spring 1993): 44–51.

HOLSTEIN, JONATHAN. *Abstract Design in American Quilts.* New York: Whitney Museum, 1971.

———. *The Pieced Quilt: An American Design Tradition.* New York: Galahad Books, 1973.

———. "The American Block Quilt." In *In the Heart of Pennsylvania,* edited by Jeannette Lasansky, 16–27. Lewisburg, Pennsylvania: Union County Historical Society, 1986.

———. *Abstract Design in American Quilts: A Biography of an Exhibition.* Louisville: Kentucky Quilt Project, 1991.

———. "In Plain Sight: The Aesthetics of Amish Quilts." In *A Quiet Spirit: Amish Quilts from the Collection of Cindy Tietze and Stuart Hodosh,* by Donald Kraybill, Patricia Herr, and Jonathan Holstein, 69–121. Los Angeles: Fowler Museum of Cultural History, UCLA, 1996.

———. "Uncommon Quilts." *Heritage: The Magazine of the New York State Historical Association* 12, no. 4 (summer 1996): 4–13.

HOLSTEIN, JONATHAN, AND CAROLYN DUCEY. *Masterpiece Quilts from the James Collection.* Tokyo: Nihon Vogue, 1998.

HOPKINSON, DEBORAH. *Sweet Clara and the Freedom Quilt.* New York: Alfred A. Knopf, 1993.

HORNBACK, NANCY. "Nineteenth Century Red and Green Appliqué Quilts." In *Kansas Quilts and Quilters,* ed. Barbara Brackman, 67–91. Lawrence: University of Kansas Press, 1993.

HOUCK, CARTER. *The Quilt Encyclopedia Illustrated.* New York: Harry N. Abrams, 1991.

HUGHES, ROBERT, AND JULIE SILBER. *Amish: The Art of the Quilt.* New York: Alfred A. Knopf, 1990.

IMPORTANT AMERICANA, JANUARY 28–30, 1988. New York: Sotheby's, 1988.

IMPORTANT AMERICANA, JANUARY 24–30, 1995. New York: Sotheby's, 1995.

INDIANA QUILT REGISTRY PROJECT. *Quilts of Indiana.* Bloomington: Indiana University Press, 1991.

IRWIN, JOHN, AND KATHARINE BRETT. *Origins of Chintz, with a Catalogue of Indo-European Cotton-Paintings in the Victoria and Albert Museum, London, and the Royal Ontario Museum, Toronto.* London, H.M.S.O., 1970.

JAMES, ARDIS, AND PENNY MCMORRIS. *Quilts in the James Collection.* Tokyo: Kokusai Art, 1990.

JAMES, MICHAEL. *The Quiltmaker's Handbook: A Guide to Design and Construction.* Englewood, New Jersey: Prentice Hall, 1978.

———. "Getting Our Bearings: Quilt Art at Century's End." *American Quilter,* fall 1992, 52–53.

———. *Michael James: Art and Inspirations.* Lafayette, California: C & T Publishing, 1998.

JAMES, MICHAEL, AND DAVID HORNUNG. *Michael James: Iconographies.* Neuchatel, Switzerland: Éditions Victor Attinger, 1999.

JOHNSON, JAY, AND WILLIAM C. KETCHUM. *American Folk Art of the Twentieth Century.* New York: Rizzoli International, 1983.

JONES, STELLA. *Hawaiian Quilts.* Honolulu: Honolulu Academy of Arts, 1930.

JURGENA, MELISSA, AND PATRICIA COX CREWS. "The

Reconciliation Quilt: Lucinda Ward Honstain's Pictorial Diary of an American Era." *Folk Art* (2003, in press).

KILE, MICHAEL. "The Collector: On the Road." *Quilt Digest* 4 (1986): 85–86.

KIRAKOFE, RODERICK. *The American Quilt.* New York: Clarkson Potter, 1993.

KRAYBILL, DONALD, PATRICIA HERR, AND JONATHAN HOLSTEIN. *A Quiet Spirit: Amish Quilts from the Collection of Cindy Tietze and Stuart Hodosh.* Los Angeles: Fowler Museum of Cultural History, UCLA, 1996.

LADIES' ART COMPANY. *Quilt Patterns: Patchwork and Applique.* 1928. Reprint, Wichita, Kansas: Vanderkellen Galleries, 1996.

LANKFORD, JOHN, AND RICKEY SLAVINGS. "Gender and Science: Women in American Astronomy, 1859–1949." *Physics Today,* March 1990, 58–65.

LAPORTE, GUL. *Quilts from Europe: Projects and Inspiration.* Lafayette, California: C & T Publishing, 2000.

LASANSKY, JEANNETTE. *Pieced By Mother.* Lewisburg, Pennsylvania: Union County Historical Society, 1987.

LAURY, JEAN RAY. *Quilts and Coverlets: A Contemporary Approach.* New York: Van Nostrand Reinhold, 1970.

LEARS, T. J. JACKSON. *No Place of Grace: Antimodernism and the Transformation of American Culture, 1880–1920.* New York: Pantheon Books, 1981.

LEON, ELI. *Who'd A Thought It: Improvisation in African-American Quiltmaking.* San Francisco: San Francisco Craft and Folk Art Museum, 1987.

LILES, JAMES. "Dyes in American Quilts Made Prior to 1930, with Special Emphasis on Cotton and Linen." *Uncoverings* 5 (1984): 29–40.

LIPSETT, LINDA OTTO. *Pieced from Ellen's Quilt: Ellen Spaulding Reed's Letters and Story.* Dayton, Ohio: Halstead and Meadows, 1991.

———. *Elizabeth Roseberry Mitchell's Graveyard Quilt.* Dayton, Ohio: Halstead and Meadows, 1995.

LOCKLAIR, PAULA. *Quilts, Coverlets, and Counterpanes: Bedcoverings from the MESDA and Old Salem Collections.* Winston-Salem, South Carolina: Old Salem, 1997.

LOWENTHAL, DAVID. *The Past Is a Foreign Country.* Cambridge: Cambridge University Press, 1985.

LYONS, MARY. *Stitching Stars: The Story Quilts of Harriet Powers.* New York: Aladdin Paperbacks, 1997.

MAASEN, RUTH. "Centennial and Bicentennial Quilts." Research paper for class on "Quilts: A Social and Feminist History," University of Missouri–St. Louis, April 1997.

MACDOWELL, MARSHA. "Quilts and Their Stories: Revealing a Hidden History." *Uncoverings* 21 (2000): 155–66.

MACDOWELL, MARSHA, ED. *African American Quiltmaking in Michigan.* East Lansing: Michigan State University Press, 1997.

MACDOWELL, MARSHA, AND C. CURT DEWHURST. *To Honor and Comfort: Native Quilting Traditions.* Santa Fe: Museum of New Mexico Press, 1997.

MACDOWELL, MARSHA, AND RUTH FITZGERALD. *Michigan Quilts: 150 Years of a Textile Tradition.* East Lansing: Michigan State University Museum, 1987.

MACK, PAMELA. "Straying from Their Orbits: Women in Astronomy in America." In *Women of Science,* edited by G. Kass-Simon and P. Farnes, 72–116. Bloomington: Indiana University Press, 1990.

MAINARDI, PATRICIA. "Quilts: The Great American Art." *Feminist Art Journal* 2, no. 1 (1973): 1, 18–23.

MAINES, RACHEL. "Fancywork: The Archaeology of Lives." *Feminist Art Journal* 3, no. 4 (1974–75): 1–3.

———. "Paradigms of Scarcity and Abundance: The Quilt As an Artifact of the Industrial Revolution." In *In the Heart of Pennsylvania,* edited by Jeanette Lasansky, 84–89. Lewisburg, Pennsylvania: Union County Historical Society, 1986.

———. "The Tools of the Workbasket." In *Bits and Pieces: Textile Traditions,* edited by Jeannette Lasansky, 110–19. Lewisburg, Pennsylvania: Union County Historical Society, 1991.

MARRIOTT, ALICE, AND CAROL RACHLIN. *Dance around the Sun: The Life of Mary Little Bear Inkanish.* New York: Thomas Y. Crowell, 1977.

MARSH, BETSA. "Storytelling, Stitch by Stitch." *Creative Ideas for Living,* May 1987, 12–13.

———. "With Brush and Needle." *Creative Ideas for Living,* July–August 1988, 14–15.

MARTIN, CHRISTOPHER. *Native Needlework: Contemporary Indian Textiles from North Dakota.* Fargo: North Dakota Council on the Arts, 1988.

MASOPUST, KATIE PASQUINI. *Fractured Landscape Quilts.* Lafayette, California: C & T Publishing, 1996.

———. *Ghost Layers and Color Washes.* Lafayette, California: C & T Publishing, 2000.

MAUERSBERGER, HERBERT R., ED. *Matthews' Textile Fibers.* 5th ed. New York: John Wiley, 1947.

MAZLOOMI, CAROLYN. *Spirits of the Cloth: Contemporary African American Quilts.* New York: Clarkson Potter, 1998.

MCMORRIS, PENNY. *Crazy Quilts.* New York: E. P. Dutton, 1984.

———. *The Art Quilt.* San Francisco: Quilt Digest Press, 1986.

———. *Nancy Crow: Work in Transition.* Paducah, Kentucky: American Quilter's Society, 1992.

MCMORRIS, PENNY, AND MICHAEL KILE. *The Art Quilt.* Lincolnwood, Illinois: Quilt Digest Press, 1986.

MELLER, SUSAN, AND JOOST ELFFERS. *Textile Designs: Two Hundred Years of European and American Patterns.* New York: Harry N. Abrams, 1991.

METCALF, EUGENE, AND CLAUDINE WEATHERFORD. "Modernism, Edith Halpert, Holger Cahill, and the Fine Art Meaning of American Folk Art." In *Folk Roots, New Roots: Folklore in American Life,* edited by Jane Becker and Barbara Franco, 141–66. Lexington, Massachusetts: Museum of Our National Heritage, 1988.

MONTGOMERY, FLORENCE. *Printed Textiles: English and American Cottons and Linens, 1700–1850.* New York: Viking Press, 1970.

MOONEN, AN. *Quilts: en Nederlandse traditie/The Dutch Tradition.* Arnhem, Nederlands: Nederlands Openluchtmuseum, 1992.

NELSON, CYRIL, AND CARTER HOUCK. *Treasury of American Quilts.* New York: Greenwich House, 1982.

THE NEW QUILT 2, DAIRY BARN: QUILT NATIONAL. Newtown, Connecticut: Taunton Press, 1993.

OAKLANDER, CHRISTINE. "Pioneers in Folk Art Collecting: Elie and Viola Nadelman." *Folk Art* (fall 1992): 48–55.

OLIVER, CELIA Y. *Fifty-five Famous Quilts from the Shelburne Museum.* New York: Dover Press, 1990.

OLIVER, PAUL. *Savannah Syncopators: African Retentions in the Blues.* New York: Stein and Day, 1970.

123 JAPANESE QUILT ARTISTS COLLECTION. Tokyo: Nihon Vogue, 1998.

ORDOÑEZ, MARGARET. "Technology Reflected." In *Down by the Old Mill Stream: Quilts in Rhode Island,* edited by Linda Welters and Margaret Ordoñez, 122–60. Kent, Ohio: Kent State University Press, 2000.

ORLOFSKY, PATSY AND MYRON. *Quilts in America.* New York: McGraw-Hill, 1974.

OSHINS, LISA TURNER. *Quilt Collections: A Directory for the United States and Canada.* Washington, D.C.: Acropolis Books, 1987.

OSLER, DOROTHY. *Traditional British Quilts.* London: Batsford, 1987.

———. *North Country Quilts: Legend and Living Tradition.* County Durham: Bowes Museum, 2000.

PARKER, ROZSIKA. *The Subversive Stitch: Embroidery and the Making of the Feminine.* New York: Routledge Press, 1989.

PASQUINI, KATIE. *Mandala.* Eureka, California: Sudz Publishing, 1983.

———. *Three-Dimensional Design.* Lafayette, California: C & T Publishing, 1988.

PECK, AMELIA. *American Quilts and Coverlets in the Metropolitan Museum.* New York: Metropolitan Museum of Art, 1990.

PERRY, REGENIA. *Harriet Powers's Bible Quilts.* New York: Rizzoli Art Series, 1994.

PERRY, ROSALIND WEBSTER, AND MARTY FROLLI. *A Joy Forever: Marie Webster's Quilt Patterns.* Santa Barbara, California: Practical Patchwork, 1992.

PICTON, JOHN. "Africa and African American Quilts." *Quilters' Review* 26, winter 1998, 2–3.

POWERS, MARLA N. *Oglala Women: Myth, Ritual, and Reality.* Chicago: University of Chicago Press, 1986.

PRZYBYSZ, JANE. "Quilts, Old Kitchens, and the Social Geography of Gender at Nineteenth Century Sanitary Fairs." In *The Material Culture of Gender/The Gender of Material Culture,* edited by Katharine Martinez and Kenneth Ames, 411–41. Winterthur, Delaware: Winterthur Museum, 1997.

PULFORD, FLORENCE. *Morning Star Quilts.* Los Altos, California: Leone Publications, 1989.

QUILTING IN AMERICA 1994: A COMPREHENSIVE STUDY OF THE U.S. QUILTING MARKET. Golden, Colorado: Leman Publications, 1994.

QUILTING IN AMERICA 2000. Golden, Colorado: Leman Publications, 2000.

QUILT NATIONAL: CONTEMPORARY DESIGNS IN FABRIC. Ashville, North Carolina: Lark Books, 1995.

RAE, JANET. *The Quilts of the British Isles.* New York: E. P. Dutton, 1987.

RAE, JANET, ET AL. *Quilt Treasures of Great Britain.* Nashville: Rutledge Hill Press, 1995.

RAMSEY, BETS. "The Land of Cotton: Quiltmaking by African-American Women in Three Southern States." *Uncoverings* 9 (1988): 9–28.

RAMSEY, BETS, AND MERIKAY WALDVOGEL. *Southern Quilts: Surviving Relics of the Civil War.* Nashville: Rutledge Hill Press, 1998.

RICHTER, PAULA BRADSTREET. *Painted with Thread: The Art of American Embroidery.* Salem, Massachusetts: Peabody Essex Museum, 2000.

RINDER, LAWRENCE, ED. *Whitney Biennial 2002.* New York: Whitney Museum and Harry N. Abrams, 2002.

ROSS, DORAN. *Fighting with Art: Appliquéd Flags of the Fante Asafo.* Los Angeles: UCLA Museum of Cultural History, 1979.

ROWE, ANN. *A Century of Change in Guatemalan Textiles.* New York: Center for Inter-American Relations, 1981.

RUBIN, CYNTHIA. "Southern Exposure: One Curator in Search of an Exhibition." *The Clarion,* spring/summer 1985, 34.

RUMFORD, BEATRIX. "Uncommon Art of the Common People: A Review of Trends in the Collecting and Exhibiting of American Folk Art." In *Perspectives on American Folk Art,* edited by Ian Quimby and Scott Swank, 13–53. Winterthur, Delaware: Winterthur Museum, 1980.

SAFFORD, CARLETON, AND ROBERT BISHOP. *America's Quilts and Coverlets.* New York: E. P. Dutton, 1980.

SCHAPIRO, MIRIAM. "Notes from a Conversation on Art,

Feminism, and Work." In *Working It Out,* edited by Sara Ruddick and Pamela Daniels, 283–305. New York: Pantheon Books, 1977.

———. "Geometry and Flowers." In *The Artist and the Quilt,* edited by Charlotte Robinson, 26–31. New York: Alfred A. Knopf, 1983.

SCHAPIRO, MIRIAM, AND MELISSA MEYER. "Femmage." *Heresies* 4 (1978): 66–69.

SELECTIONS FROM THE AMERICAN FOLK ART COLLECTION OF MR. AND MRS. ROBERT P. MARCUS, OCTOBER 14, 1989. New York: Sotheby's, 1989.

SHANKEL, CAROL, ED. *Quilts from the Shelburne Museum.* Tokyo: Kokusai Art, 1996.

SHAW, ROBERT. *Quilts: A Living Tradition.* New York: Hugh Lauter Levin Associates, 1995.

———. *The Art Quilt.* New York: Hugh Lauter Levin Associates, 1997.

SHOWALTER, ELAINE. "Common Threads." In *Sister's Choice: Tradition and Change in American Women's Writing.* Oxford: Clarendon Press, 1991.

SIENKIEWICZ, ELLIE. *Baltimore Beauties and Beyond.* Vol. 2. Lafayette, California: C & T Publishing, 1991.

SLACK, NANCY. "Nineteenth-Century American Women Botanists: Wives, Widows, and Work." In *Uneasy Careers and Intimate Lives: Women in Science, 1789–1979,* edited by Pnina Abir-Am and Dorinda Outram, 78–103. New Brunswick, New Jersey: Rutgers University Press, 1987.

SMITH, ROBERTA. "Bad News for Art, However You Define It." *New York Times,* Sunday, March 31, 2002, section 2.

SMITH, WILENE. "Quilt History in Old Periodicals: A New Interpretation." *Uncoverings* 11 (1990): 188–213.

SMITH-ROSENBERG, CAROLL. "The Female World of Love and Ritual." In *Disorderly Conduct: Visions of Gender in Victorian America,* 53–76. Oxford: Oxford University Press, 1985.

SOTHEBY'S ART AT AUCTION: THE ART MARKET REVIEW, 1991–92. New York: Rizzoli International Publications, 1992.

STRICKLER, CAROL. *American Woven Coverlets.* Loveland, Colorado: Interweave Press, 1987.

THOMPSON, ROBERT FARRIS. *Flash of the Spirit: African and Afro-American Art and Philosophy.* New York: Random House, 1983.

TOBIN, JACQUELINE, AND RAYMOND DOBARD. *Hidden in Plain View: The Secret Story of Quilts and the Underground Railroad.* New York: Doubleday, 1999.

TORSNEY, CHERYL, AND JUDY ELSLEY. *Quilt Culture: Tracing the Pattern.* Columbia: University of Missouri Press, 1994.

TOWNSEND, LOUISE. "Kansas City Star Quilt Patterns." *Uncoverings* 5 (1984): 115–25.

TROLLOPE, FRANCES. *Domestic Manners of the Americans.* 1832. Reprint, New York: Alfred A. Knopf, 1949.

TYLER, AMY. "Quilts: Piecing the Market Back Together." *Antique Monthly,* June 1993, 28–31.

ULRICH, LAUREL THATCHER. *The Age of Homespun: Objects and Stories in the Creation of an American Myth.* New York: Alfred Knopf, 2001.

VALENTINE, FAWN. *West Virginia Quilts and Quiltmakers.* Athens: Ohio University Press, 2000.

VLACH, JOHN MICHAEL. *The Afro-American Tradition in Decorative Arts.* Cleveland, Ohio: the Cleveland Museum of Art, 1978.

———. "Holger Cahill as Folklorist." *Journal of American Folklore* 98, no. 388 (1985): 148–62.

WAHLMAN, MAUDE. "The Art of Afro-American Quiltmaking: Origins, Development, and Significance." Ph.D. diss., Yale University, 1980.

———. "The Aesthetics of Afro-American Quilts." In *Something to Keep You Warm,* edited by Roland Freeman, 6–8. Jackson: Mississippi Department of Archives and History, 1981.

———. *Ten Afro-American Quilters.* Oxford: Center for Southern Culture, University of Mississippi, 1983.

———. *Signs and Symbols: African Images in African American Quilts.* New York: Studio Books in association with the Museum of American Folk Art, 1993.

WAHLMAN, MAUDE, THEOPHUS SMITH, ROBERT HOBBS, WILLIAM ARNETT, AND PAUL ARNETT. "The Hidden Charms of the Deep South." In *Souls Grown Deep: African-American Vernacular Art of the South.* Vol. 1. Atlanta: Tinwood Books, 2000.

WALDVOGEL, MERIKAY. *Soft Covers for Hard Times: Quiltmaking and the Great Depression.* Nashville: Rutledge Hill Press, 1990.

———. "The Origin of Mountain Mist Patterns." *Uncoverings* 16 (1995): 95–105.

———. "The Mountain Mist Historical Quilt Collection." *Mountain Mist Blue Book of Quilts.* N.p.: Stearns Technical Textiles Company, 1996.

———. "Remembering Sandra Mitchell." *Quilter's Newsletter Magazine,* November 2001.

WALDVOGEL, MERIKAY, AND BARBARA BRACKMAN. *Patchwork Souvenirs of the 1933 World's Fair.* Nashville: Rutledge Hill Press, 1993.

WALKER, MARILYN. *Ontario's Heritage Quilts.* Toronto: Boston Mills Press, 1992.

WALKER, MICHELE. *The Passionate Quilter.* London: Edbury Press, 1990.

WARD, GERALD, ET AL. *American Folk: Folk Art from the*

Collection of the Museum of Fine Arts, Boston. Boston: Museum of Fine Arts, 2001.

WASS, JANICE TAUER. *Weaver's Choice: Patterns in American Coverlets.* Springfield: Illinois State Museums, 1988.

WATTS, KATHERINE, AND ELIZABETH WALKER. "Joyful Improvisations: The Quiltmaking of Anna Williams." *American Quilter,* winter 1997, 36–40.

WEBSTER, MARIE. *Quilts: Their Story and How to Make Them.* New York: Doubleday and Page, 1915.

WELTERS, LINDA, AND MARGARET ORDOÑEZ, EDS. *Down by the Old Mill Stream: Quilts in Rhode Island.* Kent, Ohio: Kent State University Press, 2000.

WETTRE, ASA. *Old Swedish Quilts.* Loveland, Colorado: Interweave Press, 1995.

WHAT'S AMERICAN ABOUT AMERICAN QUILTS. Washington, D.C.: National Museum of American History, Smithsonian Institution, 1995.

WILSON, ERICA. *Erica Wilson's Quilts of America.* Birmingham, Alabama: Oxmoor House, 1979.

"THE WINTER ART SHOW." *American Heritage Magazine,* February–March 1992, 60.

WOODARD, THOMAS, AND BLANCHE GREENSTEIN. *Twentieth Century Quilts: 1900–1950.* New York: E. P. Dutton, 1988.

WRIGHT, GILES R. Review of *Hidden in Plain Sight.* Posted June 2001 on the Web site of the Camden County Historical Society, *HistoricCamdenCounty.com.*

YEAROUS, JENNY. "Stitches in Time: The Development of Sewing Threads in the Nineteenth Century and Beyond." *Uncoverings* 19 (1998): 155–78.

ZEGART, SHELLY. *American Quilt Collections, Antique Quilt Masterpieces.* Tokyo: Nihon Vogue, 1996.

CONTRIBUTORS

Janet Catherine Berlo is Professor of Art History and Visual and Cultural Studies at the University of Rochester in New York, where she held the Susan B. Anthony Chair of Gender Studies from 1997 to 2002. She received her Ph.D. in History of Art from Yale University in 1980. Berlo is the author of numerous books and articles about the indigenous arts of North America, including *Native North American Art* (with Ruth Phillips, Oxford University Press, 1998) and a memoir, *Quilting Lessons* (University of Nebraska Press, 2001). She has received grants for her research from the Guggenheim Foundation, the Getty Trust, and the National Endowment for the Humanities. Berlo has also taught at Harvard, Yale, the University of Missouri, and UCLA. A member of the founding board of the International Quilt Study Center (1998–2001), she teaches a course on the social history of the American quilt.

Patricia Cox Crews is Professor of Textiles and Director of the International Quilt Study Center at the University of Nebraska–Lincoln. She received her Ph.D. in Textile Science and Conservation from Kansas State University in 1984. She served as primary editor for *Nebraska Quilts and Quiltmakers* (University of Nebraska Press, 1991), which won the Smithsonian's Frost Prize for Distinguished Scholarship in American Crafts in 1993. More recently she edited the exhibition catalogue *A Flowering of Quilts* (University of Nebraska Press, 2001). Crews has published more than fifty technical papers about the history, conservation, and performance of textiles.

Carolyn Ducey is Curator of the International Quilt Study Center at the University of Nebraska–Lincoln, where

she has organized exhibitions including *Fanciful Flowers: Botany and the American Quilt* and *African American Quilts from the Robert and Helen Cargo Collection*. In addition, Ducey manages collection care of the more than 1,250 quilts in the IQSC's permanent collection and supervises a dynamic docent program. She is co-author of *Masterpiece Quilts from the James Collection* (University of Nebraska Press, 1998) and a contributing author of *A Flowering of Quilts* (University of Nebraska Press, 2001). Ducey earned her M.A. in Art History from Indiana University in 1998.

Jonathan Holstein's interest in quilts began in the late 1960s, when he and Gail van der Hoof began to collect them across the United States. In 1971 they curated the exhibition *Abstract Design in American Quilts* at the Whitney Museum of American Art in New York and many subsequent exhibitions in museums here and abroad, including the first exhibitions of American quilts in Japan (1975 and 1976) and the first exhibitions of Amish quilts. Holstein has lectured on quilts for more than three decades and has juried many quilt contests and exhibitions around the world. Some of his books and catalogues are *American Pieced Quilts* (Viking Press, 1972), *The Pieced Quilt: An American Design Tradition* (Galahad, 1973), and *Abstract Design in American Quilts: A Biography of an Exhibition* (Kentucky Quilt Project, 1991). Holstein was co-founder and editor of *The Quilt Journal* and one of the first four people elected to the Quilters' Hall of Fame. He was a founding board member of the International Quilt Study Center.

Michael James, Senior Lecturer in the Department of Textiles, Clothing, and Design at the University of

Nebraska–Lincoln, earned his M.F.A. in Painting and Printmaking from the Rochester Institute of Technology in 1973 and his B.F.A. in Painting from the University of Massachusetts at Dartmouth, which in 1992 conferred on him an Honorary Doctor of Fine Arts degree for his work in the area of studio quilt practice. A Fellow of the American Craft Council, James's work is in numerous collections, including the Renwick Gallery of the Smithsonian Institution, the American Craft Museum, the Indianapolis Art Museum, and the Newark Museum. He is a recipient of several National Endowment for the Arts Visual Artist Fellowships. His work is the subject of the monograph *Michael James Studio Quilts* (Éditions Victor Attinger, 1995), and he is the author of two books, *The Quiltmaker's Handbook* (Prentice-Hall, 1978) and *The Second Quiltmaker's Handbook* (Prentice-Hall, 1981). James has lectured widely and led workshops on quilt design throughout North America, Europe, and Japan.